Study Guide and Anthology *for* INTRODUCTION TO MODERN ENGLISH AND AMERICAN LITERATURE II: THE TWENTIETH CENTURY

edited by
Emily Auerbach, University of Wisconsin–Madison

with material from

William L. Andrews, University of Wisconsin–Madison/University of Kansas

Jay Clayton, University of Wisconsin–Madison/ Vanderbilt University

Terrence Doody, Rice University

Julie Rivkin, Connecticut College

Developed Through University of Wisconsin–Extension, WHA Radio and Independent Study, and University of Wisconsin–Madison

 Funding Provided by the Annenberg/CPB Project
Providing Opportunities for Higher Education
Through Telecommunications

THE AUDIO-PRINT COURSE COLLECTION
of
The Annenberg/CPB Project

This course is part of the Annenberg/CPB Audio-Print Course Collection under development through University of Wisconsin—Extension, WHA Radio and Independent Study, and University of Wisconsin–Madison. The Annenberg/CPB Project is producing a library of integrated audio-print courses to serve a national market of degree-oriented distance learners. National teams of scholars are developing these courses to fit the basic freshman/sophomore curriculum of most institutions of higher learning.

Project Director
Linda Clauder, WHA Radio

Independent Study Program
Sylvia Rose, Director

Academic Advisory Council Chair
Howard Martin, Dean
Division of University Outreach
University of Wisconsin–Madison

Study Guide Coordinator
Nancy Gaines

Study Guide Editor
Elsie Ham

Composition
Bonnie Sundal, Shirley Gleichauf

Audio Editor/Design Coordinator
Judith Strasser

Technical Producer
Marv Nonn

Audio Script Writers
Judith Strasser, James Tucker,
Kristine Rusch, Sara Rath

Audio Producers
Judith Strasser, Stuart Brooks
Ralph Johnson

Permissions/Credits

Josef Albers: *Gray Instrumentation I.* Elvehjem Museum of Art, University of Wisconsin–Madison. Gift of Bruce E. and Derene Wise Cohan.

Elizabeth Bishop: Selections from *The Complete Poems 1927-1979*, ©1979 by Elizabeth Bishop, © 1983 by Alice Helen Methfessel, used by arrangement with Farrar, Straus & Giroux, Inc.

Robert Frost: "The Road Not Taken," "Birches," "Mending Wall," and "'Out, Out—'" from *The Poetry of Robert Frost* edited by Edward Connery Lathem. ©1969 by Holt, Rinehart and Winston, Inc. ©1962 by Robert Frost. ©1975 by Lesley Frost Ballantine. Reprinted by permission of Henry Holt and Company, Inc.; and Jonathan Cape Ltd., London, England, on behalf of the Estate of Robert Frost.

Toni Morrison: Excerpts reproduced from an interview with Toni Morrison, by permission from The American Prose Library Inc., 1015 E. Broadway, Suite 284, Columbia, MO 65205. Copies of the full interview are available on cassette from The American Prose Library.

Philip Roth: Excerpts from *The Ghost Writer* by Philip Roth, ©1979 by Philip Roth, used by arrangement with Farrar, Straus & Giroux, Inc.

Karl Schmidt-Rottluf: *Junger.* Elvehjem Museum of Art, University of Wisconsin–Madison. Oscar Rennebohm Foundation Fund and Edna G. Dyar Fund purchase.

Joseph Severn: *John Keats.* Portrait of John Keats by Joseph Severn, © XXXX (NPG 1605). National Portrait Gallery, London, England.

Peter Taylor: ©1963 by Peter Taylor. Reproduced from *A Wife of Nashville* by Peter Taylor, with permission from the author.

Alice Walker: "In Search of Our Mothers' Gardens," ©1974 by Alice Walker. Reprinted from her volume *In Search of Our Mothers' Gardens* by permission of Harcourt Brace Jovanovich, Inc. "Women," ©1979 by Alice Walker. Reprinted from her volume *Revolutionary Petunias & Other Poems* by permission of Harcourt Brace Jovanovich, Inc. "Strong Horse Tea," ©1968 by Alice Walker. Reprinted from her volume *In Love & Trouble* by permission of Harcourt Brace Jovanovich, Inc.

Eudora Welty: "Petrified Man," ©1939, 1967 by Eudora Welty, reprinted from her volume *A Curtain of Green and Other Stories* by permission of Harcourt Brace Jovanovich, Inc.

W. B. Yeats: "Adam's Curse," from *The Poems of W. B. Yeats: A New Edition,* edited by Richard J. Finneran (New York: Macmillan, 1983). "Lake Isle at Innisfree," "Wild Swans at Coole," "Easter 1916," "The Second Coming," "Among Schoolchildren," "The Circus Animals' Desertion," taken from *The Collected Poems of W B Yeats*, recorded by permission of A. P. Watt Ltd., London, England, on behalf of Anne Yeats and Michael Yeats.

CONTENTS

Study Guide

GENERAL INTRODUCTION / i

PART I: LITERATURE 1900-1944

    Introduction / 3
    Chronology / 7
1   T. S. Eliot and an Introduction to Modernism / 11
2   Ernest Hemingway / 21
3   William Butler Yeats / 29
4   Virginia Woolf / 47
5   Robert Frost / 55
6   William Faulkner / 66

PART II: LITERATURE 1945-PRESENT

    Introduction / 75
    Chronology / 77
7   Contemporary Southern Writers / 81
       (Eudora Welty; Peter Taylor; Alice Walker)
8   Malcolm X and the Autobiography Genre/ 88
9   Nadine Gordimer / 96
10   Elizabeth Bishop / 104
11   Toni Morrison / 117
12   Philip Roth / 123

CONCLUSION / 136

SUGGESTIONS FOR ADDITIONAL READING / 140

OPTIONAL ASSIGNMENT 13 / 145

GLOSSARY / 147

Anthology / 163

NOTES ON CONTRIBUTORS / 233

STUDY GUIDE

GENERAL INTRODUCTION

Phone conversations leave no trace. Grocery lists and phone books fail to interest us once they have served their purpose. In contrast, literature--the imaginative use of written language--offers us a permanent and meaningful record of a writer's thoughts, emotions, and visions.

In 1854 American writer Henry David Thoreau wrote:

> We should read the best that is in literature. . . . There are probably words addressed to our condition exactly, which, if we could really hear and understand, would be more salutary than the morning or the spring to our lives, and possibly put a new aspect on the face of things for us. How many a man has dated a new era in his life from the reading of a book!

"How many a man" [and woman] has indeed experienced a profound sense of change after reading works of fiction, nonfiction, or poetry. Through reading we can enter new countries and regions, change gender, move backward to earlier eras or even ahead to imagined times in the future. We can be reminded of events in our own life or share in situations and conflicts we have never had.

Like the other arts, literature can be both enjoyable and disturbing, understandable or confusing. Twentieth-century literature is perhaps the easiest and hardest literature to read--easiest because of our closeness to the language and events; hardest because of its diverse, experimental nature. We have no trouble understanding a slang-filled poem such as Gwendolyn Brooks's "We Real Cool":

> We real cool. We
> left school. We
> lurk late. We
> Strike straight . . .
> (1960)

On the other hand, a modern poem studded with allusions, foreign words, and fragmented thoughts, like T. S. Eliot's *The Waste Land*, can send us looking for an answer key or guide:

Introduction

London Bridge is falling down falling down
    falling down
Poi s'ascose nel foco che gli affina
Quando fiam uti chelidon--O swallow swallow
Le Prince d'Aquitaine a la tour abolie
These fragments I have shored against my ruins
Why then Ile fit you. Hieronymo's mad againe.
Datta. Dayadhvam. Damyata.
    Shantih shantih shantih. (1922)

The goal of this course is to bring you closer to twentieth-century writers and their works and to give you an opportunity to respond to what you read.

Introduction to Modern Literature II, the second of a two-part sequence, provides an introduction to English and American literature of the twentieth century. The first course explored how nineteenth-century writers achieved a revolution in literature. It is worth looking back briefly at these earlier poets and novelists to see how movements they began were continued or rejected by later writers.

THE NINETEENTH CENTURY AND ITS LEGACY

Revolution swept the Western world in the late eighteenth century and early nineteenth century, resulting in political upheavals (American Revolution, 1776; French Revolution, 1789), new economic philosophies, and religious and social reforms. In the arts this revolutionary impulse resulted in a movement we call **romanticism** (Boldface terms are defined in the Glossary).

Romantic artists celebrated freedom, imagination, individual feelings, originality, and creativity. Blake, Wordsworth, Keats, and other romantic poets insisted that literature should record powerful emotions, dreams, or imagined visions. They rejected the style and subject matter of earlier writers. Painter-poet Blake refused to paint bowls of fruit or portraits of noblemen like his contemporaries, choosing instead to produce visionary canvases with titles such as *The Ghost of a Flea* or *The Angel of the Divine Presence*. Wordsworth rejected the stilted, artificial language of earlier poets, noting that "Poets do not write for Poets alone, but for men." Poetic forms and images previously used for religious subjects became for Keats a way of describing human sexuality and dreams.

American writers of the nineteenth century shared the romantic embrace of freedom and originality, but they also injected into literature a new vein of Yankee irreverence and humor. Walt Whitman boldly asserted in his "Song of Myself," 1854, that the smell of his armpits was "aroma finer than prayer." A decade later Emily Dickinson labeled the Bible "an antique volume/written by faded men" and imagined herself being kicked out of heaven for singing too loudly. Both poets chose styles totally unlike anything done before, with unconventional use of punctuation, rhyme, and imagery. American fiction writer Mark Twain poked fun at hypocrites and impostors of all sorts and sought to capture in his tales the richness of American colloquial speech. "Well, this-yer Smiley had a yaller one-eyed cow that didn't have no tail, only just a short tail like a bannanner ..." begins a Twain character.

Nineteenth-century writers sometimes felt that their world was changing too quickly. Victorian poet Matthew Arnold described feeling as if he were

> Wandering between two worlds, one dead,
> The other powerless to be born,
> With nowhere yet to rest my head.
> (1862)

"I felt a Cleaving in my Mind/As if my Brain had split," wrote Emily Dickinson. The theories of Darwin and other scientists had challenged traditional religion, leaving people less sure of their place in the universe. Were we special creations, blessed by divine Providence and governed by an unseen moral force? Or were we animals governed by instincts and natural laws, placed on a planet without apparent purpose or direction?

Although they questioned old beliefs, most nineteenth-century writers remained optimistic about human nature and convinced that an underlying order and benevolent power existed. They believed in *continuity*, in the connectedness of all aspects of human life. Romantic poet Wordsworth discovered in Nature a "divine presence," a "blessed power/That rolls through all things." Human beings had a rightful and secure place in Nature, for "Nature never did betray/The heart that loved her." American poet Whitman celebrated both his individuality and his ability to feel connected to others:

> I celebrate myself, and sing myself,
> And what I assume you shall assume,
> For every atom belonging to me as good belongs to
> you.

Victorian poet Robert Browning wrote poems about evil characters at times, but he also could take the stance that "God's in his Heaven/All's right with the world!" Victorian novelist Charles Dickens sketched a world of corruption and abuse, yet his novels invariably move toward happy endings, with characters resolving conflicts, marrying, receiving appropriate punishments, and reaching understanding.

In addition, nineteenth-century literature remained primarily the province of white men. As the century progressed, other voices invaded this province, demanding inclusion. The Brontë sisters, George Eliot, Harriet Beecher Stowe, and other women found the novel a genre suited to their experiences as observers of daily human behavior and relationships. Elizabeth Barrett Browning, Emily Dickinson, and others used poetry to capture intense emotions and moments of vision. Obstacles still thwarted women who wanted to write, though. Denied proper education, legal rights, voting rights, or access to a world beyond home and family, these women writers often adopted male pseudonyms or withdrew from conventional society in order to gain the freedom to write.

Black writers faced even harsher, more impassable obstacles. For half of the nineteenth century blacks in America remained slaves, forced to live in appalling conditions and denied all rights basic to human experience. Even after the Emancipation freed them, blacks remained politically, economically, and socially oppressed. Blacks who had not been taught to read and write developed an oral tradition of storytelling, sermons, and songs that gradually began to be heard. Slave narratives, like Frederick Douglass's *Narrative of the Life of Frederick Douglass, an American Slave*, 1845, found their way into print and began to shake the complacency of white readers.

In general, writers at the end of the nineteenth century sought to expose parts of life that were hidden or covered up by their predecessors. Happy endings seemed to mock lives filled with hardship and unresolved problems. Intricate poetic structures implied an ordered life rather than one characterized by randomness and chaos. Fiction with a clearly defined beginning, middle, and end gave an artificial shape to experiences based on fluid impressions and moods. Literature of the late nineteenth century and, as we see in this course, early twentieth century rejected earlier forms in order to capture reality in a more complex and fluid way. Novels by late nineteenth-century writers such as Thomas Hardy, Henry James, and Joseph Conrad often end tragically. The social order does not automatically guarantee a place for each individual, and characters become victims to impersonal forces beyond their control. Evil is not always punished, nor good rewarded. Understanding, if it comes at all, often comes too late.

The last work studied in Introduction to Modern Literature I: The Nineteenth Century was Joseph Conrad's *Heart of Darkness*, written in 1899. Conrad's short novel journeys into a dark, horrifying part of humanity. Rather than a neat plot, clear division of heroes and villains, linear progression of events, and comforting ending, Conrad chooses a fragmented and rambling prose narrative that moves toward no definite conclusion. The main character observes skeptically, "Destiny. My destiny! Droll thing life is--that mysterious arrangement of merciless logic for a futile purpose." With Conrad's *Heart of Darkness*, we head directly into the literature of our own century.

THE TWENTIETH CENTURY

In a chapter of Philip Roth's *The Ghost Writer*, one of the works included in this course, aspiring young writer Nathan Zuckerman stands on a book by nineteenth-century novelist Henry James in order to reach higher. This image illustrates the way twentieth-century writers have continued, expanded, built on the ideas and styles of their predecessors. The romantic insistence on originality and freedom, the American writers' insistence on informality and rebelliousness, the Victorian writers' fascination with human behavior and social ills all continue to be concerns of twentieth-century writers.

At the same time, we see twentieth-century writers reacting violently against the smugness, morality, and idealism of the writers before them. Death for Victorian Charles Dickens was an opportunity for a sentimental outpouring: Little Nell (a character in Dickens's *The Old Curiosity Shop*, 1840) dies hearing the music of the spheres, and Dickens writes, "She seemed a creature fresh from the hand of God, and waiting for the breath of life; not one who had lived and suffered death. . . . Dear, gentle, patient, noble Nell was dead." Contrast that with contemporary American Poet Laureate Howard Nemerov's attitude toward death in "The Vacuum," 1955:

> . . . when my old woman died her soul
> Went into that vacuum cleaner, and I can't bear
> To see the bag swell like a belly, eating the dust
> And the woolen mice. . . .

Twentieth-century writers have refused to be limited to subjects "suitable for family reading," to gloss over life's uncertainties or dark moments, to reach pat conclusions or offer trite moral sayings. Influenced by Freud's exposé of our motivations, drives, dreams, and nightmares and by Einstein's discovery that "reality" depends on one's point of view, modern writers have experimented with a variety of forms and styles to create a literature more in step with their world and its changed attitudes.

Introduction

Instead of viewing their world as a connected, ordered whole, writers at the beginning of the twentieth century sensed a **discontinuity**, or a feeling that parts of their life were fragmented, broken, ruptured. World War I, with many nations at war against each other, illustrated a widespread sense that the world was coming apart at the seams, pulled in many directions and divided into conflicting factions. "Things fall apart; the centre cannot hold," wrote William Butler Yeats. The international movement in all the arts at the beginning of the twentieth century to rebel against old forms and experiment with new styles is sometimes called **modernism** (see Glossary for more complete discussion).

In music, modernism led to the breakdown of traditional harmony and form. Beethoven's symphonies and sonatas possess a clear sense of structure, movement, and major and minor key. The audience has no doubt when a Beethoven symphony ends: the clear chord progressions signal resolution. In contrast, much modernist music has **atonality**, or an absence of an underlying key. Composers have experimented with new types of sound, often dissonant ones, and new instrumentation. Three pieces by contemporary American composer John Cage illustrate the radical nature of this experimentation: *Imaginary Landscape No. 4* calls for twelve radios, twenty-four musicians, and a conductor, with the multiple radios each tuned to a different station; *Variations IV* calls for "any number of players, any sounds or combinations of sounds produced by any means, with or without other activities"; and a piece entitled *4'33"* asks the performer to walk out on stage and time four minutes and thirty-three seconds of complete silence.

We may begin to wonder, is a piece consisting of silence "music"? Similarly, pictorial artists have forced us to reconsider what is and is not art. A nineteenth-century portrait like Joseph Severn's *John Keats*, 1819, (See Figure 1) can be judged by clear standards: is it a good likeness of Keats? has the artist demonstrated skillful use of materials? But how do we judge a modernist portrait such as *Disciple-Junger* by the cubist artist Karl Schmidt-Rottluff, 1918 (Figure 2)? And, pushing the arts even further, how do we judge or even respond to an abstract work like *Gray Instrumentation, 1C* by Josef Albers, 1974 (Figure 3)?

Modernist literature also has shocked its public and violated its expectations. Poet e. e. cummings chose unconventional punctuation for his name as well as his poetry, writing lines such as

```
in Just-
spring    when the world is mud-
luscious the little
lame balloonman
whistles    far    and wee . . .
("chanson innocente," 1923)
```

James Joyce, Virginia Woolf (discussed more in Unit 4), William Faulkner (Unit 6), and other modernist fiction writers experimented with new prose styles to capture the inner workings of the mind. In *Ulysses*, banned as obscene for a time, Molly Bloom considers her own sexuality:

> . . . Poldy pig-headed as usual like the soup but I could see him looking very hard at my chest when he stood up to open the door for me it was nice of him to show me out in any case Im extremely sorry Mrs Bloom believe me without making it too marked the first time after him being insulted and me being supposed to be his wife I just half smiled I know my chest was out that way at the door when he said Im extremely sorry and Im sure you were . . .

No commas or paragraphs guide the reader's way.

Modern literature, like modern art and music, seems as varied as the men and women who create it. Some artists have abandoned all conventions; others have adapted old forms to new uses. Some have sought simplicity and realism; others have deliberately created complexity, ambiguity, and artifice.

Twentieth-century writers from outside the mainstream have built on the pioneering work of earlier women and minorities and have pushed their way to the forefront of literature. Of the fourteen writers included in this course, six are women and three are black. Several others write from the standpoint of religious or political minorities. In the works of this course we meet Irish soldiers dying in their struggle against British authorities, an uneducated rural black woman fighting to get medical care for her dying son, a Jewish-American man confronting the legacy of the Holocaust, a black writer assassinated for the extremity of his beliefs, and a white South African family discovering the horror of apartheid. We discover through these and other works that one of the prime characteristics of modern literature is its variety--variety of viewpoint, ethnic and regional background, style, and subject.

Figure 1

Figure 2

Figure 3

COURSE OVERVIEW

This course examines twentieth-century English and American literature. What a vast area! By definition, any survey course, like this one, must omit many important writers, works, genres, and ideas. We aim not to *cover* twentieth century literature but to introduce it.

Fourteen important writers are included in the course: poets T. S. Eliot, William Butler Yeats, Robert Frost, and Elizabeth Bishop; fiction writers Ernest Hemingway, Virginia Woolf, William Faulkner, Eudora Welty, Peter Taylor, Alice Walker, Nadine Gordimer, Philip Roth, and Toni Morrison; and nonfiction writer Malcolm X. We have also tried to introduce major trends of modern literature and their relationship to developments in other arts, philosophy, science, and world history.

We have, however, excluded so many other important twentieth-century writers: W. H. Auden, James Baldwin, John Barth, Saul Bellow, Willa Cather, Ralph Ellison, F. Scott Fitzgerald, Ford Madox Ford, Langston Hughes, James Joyce, Maxine Hong Kingston, D. H. Lawrence, Doris Lessing, Robert Lowell, Bernard Malamud, Flannery O'Connor, Eugene O'Neill, Harold Pinter, Sylvia Plath, Ezra Pound, Thomas Pynchon, Adrienne Rich, George Bernard Shaw, Gertrude Stein, John Steinbeck, Wallace Stevens, Dylan Thomas, Anne Tyler, Tennessee Williams, William Carlos Williams, Richard Wright . . . and obviously the list goes on and on. In the concluding chapter of this Study Guide you will find an optional assignment that encourages you to read and respond to a recent work of literature *not* included in the course. We sincerely hope that your study of modern literature will inspire you to go on and read more poems, novels, short stories, autobiographies, essays, and plays.

The course material is divided into two major sections: Part I explores major figures of the first part of the century, roughly 1900-1944; Part II examines topics, issues, and trends facing important writers after World War II. Together these sections suggest the varied and rich nature of twentieth-century literature.

For many students, literature can seem intimidating. "I've always hated English, especially poetry." "I think you need a Ph.D. to figure that writer out." "English professors are weirdos who like tearing apart poems and finding hidden meanings and symbols." "Modern literature is always depressing, with characters killing themselves or going insane and talking nonsense." "I liked the book until I had to write a term paper about it." So remarked some introductory literature students on a college campus.

These views often change. Because literature deals with issues such as marriage and divorce, illness, parenthood, war, crime, religion, sexuality, loneliness, and suicide, it can touch readers in a personal way that goes well beyond college requirements, credits, and grades. Reading literature becomes for many students an adventure; literary analysis, a form of discovery. As modern poet Ezra Pound observed in his essay "How to Read," "Literature is *news* that stays *news*."

COURSE COMPONENTS

This course will ask you to read, to listen, and to write. The descriptions below explain the purpose of each component of *Introduction to Modern English and American Literature II*.

Study Guide

The Study Guide provides a general introduction to literature, a brief introduction to the two major sections of the course (Literature 1900-1944; Literature 1945-Present), chronologies indicating key developments in world history and the arts, twelve chapters on each of the major writers/issues of the course, and a concluding chapter containing a reading list of contemporary works and an optional assignment.

Each unit (e.g., Robert Frost) begins by listing the reading and listening assignment and providing a brief overview summarizing the unit's major points. The chapter continues with a biographical sketch of the writer or writers, critical comments on the assigned reading, a bibliography of relevant secondary works, and the written assignment.

Following the conclusion to the Study Guide, you will find a Glossary of Literary Terms. The glossary includes stylistic terms such as **alliteration** or **villanelle** and thematic terms such as **modernism** or **romanticism**. These definitions are included in order to clarify references in the Study Guide or audio programs and in order to acquaint you with terms you may need to use in your own written analyses of literary texts. Note: Terms that are defined in the Glossary are written in **boldface** type when they are mentioned in your Study Guide. You may also find it helpful to consult the glossary included in *Modern Poems*, one of the textbooks for the course (see Literary Texts below).

The final section of the Study Guide is an Anthology designed specifically for this course. It includes the assigned reading for the Contemporary Southern Writers unit (stories/essays by Eudora Welty,

Peter Taylor, Alice Walker) and a few poems by Yeats, Frost, and Bishop not included in *Modern Poems*.

Several faculty members contributed to the design of this course and to the Study Guide; additional scholars and writers from all over the country participated in the twelve audio programs. At the back of the Study Guide you will find photographs and brief descriptions of these contributors.

Audio Programs

The twelve 30-minute audio programs, produced with funding from the Annenberg/CPB Project, are an integral part of the course, providing an additional dimension to the study of literature. Through lecture, discussion, and reading, these programs are designed to help you appreciate modern literature, to encounter a variety of techniques and viewpoints, and to share in the excitement of the college experience.

The many literary scholars you will hear are included not to impress or intimidate you, but rather to enable you to profit from both their expertise and enthusiasm, Some, like James Merrill and Rosellen Brown, are writers commenting about fellow writers. Others are professors of English at the University of Wisconsin, Yale University, Vassar College, Rice University, and many other universities throughout the United States. These scholars and writers have one thing in common: they love literature.

We hope these programs will help make the literature come alive for you.

Literary Texts

The core of Introduction to Modern English and American Literature II: The Twentieth Century is not the audio programs, nor is it the Study Guide. It is the literature itself. In addition to the Anthology included as part of the Study Guide, you will need the following texts:

Three Famous Short Novels, by William Faulkner (New York: Vintage, 1958).

Modern Poems, ed. Richard Ellmann and Robert O'Clair (New York: Norton, 1976).

July's People, by Nadine Gordimer (New York: Penguin, 1981).

In Our Time, by Ernest Hemingway (New York: Scribners, 1987).

The Autobiography of Malcolm X, by Malcolm X (New York: Ballantine, 1986).

Song of Solomon, by Toni Morrison (New York: Signet/New American Library, 1978).

The Ghost Writer, by Philip Roth (New York: Fawcett, 1982).

To the Lighthouse, by Virginia Woolf (San Diego: Harcourt Brace Jovanovich, 1964).

Each Study Guide unit includes a reading assignment from one of these texts and/or from the Anthology. You also will need a good college dictionary to look up all new words you encounter in your reading.

RECOMMENDED PROCEDURE

Since this course has both audio and print materials, a natural question is where to begin: with the Study Guide chapter, the audio program, or the literature itself. In some instances, the comments in the Study Guide and audio programs deal directly with the endings of assigned poems, short stories, and novels. In other words, if you read the Study Guide chapter or listen to the audio program first, you will know in advance whether a character marries, commits suicide or murder, or becomes a hero or heroine. Why spoil the plot in this way when suspense, uncertainty, and involvement with fictional characters are part of the joy of reading?

It is our feeling that you should first encounter a work of literature without preconceptions--fresh, in your own way. Then you can add to that original response the insight you gain from further study and from encountering the ideas of others. We thus recommend the following procedure for this course:

1. If you are beginning a section (Part I or II), **read the introductory material in the Study Guide** and consult the **Chronology** in order to get a sense of the important historical, social, and cultural movements of the time.

2. For each unit, **note the reading/listening assignment and unit overview** in the Study Guide.

3. Before reading the rest of the Study Guide chapter, **read the assigned literature yourself**. As you read on your own, try to

absorb and respond to the ideas, emotions, and vision of the writer. You may wish to make note of questions and problems you have as you read. If you are reading poetry, you may wish to **consult the annotations in** *Modern Poems*. Whether reading poetry or prose, **have a dictionary handy** to look up unfamiliar words or words used in unusual ways.

4. **Read the entire Study Guide unit.** You may wish to **consult the Glossary** for help with literary terms. Glance at the written assignment questions at the end of the Study Guide unit so you can keep these in mind while listening to the audio program.

5. **Listen to the audio program.** The purpose of the audio program is to highlight, clarify, and expand on the main points of the unit and to make the writers and their works more real. You may find it helpful to take notes as you listen and, if you are listening to the program on your own cassette player, to stop the tape, rewind, and listen again to important or difficult sections before proceeding.

6. **Complete the written assignment.** In order to answer the questions well, you will need to reread the literary texts, looking carefully for specific details to use as you develop your essays. After benefiting from the Study Guide chapter and audio program, you will probably be able to reread the material with increased understanding and appreciation.

7. (optional) **Consult the bibliography** at the end of the Study Guide chapter if you need additional information about a writer or work. *Caution*: Secondary reading is not required and should in no instance be a substitute for your own careful reading. If you do consult outside sources and use this information in your written assignment, be sure to footnote all material carefully.

8. (optional) **Complete the optional written assignment** at the end of the concluding chapter. This assignment gives you a chance to read and respond to a recent literary work not included in the course.

This list of steps is one suggested order; you are welcome to use the audio and print materials in whatever way works the best for you.

We hope that the combination of Study Guide, audio programs, and literary texts will provide you with an exciting introduction to English and American literature of the twentieth century.

PART I

1900-1944

PART I: 1900-1944

The years 1900-1944 saw major changes in all areas of human life: in politics, philosophy and religion, science and technology, economics, social trends, and the arts. The Chronology highlights some of these important developments.

Two world wars (World War I, 1914-1918; World War II, 1939-1945) scarred the first half of the twentieth century. These international conflicts stood as glaring indicators that all was not well, and that the world was in danger of fragmentation or even extinction.

Sometimes called the Great War, World War I began with German submarine attacks on Atlantic shipping but evolved into large-scale warfare among many nations of the world. The Allied Powers (France, Great Britain, and Russia, later joined by Japan, Italy, and the U.S.) battled the Central Powers (Germany, Austria-Hungary, and Turkey) on land, in the sea, and, for the first time, in the sky as well. Technological advances made World War I a war of a very different sort, with fighter aircraft, machine guns, submarines, poison gas, and bombing.

Many Europeans and Americans who fought in World War I began with lofty ideals and a sense that they were involved in a holy, righteous mission to stop German expansion. As with all wars, though, millions of innocent men and women lost their lives for the sake of ideological differences. Great Britain in particular was hard hit: over a million young British soldiers died in World War I, wiping out the intelligence and creativity of nearly an entire generation. In addition, Britain faced huge war debts and declining international prestige. A war that initially seemed a noble and heroic effort came to be viewed as an incomprehensible tragedy.

The works of American, English, and other European writers captured this disillusionment, terror, and lost innocence. A world torn apart by war and dissension seemed to negate romantic notions of a divine presence, a kindly Mother Nature, heroic honor, and shared communal values. Instead of writing romantic lyrics about his worship of Nature, as Wordsworth had done, World War I poet and victim Wilfred Owen (1893-1918) described the sight of a dead soldier:

In all my dreams, before my helpless sight,
He plunges at me, guttering, choking, drowning.

If in some smothering dream you too could pace
Behind the wagon that we flung him in,
And watch the white eyes writhing in his face,
His hanging face, like a devil's sick of sin;
If you could hear, at every jolt, the blood
Come gargling from the froth-corrupted lungs
Obscene as cancer, bitter as the cud
     Of vile, incurable sores on innocent
  tongues,--
My friend, you would not tell with such high zest
To children ardent for some desperate glory,
The old Lie: *Dulce et decorum est*
Pro patria mori. [It is sweet and proper
to die for one's country.]
"Dulce Et Decorum Est," 1917

Three years later Ezra Pound looked back at the millions of slain men and women and concluded cynically that they had died "For an old bitch gone in the teeth,/ For a botched civilization." ("There Died a Myriad," 1920). The war triggered for many individuals a profound spiritual crisis--a loss of faith in any institution, country, or belief. "We are the lost generation," wrote expatriate novelist Gertrude Stein.

Although many people had entered World War I hoping it would be "the war to end all wars," it was not. Disputes over national boundaries, economic markets, and ideologies continued, finally erupting in World War II. Germany attacked Poland in 1939; Japan battled China, established troops in Southeast Asia, and bombed the U.S. Pacific fleet in Pearl Harbor. War broke out throughout the world--Paris, London, Stalingrad, North Africa, on tropical Pacific islands such as Iwo Jima and Okinawa, and elsewhere. The success of D-day and other Allied operations in Europe ended the war with Germany; the U.S. bombing of Hiroshima and Nagasaki (August 1945) ended war with Japan. The atomic bombs that annihilated the two Japanese communities provided an ominous warning of where the world could be heading. What might a World War III be like?

This strife-ridden climate profoundly affected writers of the first half of the century. Traditional forms, plots, characters, and styles seemed anachronistic, or out of date, in a world torn into pieces. If the greed for power in so-called Christian nations could result in so much killing, why have faith in Christianity or in any religion? If political dictators could convince masses of people to sanction unconscionable acts--as with Hitler's horrifying murder of millions of Jews--why believe in government? If scientific exploration only led to the invention of new and more destructive weaponry, why believe in progress or education? If fortunes could be lost overnight, as they were in the U.S. Stock Market Crash (1929) and Depression, why believe in capitalism or the American Dream?

A tone of cynicism and despair pervades much of the literature of these decades. "I grow old. I grow old," bemoans Eliot's Prufrock, ". . . It is impossible to say just what I mean." "Innocence is drowned," observes William Butler Yeats, and he asks of the frightening future, "What rough beast . . . slouches toward Bethlehem to be born?" "It isn't fun any more. Not any of it," comments Hemingway's Nick Adams. "Life is too much like a pathless wood," remarks Robert Frost in "Birches." "There was no beauty anywhere. . . . Nothing seemed to have merged," concludes Virginia Woolf's Mrs. Ramsay. In "The Bear" Faulkner notes that "We were all born lost" and have been "dispossessed of Eden."

The literature you will read in this first part of the course is often labeled "modernist" to suggest its reaction against the traditional values and visions of the nineteenth century. By the outbreak of World War I, **modernism** was a recognized and self-conscious movement. The war added to the modernists' sense that they had departed from Victorian security into an uncharted world. There had never been anything on the universal scale of World War I to mark and underline what had already been taking place in the minds of various artists and thinkers for some time--the realization that many of the securest assumptions of the nineteenth century no longer held.

Although the six writers included in Part I reflect the general despair of their era, each writer also achieves a means of coping with or overcoming this gloom. Modernism attempted to find new values, new definitions, new solutions. Running through works of the time is the hope that art can replace both religion and society as the source of our ultimate values. For if art itself cannot change the world, it can alter the ways in which we understand it.

Modernist writers sought new ways to create order out of the chaos surrounding them. Poets T. S. Eliot, William Butler Yeats, and Robert Frost all explored earlier traditions in search of new understanding. Eliot focused on the literary tradition, filling his poems with allusions to Shakespeare, Milton, Dante, and many other writers. Yeats turned to the myths and fairy tales of his native Ireland for inspiration, while Frost drew from the down-to-earth sayings and customs of New Englanders. Fiction writers Hemingway, Woolf, and Faulkner experimented with new styles of storytelling, character-ization, and description in an attempt to capture "reality" more accurately. Hemingway altered fiction by adopting a reporter's objective tone and by relying on dialogue and carefully selected images to reveal his characters' emotional states. Woolf, reflecting the growth of the women's movement, expanded fiction to include the unique perspective, language, and thought processes of each gender. Faulkner sought understanding of the present American South by turning to its past, examining the effect of heredity, traditions, and environment on a character's behavior. Together these six major writers illustrate the struggles and triumphs of modernism.

CHRONOLOGY

FOR

PART I

Part I
CHRONOLOGY 1900-1945

	COURSE LITERATURE	THE OTHER ARTS	SCIENCE & TECHNOLOGY	WORLD HISTORY
1900	Yeats, "Lake Isle of Innisfree" (1892)	Debussy, *Nocturnes* Mahler, *Fourth Symphony* Rachmaninov, *Second Piano Concerto* Monet, *Waterloo Bridge*	Freud, *Interpretation of Dreams* Planck, quantum theory Wright brothers, first successful airplane flight First transatlantic radio	Theodore Roosevelt administration (1901-1909) Queen Victoria dies (1901); replaced by King Edward VII Boer War Boxer Rebellion U.S. Steel becomes first billion-dollar corporation
1905		Schoenberg, *Kammersymphonie* First music broadcast Bartok, *First Quartet* Picasso, *Les Demoiselles d'Avignon* Matisse, *Le Luxe* Frank Lloyd Wright, Robie House	Peary visits North Pole Development of novacaine Congress passes Pure Food and Drugs Act	San Francisco earthquake/fire U.S. restriction of Japanese immigration
1910	Frost, "Mending Wall"; "After Apple-Picking"	Stravinsky, *The Rite of Spring* Woolworth Building Ziegfeld Follies Strauss, *Der Rosenkavalier* Sibelius, *Fourth Symphony*	Einstein, special relativity theory Model "T" Ford produced Rutherford creates a model of the atom Bohr identifies electron orbits	Woodrow Wilson's Administration (1913-21) World War I (1914-17) Titanic sinks Panama Canal opens Suffragette demonstration in London
1915	Frost, "Birches"; "The Road Not Taken"; "Out,Out—" Yeats, "The Wild Swans at Coole," "Easter 1916" Eliot, "The Love Song of J. Alfred Prufrock"	Matisse, lithographs Tiffany patents stained glass lampshade Bartok, *Piano Sonatina*	Auto assembly lines Morgan, theory of the gene	U.S. enters World War I (1917) Margaret Sanger arrested for opening birth control clinic Treaty of Versailles Bolshevik Revolution

Year	Literature	Arts	Science & Technology	History
1920	Frost, "Stopping by Woods on a Snowy Evening"; Yeats, "The Second Coming"; Hemingway, *In Our Time*	Schoenberg, *Suite for Piano*; Gershwin, *Rhapsody in Blue*; Holst, *The Planets*	Banting isolates insulin; Oehmichen develops helicopter; King Tut's tomb discoverd; First commercial radio broadcasts	Harding's administration (1921-23); Irish Free State established; League of Nations forms; Prohibition begins in U.S.; U.S. women win suffrage
1925	Frost, "Acquainted with the Night"; Yeats, "Sailing to Byzantium"; "Among Schoolchildren"; Woolf, *To the Lighthouse*	Copland, *Piano Concerto*; Ravel, *Bolero*; Miro, *The Hair*; First Mickey Mouse cartoon	Regular TV broadcasts begin in U.S.; Scopes trial: creation vs. evolution; Lindbergh flight; Eastman develops color motion picture	Stalin begins 5-Year Plan; Coolidge administration (1923-29); Stock Market crash (1929)
1930		Rockefeller Center, Empire State Building; Mondrian, *Composition with Red, Blue & Yellow*; Grant Woods, *American Gothic*; "Star Spangled Banner" becomes national anthem; Prokofiev, *Fourth Symphony*	Transatlantic telephone; Earhart flies Atlantic; Lawrence invents cyclotron	U.S. Depression (1929-33); Hoover administration (1929-33); Inauguration of FDR (1933-45); Hitler comes to power
1935	Frost, "Design"; "Desert Places"; Yeats, "The Circus Animals' Desertion"	Frank Lloyd Wright, *Falling Water House*; Picasso, *Guernica*; Dali, *Premonition of the Civil War*; Gershwin, *Porgy & Bess*; Calder, mobile sculptures	Regular air service; Carlson completes xerox machine; Carothers develops nylon; First artificial heart; Golden Gate Bridge	FDR & New Deal era; Spanish Civil War; World War II begins (1939-45); Hindenburg dirigible crashes; Stalin's purge trials
1940	Faulkner, *The Bear*; Welty, "Petrified Man" (included in Part II)	National Gallery of Art opens in Washington, DC; Grandma Moses, New England Primitives; Movies: *Fantasia, Casablanca, Gone with the Wind*; Shostakovich, *Seventh Symphony*; Ansel Adams, *Moonrise*	Atomic fission demonstrated; Penicillin discovered; Computer technology developed	U.S. enters WWII after bombing of Pearl Harbor; FDR inaugurated for 3rd term; meets with Churchill & Stalin; D-Day invasion of Western Europe

Unit 1

T. S. Eliot

and an Introduction to Modernism

READING

"The Love Song of J. Alfred Prufrock," in *Modern Poems*

"Reading Poems," in *Modern Poems*, pages xxvii-xlviii, lxv-lxix

LISTENING

Audio Program 1, with Terrence Doody and Cyrena Pondrom   (See Notes on Contributors for a description of each participant.)

OVERVIEW

This unit introduces modernist art as an attempt to describe and interpret a world no longer ordered or connected. "The Love Song of J. Alfred Prufrock" illustrates T. S. Eliot's poetic theories: his avoidance of direct emotional address, his use of the past to understand the present, and his reliance on juxtaposition, allusion, and startling imagery to capture life's

11

complexity. Prufrock is an anti-hero whose inability to express himself captures the alienation and despair of early twentieth-century society.

T. S. ELIOT (1888-1965): A BIOGRAPHICAL SKETCH

T. S. Eliot was born Thomas Stearns Eliot in St. Louis, Missouri. After graduation from Harvard in 1910, he studied abroad and lectured on philosophy. He settled in England in 1915. While working as a bank clerk, he began polishing his first volume of poems, *Prufrock and Other Observations*. This collection was published in 1917 with the encouragement of poet Ezra Pound. A second volume, called *Poems*, was printed in 1919 by Leonard and Virginia Woolf at the Hogarth Press. At this point Eliot became committed to a vocation as a writer and critic.

Fascination with the British church and state--and the long traditions behind them--led Eliot to declare himself a British subject in 1927. Increasingly Eliot's creative writing and critical essays looked back at earlier traditions and what he saw as more noble eras. Modern life seemed sordid and trivial compared to previous epochs; modern men and women lacked grandeur compared to the heroes and heroines of other times. Eliot writes unflatteringly in his poem "The Hollow Men":

> We are the hollow men
> We are the stuffed men
> Leaning together
> Headpiece filled with straw . . .

Eliot saw the task of the artist to recover a sense of heroism and purpose, to draw from and synthesize the writings of the past in order to create a new way of viewing the present.

Eliot's early poetry, including his masterpiece *The Waste Land* (1922), makes extensive use of allusions, quotations in foreign languages, songs, and references to myths and historic events. These characteristics gained for Eliot the reputation of a "difficult" poet--one whose works were accessible only to a literary elite. Eliot himself seemed to cultivate a sense of distance from his readers, refusing to offer guidance. In 1929 at a meeting of the Oxford Poetry Club, an undergraduate student asked Eliot, the guest of honor, "Please, sir, what do you mean by the line, 'Lady, three white leopards sat under a juniper-tree'?" Replied Eliot, "I mean, 'Lady, three white leopards sat under a juniper-tree.'"

In later poems and plays, Eliot became more traditional in viewpoint, expressing his deep faith in the Anglican church and its continuing relevance to postwar society. Eliot declared himself "Anglo-Catholic in religion, royalist in politics, and classicist in literature." Later works by Eliot include the poems "Ash Wednesday" and *Four Quartets* and verse dramas such as

Murder in the Cathedral and *The Cocktail Party*. Eliot was awarded the Nobel Prize for Literature in 1948 in recognition of his status as a major poet and commentator of the twentieth century.

When Eliot was born in 1885, Queen Victoria was on the throne and electricity was a novel invention; when he died in 1965, the space age had begun, President Kennedy had been assassinated, and American troops were entering Vietnam. T. S. Eliot captures in his long life and varied works the enormous complexity of this time period. An American-born British subject who quotes foreign writers, Eliot demonstrates the cosmopolitan nature of modernism. He also illustrates both the radical and reactionary nature of modern art. Eliot is **avant-garde** in his experimentation with radically new styles of expression, yet conservative in his turning to the past as a reaction against modern chaos.

ELIOT'S POETIC THEORIES

T. S. Eliot wrote numerous critical works explaining the methods he adopted in his poetry. In his famous essay of 1920, "Tradition and the Individual Talent," perhaps still the most influential statement on modernist poetry, Eliot says:

> . . . the mind of the mature poet differs from that of the immature one not precisely in any valuation of 'personality,' not being necessarily more interesting, or having 'more to say,' but rather by being a more finely perfected medium in which special, or very varied, feelings are at liberty to enter into new combinations.

The mind of the poet is a space in which emotions and ideas meet. The poet acts, Eliot says, like a catalyst in a chemical reaction. Eliot notes that when a filament of platinum is present, hydrogen and sulphur dioxide combine to form sulphurous acid. Though the platinum remains unchanged and the acid contains no part of it, the reaction cannot occur without it:

> The mind of the poet is the shred of platinum. It may partly or exclusively operate upon the experience of the man himself; but, the more perfect the artist, *the more completely separate in him will be the man who suffers and the mind which creates,* the more perfectly will the mind digest and transmute the passions which are its material.

In other words, the poet is *not* trying to *express self*. The poet is, it is fairer to say, trying to make poetry. And the poet prepares for this task, Eliot says in the essay, by studying the whole preceding tradition to discover how the past affects the poet and where the new poems fit in the tradition. Poetry therefore requires scholarship, and this is one obvious source of its difficulty for the reader who may not have read and studied as much as the poet has.

Note in the Eliot section of your *Modern Poems* anthology how much space must be devoted to footnotes and explanations; publications such as *The Reader's Guide to T. S. Eliot* similarly try to provide an "answer key" for confused readers.

Eliot, then, rejects the romantic poets' insistence that poetry should be "the spontaneous overflow of powerful feelings" (Wordsworth, *Preface to Lyrical Ballads*, 1798) or the record of personal thoughts and experiences. In direct contrast, Eliot writes, "Poetry is not a turning loose of emotion, but an escape from emotion; it is not the expression of personality, but an escape from personality. . . . What happens [to the poet] is a continual surrender of himself as he is at the moment to something which is more valuable." Instead of subjectivity, Eliot calls for poets to take a more objective stance, to negate self, and to write in a highly studied and complex language.

What Eliot terms his method of "Impersonal Poetry" is perhaps his most radical departure from the way in which we have been accustomed to think of the poet's practice. Yet it is a theory or method that nearly all of the great modernist writers came to embrace for themselves, in one way or another, and clearly one of the reasons we find modernist writing so difficult to read: the poets are not *talking* to us in the way we talk to one another; they are *writing* poetry that attempts to comprehend a world no longer easy to understand. As Eliot says in another essay:

> We can only say that it appears likely that poets in our civilization, as it exists at present, must be *difficult*. Our civilization comprehends great variety and complexity, and this variety and complexity, playing upon a refined sensibility, must produce various and complex results. The poet must become more and more comprehensive, more allusive, more indirect, in order to force, to dislocate if necessary, language into his meaning.

Poetry is thus deliberately difficult, complex, and allusive as a way of accurately reflecting the modern world.

Yet even Eliot admitted that a poem could be appreciated on some level without extensive research. In his essay "The Use of Poetry and the Use of Criticism," Eliot confesses that even "seasoned readers" can enjoy poetry without fully comprehending every reference at first. "I know that some of the poetry to which I am first devoted is poetry which I did not understand at first reading; some is poetry which I am not sure I understand yet. . . ." One begins with reading and simple response, then moves to a more mature understanding of a writer's vision through careful study and thought.

T. S. Eliot

"THE LOVE SONG OF J. ALFRED PRUFROCK"

Although "The Love Song of J. Alfred Prufrock" was not published until 1917, Eliot had begun work on it in as early as 1910. The poem remains one of Eliot's most widely read pieces--what some have called "everybody's favorite hard modern poem." The character of Prufrock still moves us today as he gives utterance to the hopelessness and isolation of the modern world.

Prufrock is a figure who symbolizes the lack of continuity on every level. He no longer feels that time flows smoothly from the past through the present to the future. He feels another discontinuity between his intentions and his actions and between his actions and their meaning. And finally he feels discontinuous with his own society, trapped in an isolation he cannot escape and paralyzed by his inability to improve his situation.

For Prufrock, discontinuity from the past is a burden and source of anxiety. Instead of feeling a sense of liberation--freedom from old beliefs, old rules, old thoughts--Prufrock experiences despair and confusion. Life has no clear purpose or ground for hope.

As discussed in Audio Program 1, "The Love Song of J. Alfred Prufrock," despite its title, is neither a song nor an account of love. The title is but one instance of the **irony** (see Glossary) Eliot employs throughout the poem to make us see Prufrock not as a hero but as a failed and failing human being.

Prufrock begins his "Love Song" as though he is going to make a journey. "Let us go then, you and I," he says. But he ends by going nowhere, trapped by the realization of his own paralysis and fear that life is death. He excuses his inaction, first, by saying, "For I have known them all already, known them all," by which he implies he has no need to act in any case. So he does nothing, as though he is caught between a past that leads nowhere and a future which never arrives; and he implies as well that the future somehow comes *before* the past. There is, in a sense, no *present* in this poem, no movement that flows naturally from one moment to the next, from any cause to any effect, from a past that has a useful meaning toward a future that holds promise.

Without a sense of time related to an order of cause and effect, Prufrock has great difficulty connecting his intentions to his actions, or his actions to any clear meaning. Late in the poem he asks, "Do I dare to eat a peach?" It is a question he never answers or quite explains. Earlier, however, he has asked, "Do I dare/Disturb the universe?" If his question about peach-eating is supposed to suggest the timidity of a man who has measured out his life with coffee spoons, how does he think he can "disturb the universe"? He says very forcefully, "No! I am not Prince Hamlet, nor was meant to be," clearly recognizing his lack of traditional heroic status. But he says it in a way that suggests he may have thought at one time he was like Hamlet, or somebody

15

mistook him for Hamlet, which seems preposterous. This illustrates his disproportionate sense of self. Prufrock is an **anti-hero** (see Glossary). Rather than being a larger-than-life hero who performs grand tasks or has extraordinary insight, Prufrock is a man who cannot distinguish between petty and important concerns; he seems impotent to change himself or his world.

Prufrock is not a man of action, of even the smallest actions, but one who takes comfort in knowing that there will be

> Time for you and time for me
> And time yet for a hundred indecisions,
> And for a hundred visions and revisions,
> Before the taking of a toast and tea.

The third line of this passage is another signal moment of his lack of proportion or connection. "Indecisions" suggests the opposite of the unspoken "decisions"; but "visions and revisions" are not connected in that same way. A vision is usually a significant moment of great illumination that often has a religious or metaphysical aspect to it; revisions, on the other hand, are small changes we make, usually in something we have written. "To revise" in no way means "to re-envision." And Prufrock is trapped once again in an empty space where nothing connects, nothing happens, nothing makes much sense.

But his most obvious and painful **discontinuity** is from his society. In the first line, it is not clear to whom he is talking, if to anyone at all; the rest of the poem suggests that he is really talking to himself because there is no evidence that his previous attempts at communication have been successful. In fact, the rest of the poem often indicates that contacts with other people have been painful, humiliating failures:

> And I have known the eyes already, known them all--
> The eyes that fix you in a formulated phrase,
> And when I am formulated, sprawling on a pin
> When I am pinned and wriggling on the wall,
> Then how should I begin
> To spit out all the butt-ends of my days and ways?
>   And how should I presume?
> (ll. 55-61)

He is afraid of women who do not understand him, afraid of revealing his bald spot and his thinness, of eating peaches, of growing old, of life itself, apparently. With great despair, he concludes, "I should have been a pair of ragged claws/Scuttling across the floors of silent seas." (ll. 73-74).

The whole poem is constructed as an **interior monologue**, or a speech by a single character to himself. Unlike earlier dramatic monologues by Robert Browning and others, we have no sense here of a listener, an audience, or an exact point in time. Some readers see Prufrock's reference to "you and I" as his address to parts of himself--one part wanting to act; the other holding him back--rather than to another human being. Prufrock seems unable to communicate his thoughts to anyone: "It is impossible to say just what I mean!"

Prufrock, however, is not inarticulate; he is even quite eloquent and insightful in defining his predicament, and the style of his speech is worth noting. In the first place, it is fragmentary: like his sense of time, nothing he says quite follows from anything else. The first verse paragraph and the final twenty-one lines are strongly rooted in place: they begin his journey and then suggest he has realized its failure and his own disconnection. So much of the middle, however, is arbitrary. Even the order of "There will be time" and "I have known them all already" could be reversed without destroying the sense that Prufrock chooses perpetual delay in the wake of failure, that he does not want to get to his destination, that linear time no longer makes sense in his life. There is also the suggestion in the poem's middle that there are other voices that we hear. Are we sure that Prufrock himself utters the famous, oblique, and haunting couplet: "In the room the women come and go/Talking of Michelangelo"? Or is it an echo of something he has heard? And do lines 15 to 22, about the yellow fog, sound like anything else he says, when everything else he says sounds so conversational? Does the whole poem sound anything like a love song?

Prufrock rises to his greatest eloquence in the passage that begins "No, I am not Prince Hamlet," where the **rhymes** become tight, subtle, and suave. He is most lyrical and longing in the final lines that describe the mermaids who sang to the heroic Ulysses. Ulysses could face his life, accomplish his ends, and even willingly accept danger in listening to their siren song: but anti-hero Prufrock says:

> I have heard the mermaids singing each to each
> I do not think that they will sing to me.
>
> I have seen them riding seaward on the waves
> Combing the white hair of the waves blown back
> When the wind blows the water white and black
>
> We have lingered in the chambers of the sea
> By sea-girls wreathed with seaweed red and brown
> Till human voices wake us, and we drown.

Reality, he admits, is too much not only for him but for "us." Our life is a kind of lethargy or death because significant action is unobtainable, isolation impossible to overcome, and love and human connection almost unimaginable.

Prufrock focuses on himself--his thoughts, sufferings, longings--rather than accomplishing the "extinction of personality" Eliot believed a poet needed in order to write literature of value. According to Eliot's definition, then, we might call Prufrock an immature poet. He *is* trying to express himself; he *is* trying to unite his suffering and his understanding. This alone distinguishes him from Eliot, who insists as a poet on not presenting us with his autobiographical experience. Eliot wants for himself the kind of discontinuity that Prufrock finds so painful and defeating; he wants to be liberated from his personal past so that he can use the greater past of historical literary tradition in order to write.

In "The Love Song of J. Alfred Prufrock," we do not hear the direct voice of T. S. Eliot, as we hear Wordsworth in "Tintern Abbey" or Frost in "Stopping by Woods on a Snowy Evening." We enter directly into the mind of Prufrock and must distinguish carefully between his outlook and that of his creator. Eliot was only twenty-five when he wrote most of this poem, but he chose for poetic reasons to adopt the **persona** (see Glossary) of an aging man.

The style of "The Love Song of J. Alfred Prufrock" thus illustrates some of the principles discussed above under "Eliot's Poetic Theories." It is impersonal, discontinuous, and difficult. The poem opens with a quotation in Italian from Dante, sending most of us immediately to the explanatory footnote below, and continues with references to the Bible, Shakespeare, Hesiod, Marvell, and other voices from the past. A further source of "difficulty"--which Eliot considered an essential feature of modern poetry--is the fractured time sequence. We feel that many lines could be rearranged or reversed, since we do not seem to progress from one point to another.

Instead of intervening in the poem as a guide or authority, Eliot stands back and lets his character speak. Instead of providing an artificial order to Prufrock's thoughts, Eliot simply juxtaposes them. **Juxtaposition** means placing one thing next to another, without any necessary relationship. We are used to thinking in a linear, temporal sequence: first A happened, which caused B to happen, and then C. In Eliot's poetry, D or L could just as well come before A.

This arrangement by juxtaposition is another factor that makes modernist poetry hard to read, but it is not a feature uncommon to contemporary life. Scan the front page of any newspaper, and try to see what order exists from left to right. Walk an inner-city street. Flip the television from one station to the next. Punch the buttons on a car radio. Watch commercials. Look through a magazine, which some of us read from back to front. How do you coherently order any of these phenomena? How do we read our own nightly dreams? In some ways, reality may be closer to what we find in modern poetry than to the comforting, ordered vision of earlier times.

"Juxtaposition" is a positive alternative to the term "discontinuity." It suggests that the poet at least is responding to the various and complex stimuli of the modern world in an honest way. And for the readers, juxtaposition can be a liberating perspective allowing us to see the modern world with new energy, new insight. In doing this, we do not have to see ourselves in Prufrock exactly, although many of us have and will. Instead, we can identify with Eliot, who grapples with what is painful, maybe incomprehensible, and certainly difficult. Perhaps this willingness to struggle gives us the strength to cope with ourselves and the complexities of our world.

BIBLIOGRAPHY

(Note: These secondary sources are listed in case you wish to read more about Eliot and his poetry. **Secondary reading in no way should substitute for your own careful reading of the poetry, however.** If you do consult other sources, be sure to acknowledge and document any ideas you draw from them in your written assignment.)

Matthiessen, Francis O. *The Achievement of T. S. Eliot: An Essay on the Nature of Poetry*. New York: Oxford University Press, 1958.

Spender, Stephen. *T. S. Eliot*. New York: Viking, 1976.

Williamson, George. *A Reader's Guide to T. S. Eliot: A Poem-by-Poem Analysis*. New York: Farrar, Straus and Giroux, 1953.

WRITTEN ASSIGNMENT 1

Complete both Part I and Part II.

Part I: Short Answer

Answer all three of the following exercises.

1. Read the discussion of "denotation" and "connotation" in the Glossary of this Study Guide and the one in the beginning of *Modern Poems*. Then write a few sentences discussing the **connotations** of *two* of the following words and images:

    a. ragged claws

    b. yellow fog

    c. mermaids

    d. butt-ends of my days

2. **Setting** is important in establishing the mood of the poem and revealing Prufrock's state of mind. Write one-to-two paragraphs

discussing the setting established in lines 1-23. What month is it? time of day? weather? Where is Prufrock--in the country or the city? What kind of mood does Eliot create through his choice of setting? What does the setting reveal about Prufrock?

3. Read the discussion of **allusion**, **simile**, **metaphor**, and **personification** in your Glossary and in *Modern Poems*. Find one example of each in "Prufrock." Quote each example and discuss how it adds to Eliot's characterization of Prufrock.

Part II: Essay

Choose *two* of the questions below and answer each in approximately one-to-two pages.

4. A hero is a man endowed with great courage and stength, celebrated for his bold, daring exploits and special achievements. Discuss how Prufrock fits the definition of an **anti-hero**. What examples do you find in the poem that suggest he is the opposite of a traditional hero?

5. Eliot claimed in an essay that good modern poetry should be difficult, requiring a reader to study. Discuss your own reaction to "Prufrock." Did you find it difficult? If so, why? What questions does Eliot leave unanswered? To what extent do you identify with Prufrock and his dilemma? Explain why you consider studying the poem rewarding or frustrating.

6. Audio Program 1 contrasts nineteenth-and twentieth-century music and poetry. The program opens with Chopin's piano music and excerpts from nineteenth-century poets Wordsworth, Longfellow, and Whitman. It then moves to readings from Eliot's "Prufrock," accompanied by dissonant modern music lacking harmony, structure, or resolution. The Study Guide provides a visual illustration of the difference between the two centuries: see the contrast between Figure 1 and Figures 2 and 3 in the Introduction.

Use these contrasts as a foundation for discussing how "Prufrock" is "modern." Is the poem distinctly different from the first poems on the program? How does it resemble the examples of modern music and painting? What clues do we have that this poem was written in 1917 rather than 1817?

Unit
2

Ernest
Hemingway

READING

Ernest Hemingway, *In Our Time*

LISTENING

Audio Program 2, with Jay Clayton and David Wyatt

OVERVIEW

The short-story collection *In Our Time* illustrates Hemingway's distinctive prose style and controversial code of masculine behavior. Through dialogue, compressed description, and short, understated sentences, Hemingway chronicles Nick Adams's growth to manhood. Nick Adams learns discipline, courage, and emotional restraint as a strategy for coping with the troubled, war-torn world around him.

ERNEST HEMINGWAY (1899-1961): A BIOGRAPHICAL SKETCH

Ernest Hemingway, the son of a cultivated mother and a well-to-do doctor, was born in Oak Park, Illinois, a middle-class suburb of Chicago. He lived the kind of ideal American boyhood that the painter

Norman Rockwell once depicted. Hemingway was popular, handsome, and smart; he played football in high school, engaged in amateur boxing, and took fishing trips in the backwoods of northern Michigan. He also wrote articles for the school newspaper, played the cello in the school orchestra, and attended concerts and plays with his mother.

Although he refused to go to college, he landed a job as a cub reporter on the Kansas City *Star* when he was only eighteen. His experience with newspaper writing was to become one of the first major influences on his fiction. He learned to write a clear, direct, uncluttered style that emphasized facts rather than interpretations and that avoided unnecessary adjectives. Reporting on the police beat in a large American city, he also came into close contact with the underside of life.

With the outbreak of World War I, Hemingway found himself unable to enlist for active duty because of an eye condition, but he volunteered as an ambulance driver and served in Italy. His career was short but glorious. Three weeks after his arrival at the front, he was badly wounded while saving another man's life. He later claimed to be the first American injured in Italy, and he was decorated by the Italian government. While he was recovering in an Italian hospital, he met and fell in love with a nurse who became the model for Catherine in his novel *A Farewell to Arms*.

His return to the United States in 1919 left him uncertain about his future, even though he had initially been greeted with a hero's welcome. His aimlessness may well have given him insight into the characters that populate some of the stories in the middle part of *In Our Time*. He worked for a while for the Toronto *Star* and married the first of what were to be four wives, Hadley Richardson. Soon, however, he returned to Europe, this time to Paris, armed with a letter of introduction to Gertrude Stein, whose literary salons formed the center of an impressive and increasingly celebrated group of artists, writers, and expatriate intellectuals.

Hemingway's goal, by this time, had become clear: he wanted to be a writer. He supported himself by composing occasional articles for the Toronto newspapers and taking other journalism jobs, but he saved his best, most disciplined efforts for fiction. He lived among the expatriate population of Paris, meeting frequently with some of the most famous artists, poets, novelists, composers, and intellectuals of his day. His acquaintances included Ezra Pound, Ford Madox Ford, and F. Scott Fitzgerald, who had already become famous by this time. They spent long afternoons in cafés, bookstores, and Stein's salons; they affected an alienated, world-weary pose, as people who had seen the end of an era in World War I and who did not like what was developing in the new world led by the United States. Hemingway himself, however, was anything but world-weary. He was convinced of his genius; he had great energy and an almost ruthless concentration; and he had the rare ability to locate and seize precisely what was needed for his artistic growth. By the age of twenty-four he had already published his first major book, the collection of short stories *In Our Time* (1924).

Out of this period came Hemingway's best work. Two years after *In Our Time* he published one of his finest novels, *The Sun Also Rises* (1926). This story of the carefree café society in Paris and of the bull ring in Spain achieved immediate popular and critical success. *A Farewell to Arms* (1929) followed three years later, another excellent novel that reached a wide readership. After these books, however, his fiction began to decline, and *For Whom the Bell Tolls* (1940) lacks the power and authenticity of the earlier works, even though it was more popular still. Aside from some nonfiction, only *The Old Man and the Sea*, for which he received the Pulitzer Prize in 1953, and parts of two posthumous novels, *Islands in the Stream* (1970) and *The Garden of Eden* (1984), lived up to the potential of his early work.

Out of this early period also came the famous Hemingway **persona**, appearing in all his books, which is the secret of his greatness as well as the ultimate limitation of his art. Hemingway was the first of the modern writers to use his personal life almost as an extension of his writing. Over the years a legend built up around him, a legend that he cultivated and helped publicize. He was known as a boxer, an expert fly fisherman, a big-game hunter, an unerring shot, a bull ring aficionado (fan), and a ladies' man. These occupations were, of course, the subject matter of his fiction, so readers were never able to tell where the glamorous life left off and the art began. Eventually, Hemingway himself may not have been able to tell either. Near the end of his life, the public image seemed to subsume both the man and the writer. He came to believe in his own legend, to imitate his own fiction in his life. But in the process he became immensely famous. His works were monumental best sellers; he had his picture on the cover of *Time* magazine; *Life* did picture stories of him big-game hunting in Africa and fishing for marlin off Cuba; he was a close associate of John F. Kennedy; his novels were turned into successful movies; and he was awarded the Nobel Prize for literature in 1954.

One might almost say that the public Hemingway succeeded too well. Because he felt he had to live up to his well-known image, he let his life harden into a set of postures. His writing, too, acquired a certain falsity. It was almost as if he had begun to imitate himself, to try to recapture his past successes. Always a competitive man, he could not bear to observe his own decline, which by the fifties was beginning to affect his health as well. He suffered from an emotional breakdown that required hospitalization. His death was as violent as the life he led and wrote about. On Sunday morning, July 2, 1961, he shot himself in the head with a shotgun.

HEMINGWAY'S STORIES: *IN OUR TIME*

In Our Time is both an autobiographical work and the record of a turbulent era in the twentieth century. Like much modern literature, large historical events and political changes are focused through the lens of an immediate, personal story. This story is the tale of Nick Adams, who grows up with the century and who suffers through many of the century's most terrifying events.

The book forms a unity, even though it is divided into a number of stories and vignettes, which at times seem unconnected to one another. But the unity of the collection can best be perceived by viewing the bewildering array of people, settings, and times as forming a composite portrait of Nick Adams. We might divide the work into three sections. Section One might be called "The Development of the Hemingway Code." These stories about Nick's childhood, adolescence, and departure from home give us a glimpse into the forces that led Nick to create a code of behavior that emphasized discipline, practical skills, an abhorrence of sentimentality, and a refusal to cheapen one's feelings by talking about them. This code defined courage as grace under pressure and honor as facing up to the hard truths about the meaninglessness of life. These stories, unlike later works by Hemingway, present this code in a critical light; they see it not as an ideal mode of behavior but as a defensive and even desperate way of dealing with the almost overwhelming pain of life in our time.

Audio Program 2 discusses the origin of the Hemingway code in the traumatic events of "Indian Camp." Nick's brutal awakening to the way life leads to death led him to forge a mode of behavior that would allow him to deal with painful experiences. Later stories in this section deal with the way Nick refines this mode of behavior. The end of the next story, "The Doctor and the Doctor's Wife," shows Nick ready to retreat from engagement with life, to go with his father to a secluded place in the woods where they can be beyond the touch of unpleasantness and humiliation. "The Three Day Blow," like "The End of Something" (discussed in the audio program), presents Nick as an adolescent. But Nick is still not ready to assume the responsibilities of life. He hates giving up a certain kind of freedom.

He doesn't want to wear socks; he doesn't want the summer to end; and he still doesn't want to commit himself to a serious relationship with a woman. His inability to commit himself stems ultimately from his fear that relationships will not work out. He has had a taste of what endings are like, of what full, committed love can lead to, and it scares him.

The italicized vignettes that introduce each story all date from the time of World War I, and they show the horror and brutality of the world where Nick is growing up. They set a tone of foreboding and form an adult context for the stories about the problems of boyhood and adolescence. If they do not justify Nick's defensive behavior, they at least show the painful possibilities of the world he is defending against. Underlying everything, according to these interchapters, is the horror of a civilization falling apart, the senseless violence and death of a world at war.

In Section Two of the book, which we might call "The Breakdown of Values," we see the meaninglessness and loss of values that Hemingway's code of behavior is meant to defend against. The first thing that every reader notices about the stories in this section is that Nick has disappeared from them. The careful reader also notices that Nick reappears in interchapter VI. As Nick and the stories approach the time of World War I, Nick is absorbed into historical events that are beyond his control. He becomes anonymous, another faceless figure in the chaos, and his disappearance from the book symbolizes his helplessness about his own life. His individual story becomes lost in the vortex of history, and as a unique character Nick is lost too. He shows up only as one of the almost anonymous figures in the italicized passages. In turn, the characters such as Krebs or Mr. and Mrs. Elliot that we meet in the stories in this section can be seen as surrogates for Nick. They are alternative lives for Nick, visions of what his adult life might become in this time of crudity, failure, loss of will, ugliness, and corruption. The main stories and the italicized vignettes seem almost interchangeable now. We meet gangsters from the roaring twenties, revolutionaries, untalented matadors, and bored expatriates. No one seems to possess any of the grace--the skill and courage under pressure--that the Hemingway code has relied upon as a defense.

Section Three, which we might call "The Recovery," gives us back Nick as our central focus. Nick has been injured spiritually as well as physically during the war years, just as society has. The concluding stories of the book show Nick making a slow, cautious recovery, pulling himself back together by means of a more rigid adherence to the code than any we have seen before. "Cross-Country Snow" announces his return, and the story seems to renew the preoccupations of the early stories as well. Once again, we see two young men out in nature, having a conversation about one of their relationships with a woman. But this time there is a difference--the stakes have been raised. Rather than being burdened by a relationship with a teenage girl, Nick now feels pinned down by a woman who is bearing his child. The callousness of the code shows up, once again, in the way Nick seems to see this woman only as an impediment, something that might prevent him from going skiing again in the future. Regardles of how we view Nick's position, we know now why he needs this defense; we have seen what a world without some code of behavior looks like.

The final two stories, the classic "Big Two-Hearted River" Parts I-II, expose once and for all the compensatory, defensive nature of Hemingway's celebrated code. These beautiful, soothing stories represent a form of therapy for Nick, a slow recovery from events that have burnt out his life as completely as the forest fire has scorched the hillside near the stream.

Hemingway's fiction has given us an enduring myth of masculinity and a legacy of pure, direct prose that has often been imitated but never equaled. In his early fiction, and above all, in the stories that make up *In Our Time*, he understood the limits of his myth and his style, and they became all the more powerful for that understanding. As readers, we must be critical too. In today's world, only the reader who can see through the code--acknowledge its flaws but also recognize what made it seem necessary at the time--only such a reader can be said to have learned the lesson of Hemingway's best fiction.

BIBLIOGRAPHY

Baker, Carlos. *Ernest Hemingway: A Life Story*. New York: Scribner's, 1969.

_____. *Hemingway: The Writer as Artist*. Princeton, NJ: Princeton University Press, 1972.

Warren, Robert Penn. "Ernest Hemingway." In *Selected Essays*. New York: Vintage, 1958, 80-117.

Wyatt, David. *Prodigal Sons: A Study in Authorship and Authority*. Baltimore: Johns Hopkins University Press, 1980.

WRITTEN ASSIGNMENT 2

Pick *three* questions to answer. Write one or two pages for each.

1. In "The Doctor and the Doctor's Wife," one of the men working for Nick's father accuses him of stealing timber. Nick, who is watching when this happens, sees his father back down. How does Nick react? Contrast his reaction with his mother's. Explain how this scene emphasizes the issues that become important to Nick and his development of the code.

2. Hemingway's story "The Battler" forms a transition between the first section of *In Our Time*, which deals with Nick as a youth, and the second section, which treats the period when Nick has grown to manhood. What lesson does the encounter with the burnt-out boxer teach Nick? Does this help shape the man that Nick will become? Explain.

3. *In Our Time*, with its fragmented, discontinuous structure, is a more experimental work than its straightforward style would seem to suggest. In what ways does this collection reflect the characteristics of the modernist movement discussed in Unit 1? Use specific passages to support your conclusions.

4. Contrast how Krebs and Nick each deal with the return from Europe in the stories "Soldier's Home" and "Big Two-Hearted River" Parts I and II. What point does Hemingway make through this contrast?

5. Hemingway's code of masculine behavior has had a profound effect on American culture. Analyze any two *female* characters in *In Our Time*. How does Hemingway portray the women? How do the men in the stories treat them? As a contemporary reader, what reaction do you have to these characterizations?

6. (*Creative*) Hemingway relies more heavily on dialogue than almost any other fiction writer. The conversations seem "real," although the dialogue is actually more condensed and suggestive than ordinary speech.

   Write one page of dialogue carefully imitating Hemingway's style. You may either pick characters from a Hemingway story and write additional dialogue for them, or create characters of your own. If you feel inspired, also try writing accompanying paragraphs of description (perhaps describing the characters' physical appearance, setting, etc.), again carefully imitating Hemingway's sentence structure and imagery. (Cont'd next page)

After you finish, write a paragraph analyzing the characteristics of Hemingway's style that you attempted to imitate. You might comment on dialogue, sentence structure, use of modifiers, word choice, imagery, and so on.

Unit 3

William Butler Yeats

READING

"Lake Isle of Innisfree," "Wild Swans at Coole," "Easter 1916," "The Second Coming," "Sailing to Byzantium," "Among Schoolchildren," "Crazy Jane Talks with the Bishop," and "The Circus Animals' Desertion" in *Modern Poems*; "Adam's Curse," in the Anthology section of this Study Guide

LISTENING

Audio Program 3, with Terrence Doody and Douglas Archibald

OVERVIEW

Yeats saw himself as a poet who represented the Irish people, their history, folklore, strong oral tradition, and above all, their political struggles with England. Selected poems from 1890 to 1939 reveal Yeats's everchanging approach to art and politics, art and love, art and nature, and art and himself.

WILLIAM BUTLER YEATS (1865-1939): A BIOGRAPHICAL SKETCH

Yeats's father, John Butler Yeats, came from an English family that had been in Ireland for over two hundred years; his mother's family, the Pollexfens, also came from England, but had lived for some generations in Sligo, in western Ireland. The differences between his parents begin to explain Yeats's commitment to reconciling in himself all the oppositions and contradictions that every one of us contains. J. B. Yeats was a painter who taught his son to love poetry and value art above all else. His mother, however, rooted him in the peasant Irish soil. As a child in Sligo, Yeats first heard the stories of the wee folk, the fairies, that interested him all his life and led him to investigate older Gaelic myths as well.

As we hear in Audio Program 3, Yeats's father was also a classical nineteenth-century skeptic and a perfectionist who rarely finished a painting. Yeats himself had a deeply religious sensibility, but found it hard, as his father did, to subscribe to any orthodoxy. He fashioned his own religious system, as he fashioned his own theory of history, out of myth, poetic symbols, and the rituals and practices of occult belief, which he often called "magic." Yeats was a perfectionist; and although he was much more productive than his father, he was never satisfied with what he had done.

At least three other people influenced themes and characteristics of Yeats's poetry: Lady Augusta Gregory, Maud Gonne, and Yeats's wife Georgie Hyde-Lees. Lady Gregory worked with Yeats in his research into Irish folklore, and she helped him to found the Abbey Theater, which Yeats intended to be a *national* theater for his nation of listeners and for which both he and Lady Gregory wrote drama based on native themes and stories. Yeats also intended the Abbey Theater to be, as his poetry was, political.

Some of his early plays were vehicles for Maud Gonne--who was a lifelong political activist on behalf of Irish independence. Yeats supposedly fell in love with Maud at first sight and continued to love her for many years; but she was not romantically interested in him, perhaps because she never understood his poetry. However, she influenced him in two very important ways: she came to embody the beautiful woman that he saw as the symbol and reward of art, and she persuaded him that the cause of the Irish rebels was just. Her importance to Yeats is evident in "Adam's Curse," "Easter 1916," and "Among Schoolchildren."

Yeats remained unmarried until he was fifty-two. In 1917 he married Georgie Hyde-Lees, and the couple had a daughter and son.

Yeats met his wife through their common interest in the occult. On their honeymoon, Mrs. Yeats attempted automatic writing, as if under hypnosis, and she inspired Yeats's long, symbolic prose work, *A Vision*. Shorter poems, such as "The Second Coming," similarly show Yeats's fascination with the occult.

Yeats received from his wife the security and support he needed to continue writing and changing well into his old age. Many of his greatest works came after he had reached sixty. Yeats, who also became a member of the Irish Senate in 1922, often thought of himself as a timid, passive man. But by every standard he remained remarkably energetic and productive until his death in 1939. By then he was the leading poet of his age and had been honored with the Nobel Prize for Literature.

SELECTED POEMS

The reading assignment for this unit asks you to sample poems from various points in Yeats's career, from "The Lake Isle of Innisfree," written in 1890 while Queen Victoria was on the throne, to "The Circus Animals' Desertion," written in 1939 as World War II erupted in Europe. The nine assigned poems share some common characteristics: a concern with Irish culture and politics, a fascination with the relationship between art and life, and an interest in blending autobiographical details with myths and images from the past.

Yeats is not always easy to grasp. He confronts modern life in what Eliot called its "great variety and complexity," and he asks more questions than he answers. Anthologies reprinting his poems (like your *Modern Poems* text) include many footnotes explaining his symbols and allusions.

Although Yeats's poetry may seem difficult, he worked all his life to make his poetic style as simple and as accessible as possible. He wanted above all to make his poetry valuable and useful to his fellow Irishmen. By referring to Irish myths and historical events, Yeats hoped to promote a sense of Irish nationalism that would help the Irish win political independence from England. The best poets, Yeats said, were not "separated individual men" but those who "spoke or tried to speak out of a people to a people."

To reach his Irish readers, Yeats made use not only of Gaelic myths but of traditional song and oratory. Yeats knew the Irish were not a nation of readers, but they did listen to their folk music and the rhetoric of the pulpit and the politician. Taking advantage of this oral tradition, Yeats chose a poetic style sometimes like song, sometimes like conversation. His poetry is intended for the Irish, whether they want it and like it or not.

As discussed in Audio Program 3, Yeats's greatness comes in part from his continual effort to grow as a man and as a poet--to change his views as he matured and adopt new poetic styles. By examining poems written at different times in Yeats's career, the reader can appreciate his search for words, images, and poetic forms to capture an inarticulate, invisible, and intangible dimension of human life.

"The Lake Isle of Innisfree" (1890)

"The Lake Isle of Innisfree" illustrates the romantic characteristics of Yeats's early poems. Like the romantic poets before him, Yeats expresses the longing to escape mundane reality to a glorious realm of the imagination.

The Isle of Innisfree is a real place in northwest Ireland, but Yeats uses it in the poem as a symbolic alternative to the daily world. By describing this journey in terms of future and present--"I *will* arise and go *now*"--Yeats unifies the present with the future and transforms Innisfree into a place of the imagination. He can have bean rows there and bees in his glade and peace. However, "midnight's all a glimmer, and noon a purple glow." These are not attributes of the natural world; they are features of a supernatural, otherworldly realm that exists finally nowhere else but "deep in the heart's core." With Innisfree in his heart, Yeats transcends the world of grey pavements and his daily rounds.

As you listen to this poem read in its entirety in Audio Program 3, you may note another characteristic of Yeats's early poetry: its beauty of sound. Rhyming, end-stopped lines create a sense of harmony--in the second stanza, for instance, we bask in rhymes like "slow"/"glow"; "sings"/"wings." By choosing four- line stanzas with a shorter last line, Yeats stays close to the ballad form of traditional song. A further musical effect comes from Yeats's use of alliteration ("lake water lapping" "hive for the honeybee"). (See Glossary for discussions of **end-stopped lines, ballad, alliteration, rhyme**.) This poem's beautiful sound and evocative mood reinforce the theme: that of the enchantment of an imagined world.

"Adam's Curse" (1902)

For a relatively short poem, "Adam's Curse" contains an unusual number of interrelated themes. The first on Yeats's mind is poetry and the great effort it takes to sound spontaneous and natural. Yet, he complains that the world constituted by "bankers, schoolmasters, and clergymen," all of them "noisy" rather than sweetly articulate, thinks poets are "idlers." Yeats casually links the writing of verse to a traditionally female activity--"stitching and unstitching"--but says it is actually harder than scrubbing pavement or breaking stones.

Secondly, Yeats considers female beauty. Three people figure in the poem--Yeats, Maud Gonne, and a "beautiful mild woman" to whom he and Maud are talking. The beautiful woman tells Yeats that all perfection is difficult and that even a beautiful woman must *labor* to be beautiful.

From this Yeats moves to consider love. He notes that everything worth accomplishing is difficult and that this is the curse placed upon Adam when he was expelled from the Garden. The curse extends to love, and Yeats remarks that lovers who have tried to love according to traditional standards of "courtesy" have also failed and now seem as "idle" as the poets. On this sad note, Yeats then notices the "last embers of daylight die" and, though still a young man, like Prufrock he defines himself and the world as old and waning. The wreckage of time, the loss of hope implicit in the image of the washed-out moon, seems to deprive Yeats even of his powers of speech. He turns to Maud but does not speak out loud; instead he thinks that though he tried to love her "in the high old way of love," he has failed to win her heart. The saddest note in the poem is not that we have to work to achieve anything fine, but that even if we do work, we sometimes fail, even at something so noble and traditionally "selfless" as love, an ideal more difficult than beautiful verse and feminine beauty.

Again, style and theme work together. Yeats chooses *heroic couplets* (see **couplet**) in the "high old way" of past literature, but his use of *near rhyme* (see **rhyme**) in the last stanza of the poem--"strove"/"love"; "grown"/"moon"--echoes the sad, dissonant sentiment of the final lines.

"Easter 1916" (1916)

"Easter 1916," like "Adam's Curse," makes use of autobiographical material concerning Yeats's relationship--or lack thereof--with Maud Gonne, and it records a change in Yeats. In "Easter 1916" we see the effects not of Maud's personal beauty but of her intense devotion to Irish nationalism. Yeats is forced to recognize the heroism and sacrifice of his contemporaries; and he even goes so far as to acknowledge and forgive the "drunken, vainglorious lout,"

Major John MacBride, who married Maud and wronged her. Yeats embraces the cause of those seeking to liberate Ireland from English domination.

The Irish chose to stage an uprising on Easter Sunday, 1916, in order to use the natural symbolism of the spring and the religious symbolism of Easter to signal their rebirth and resurrection. Independence would not come for another six years, but the poem records a turning point in Yeats's perception of the struggle. From the "terror" of the deaths came the "beauty" of a heroic Irish struggle. In short lines and refrains reminiscent of Irish song, Yeats records the fact that all has "changed, changed utterly."

The language of the poem traces Yeats's changing attitude toward the Irish Revolution. Before his conversion to the rebels' side, Yeats has for his countrymen only "polite meaningless words," "mocking tales," and "gibes." He has moreover the sense that Ireland is a place where everyone wears motley, the traditional multicolored costume of the court fool, with cap and bells; in other words, the Irish are not to be taken too seriously. But by the end of the poem, this multicolored motley has become the single color green, which refers to Irish unity, the Irish flag, and the color of the revivifying spring.

Stanza II is a catalogue of the heroes who have sacrificed their lives. In every case, Yeats refers to someone real and lists most of their names in Stanza IV (See your text's notes for their identities). Who they are is not so important to us as what they represent, and again many of them are characterized by their voices or their use of language. "That woman" ruined her sweet, aristocratic voice in shrill political arguments. "This man" kept a school and was a poet. Yeats then mentions even his rival John MacBride; and in an allusion to the notion that Ireland wears the motley of a clown, Yeats praises MacBride for having resigned his part in "the casual comedy." Nothing is casual anymore. The comedy of Ireland's caricature has taken on tragic implications: "Transformed utterly: /A terrible beauty is born."

In Stanza III Yeats turns to embracing the constant change that is at the heart of nature. Yeats seems afraid that too much revolutionary dedication, too great a focus on a single purpose, can turn the human heart to stone and decent people into murderous fanatics. This "stone" would then disrupt the continuous flow of the stream of life that changes "minute by minute." In this stanza the refrain--"Are changed, changed utterly"--is missing, perhaps because Yeats senses that not even a poet can change the deaths of the Easter uprising. The hearts that have turned to stone are no longer living hearts.

In the final and most important stanza, Yeats decides how to define his own role as poet. He can record the heroes, define their achievement, and leave a permanent artistic record of their triumph:

> I write it out in a verse--
> MacDonagh and MacBride
> And Connolly and Pearse
> Now and in time to be,
> Wherever green is worn,
> Are changed, changed utterly:
> A terrible beauty is born.

Yeats is not so naive as to think the changes these sacrificed lives have put in motion are simply beautiful, or anything else simple at all. They are a "terrible beauty"--frightening, awesome, violent, and absolute. The poem itself demonstrates a "terrible beauty" as it turns the names of dead men into pleasing rhymes. The poem's language and imagery echo the contradiction of the **oxymoron** "terrible beauty." Contrast runs throughout the poem, from direct opposites like "shrill" and "sweet," summer and winter, to the more subtle contrasts between sunlight and cloud, horse and rider, sleep and activity, night and death, heaven and poet, passion and confusion. Both stone and stream have several different meanings in Stanza III. All these contrasts illustrate that every action, every sacrifice, is more complex than it appears.

"Wild Swans at Coole" (1917)

Change--in himself, in others, in his world--fascinated Yeats. "Wild Swans at Coole" records his sense at the age of fifty-two that he is now an older man, heavier with cares and sorrows. He returns to a place he visited nineteen years earlier (Lady Gregory's estate, where wild swans swim each year), but now he is aware of his own death, his own mortality. Like Eliot in "Prufrock," Yeats chooses the month of October for "Wild Swans," creating a mood of autumnal decline and decay. "All's changed," notes Yeats, since the lighter days of his youth. Now his "heart is sore." He ends the poem with a question: after he has died (and can no longer see the beautiful, mysterious swans), where will they be? whose eyes will they delight?

Many of us find this poem virtually unequaled for its sheer beauty of sound, imagery, and mood. The poem seems so simple that only a close reading reveals its artistry. Note the sounds, not only the rhyme, but each word in relation to those surrounding it, and how Yeats captures what he hears as well as sees. The few carefully chosen adjectives contribute to the illusion that we look at a succession of photographs. As you listen to it read by professional Irish reader Brian O'Dougherty in Audio Program 3, see what images and moods come to your mind.

"The Second Coming" (1920)

"Easter 1916" records a change in Yeats's political sentiments, and "Wild Swans at Coole" expresses a change in his sense of himself. "The Second Coming" goes even further: drastic change is now a universal phenomenon. Yeats wrote this poem in 1919 in despair, for although World War I had ended, Ireland's own bloody civil conflict was not yet fully resolved. In "The Second Coming" Yeats has a vision, and it is not of one man or of one country but of the whole world. This visionary poem relies more on the practices of oratory, or political speech, than of poetry.

The first stanza is filled with powerful images that suggest humanity and nature are no longer in unison: the animal falcon cannot hear his human trainer, the falconer. But what exactly is the "blood-dimmed tide" and the "ceremony of innocence"? In this poem the vagueness of the phrases gives them a resonance perfectly apt to a speech of prophecy and warning. All we have to know to lament the situation of our world is that "The best lack all conviction, while the worst/Are filled with passionate intensity." If we had not already read "Easter 1916," we might guess that only drunken louts, and not idealistic poets, are interested in politics.

The tone of the opening lines of the second stanza is so different it is jarring: "Surely some revelation is at hand;/Surely the Second Coming is at hand." Yeats is no longer the political orator, but the visionary poet, who feels that the intensity of a moment like this must produce a vision, a reverie. And he is right. He envisions the Second Coming--the Messiah's promised return to earth--but the new shape the Savior takes is not going to comfort orthodox believers. The Second Coming is embodied in something like the ancient body of the Sphinx:

> A shape with lion body and the head of a man
> A gaze blank and pitiless as the sun.
> Is moving its slow thighs

"Is moving its slow thighs" seems to suggest a beast so huge that it has to *move* its thighs deliberately, put itself into motion in the way large trucks grind through their low gears up a hill. And yet, despite this effort, its "gaze blank and pitiless as the sun" contains no self-pity, nor any pity whatsoever for how its arrival will affect humanity.

The result of Yeats's vision is firm knowledge that a new historical cycle has begun. Four thousand years ago, Leda's encounter with the swan began the classical age of pagan Greece. Two thousand years ago, a god in the form of another bird, a dove, addressed another virgin whose offspring ushered in the next two-thousand-year epoch of European Christianity. The "indignant desert birds" in "The Second Coming" are neither Zeus nor the Holy Spirit, but they are birds nonetheless at a moment of critical historical change. Yeats wants us to note that the darkness is no longer empty. He ends with a question for us to answer: "What rough beast" is this? What has "brought round its hour at last" and why is it "slouching towards Bethlehem to be born"? Yeats's vision of the future disturbs us.

Yeats flirts with the idea of violence here because he thought violence was one condition of heroic action. Violence, if it is nothing else, is intense; and we have all seen *beautiful* slow motion explosions and car wrecks. More important, however, is the fact that Yeats does not know exactly what this beast will be or what the next two-thousand-year phase will be like. It will be violent, he is sure; it will be nothing like classical Greece or the early moments of Christian Europe. From his perspective in 1919, the rest of the twentieth century looks bleak. Many of us who read the poem toward the close of the twentieth century--after World War II, the Korean War, the Cold War, the Vietnam War, atomic, hydrogen, and neutron bombing--may feel that history has indeed fulfilled Yeats's vision.

"Sailing to Byzantium" (1927)

If we are living in a world where "things fall apart," as Yeats suggests in "The Second Coming," where do we go? what do we do? In "Sailing to Byzantium," Yeats longs for escape and transcendence, just as he did thirty-seven years earlier in "The Lake Isle of Innisfree."

Byzantium, like Innisfree, is, or was, a real place--Constantinople, which we now call Istanbul. It stands at the border of Western and Eastern Europe, across the Aegean Sea from Greece, and was for Yeats an example of a perfect political order in which the artists worked happily for a society organized around its culture. Yeats idealizes such a place because he is tired of dealing with modern Ireland where no one pays attention to the poets. Again, he is feeling old--"That is no country for old men"--and jealous of the sexual joy of both the young and the animal life that makes the seas "mackerel-crowded." Natural life, or

> Fish, flesh, or fowl, commend all summer long
> Whatever is begotten, born, and dies.

> Caught in that sensual music all neglect
> Monuments of unageing intellect.

Yeats resists death and clearly prefers the realm of permanence and art--"monuments of unageing intellect."

In Stanza II, Yeats says that the only thing an old, scarecrow-like man, "A Tattered coat upon a stick," can do is clap his hands in defiance and sing in *ironic* celebration of its "mortal dress." But singing, the art that always represents for Yeats the whole of poetry, will remind the singer that studying songs as models or "monuments" of the soul's "magnificence" is better than mere song itself. The soul is attached to a body that will die, but it can still celebrate the artistic and cultural symbols it has built against its death. Such a monument is the whole city of Byzantium, so Yeats has sailed away there.

Stanza III records his initiation into this realm, an initiation by fire not unlike the old Christian concept of Purgatory. Because his heart is so "sick with desire/And fastened to a dying animal/It knows not what it is," the only solution is being gathered into "the artifice of eternity," defined here in terms more artistic than spiritual.

> Once out of nature I shall never take
> My bodily form from any natural thing,
> But such a form as Grecian goldsmiths make
> Of hammered gold and gold enamelling.

Yeats wants to take his place not in nature, but in the realm of this imaginary court "upon a golden bough." And instead of attending to "Whatever is begotten, born, and dies," he will attend to what "is past, passing, or to come," a symmetrical phrase which emphasizes the incompleteness and endlessness of the future. In the golden court of the drowsy emperor, nothing much happens, but no one dies.

"Sailing to Byzantium" does more than *talk* about "monuments of unageing intellect"; it becomes one. With this ornate and permanent artistic form, Yeats earns his place at the court of Byzantium. Yeats chooses **ottava rima**, or an eight-line stanza with an intricate rhyme scheme. Both figurative and literal imagery describe the changing human body, the meaning of song, and the contrast between the mortal and the artistic/spiritual worlds. The action within the poem mirrors the theme: fish leaping, souls applauding, goldsmiths hammering. Part of the poem's beauty is the near invisibility of its artistry.

"Among Schoolchildren" (1927)

Written the same year as "Sailing to Byzantium," "Among Schoolchildren" raises similar questions about art and nature, but in a more ambiguous way. This difficult poem epitomizes many of Yeats's concerns and techniques.

"Among Schoolchildren" asks a very basic question: Given the fact that we have to die, is it worth being born and living? In other words, is it worth accepting life, or should we try to escape and transcend it--a possibility Yeats considered seriously in "The Lake Isle of Innisfree" and "Sailing to Byzantium." His answer in "Among Schoolchildren" is indirect. Yeats asks his readers to come up with their own interpretations, a strategy which lets him pose but not necessarily resolve hard problems.

"Among Schoolchildren" has the dramatic quality Yeats learned from his father to prize so highly. For Yeats, "dramatic" means placing one attitude or desire against its opposite. Out of this opposition or conflict comes some basic change, even if it is only a change of mind or mood. But in Yeats, who kept trying to change himself and his style all his life, the change is usually more.

In "Among Schoolchildren," we can see him begin to establish opposing principles immediately. As the "sixty-year-old smiling public man," he has authority as both a famous poet and a senator. The nun is another principle of authority, yet religious and feminine rather than artistic, political, and masculine. Yeats himself is also the opposite of the children, who "stare upon" this old man "in momentary wonder," as if to ask him who he is, what he is doing there, and what being old means.

Between the stanzas of this poem, there is usually a sharp discontinuity of subject. In Stanza II Yeats makes a great jump from the public school room into the privacy of his own mind and all it contains. He moves from the world of external events to the world of dreams, and the Ledaean body he dreams of is Maud Gonne. Yeats's poem "Leda and the Swan" explains this reference: Leda is a mortal woman raped by Zeus in the form of a swan; she gives birth to Helen of Troy: "the face that launched a thousand ships," the beautiful woman over whom the Trojan War was fought. Yeats often thought of Maud Gonne as the reembodiment of Helen of Troy because of her great physical beauty and her political importance, but here he simply remembers a story Maud has told him about her childhood. Yeats in his sixties remembers a moment in his life that happened maybe thirty years before, when Maud reminisced about a moment in her life maybe twenty years before that, when both of them would have been about ten, the age of these schoolchildren. Yeats feels united with Maud across these spans of time, which reminds him of one of Plato's parables. This idea widens the scope of time again, back another 2400 years to a mythic time before Helen and the Trojan War. The drama comes from feeling these disparate things simultaneously, from bringing all these different historical periods to bear on a single, fleeting moment.

"And thinking of that fit of grief or rage," Yeats moves his attention back into the schoolroom. He wonders if the beautiful Maud ever looked as plain as the little girls before him. "Even daughters of the swan" may have looked like ugly ducklings when they were children. But this thought immediately inspires another: "And thereupon my heart is driven wild/She stands before me as a living child." Not often in the canons of English literature are the words "thereupon" and "wild" found in a sentence as short as this. "Thereupon" is formal and precise; "wild," of course, means simply *wild*, and wildness has nothing to do with rhetorical formality or precision. Yeats's need to articulate unutterable passion gives him intensity and power.

Stanza IV records another move in time. The image of Maud as she is now, in her sixties, "floats into the mind." Indirectly, Yeats asks if he now looks as old as Maud does. As a matter of fact, Yeats aged much more gracefully; Maud's face folded into a mass of wrinkles. But before he asks this mundane question, he poses a much more startling one, which some of us may find hard to take seriously. Yeats truly believes that art can affect life; and because it can, he asks himself and us if Maud's looks, which once reminded him of the beauty of Helen of Troy, are now so decrepit because a fifteenth-century Italian painter once painted a version of an aged Helen. In other words, does Maud resemble a painting four hundred years old because both she and the painting are symbolically related to Helen of Troy? Has this Renaissance painter "created" her face as it is now? Has art made life?

In Stanza V Yeats returns to the present. Looking at the children before him, he poses another rhetorical question: would a young mother who has suffered the deep pains of childbirth think the labor worth it if she could see her child's future and old age?

Stanza VI is even more abstract. Yeats considers three very different philosophical explanations of the nature of human life, those from the ancient Greek philosophers Plato, Aristotle, and Pythagoras. But all these philosophers grew old and looked like scarecrows themselves: "Old clothes upon old sticks to scare a bird." So Yeats is suggesting that since age levels us all, he is just as qualified as anyone to offer his own explanation of the meaning of life.

He does this in Stanza VII by referring to "images" and "Presences." Nuns worship the holy figures embodied in bronze or marble statues; mothers worship the perfected images of their children. These images--like his own images of Maud--are perfect idealizations, timeless and beyond humanity, and thus impossible to attain. They remain out of reach and mock our attempts to realize or possess them.

Yeats invokes the "Presences" themselves in Stanza VII but leaves the stanza unresolved; a semicolon connects it with Stanza VIII, where Yeats changes the tone and direction of his address completely. Through the first four stanzas, Yeats has been talking softly to himself, comparing his public life to the life of his imagination, *narrating* what has been happening to him. Stanzas V through VII are more contemplative and also more abstract, as he moves away from what is happening to what it may mean in a larger scheme. Stanza VIII seems *intoned*, as though he has lifted his eyes and arms to the realm of the Presences and has started speaking or praying to them, trying to define an ideal state.

In this ideal state, unity reigns; humanity is not in conflict with itself; wisdom and beauty come effortlessly. Yeats is not sure whether the spiritual is superior to the physical, but he suggests that we cannot have one without the other: the body is necessary to the soul, for without bodily effort we cannot generate imaginative ideals.

The last four lines of "Among Schoolchildren" contain two images occurring throughout Yeats's poetry: the tree and the dance. The great-rooted, blossoming chestnut tree cannot be reduced to being merely its leaf, blossom, or trunk. It is all of these and more, an organic whole greater than any of its parts, or their sum, growing according to its own principle, and seemingly immortal. The dance, in contrast, cannot be abstracted into any immortality whatsoever. For Yeats, dance represents perfectly embodied, perfectly spontaneous art, for dance does not exist without the dancer dancing it. It is the whole body, for Yeats the female body, engaged and even "idealized" in a gesture that cannot be made in any other way. Can we know the dancer apart from her dance? Can we be happy in a situation where body and mind, life and its meaning are divided or conflicted?

Yeats's rhetorical questions ask us, demand us to participate in the poems he writes, the problems he defines. In one sense, reading Yeats is like dancing. Just as the dancer makes the dance, so we as readers make the poem by creating its meaning through an active use of our minds and imaginations. Yeats involves us by sharing the images that flashed through his mind as he visited the schoolroom. With Yeats we contrast senator and nun, age and youth, philosophy and poetry. Yeats closes the poem with an image of unity, then invites us to formulate our own meaning for a world of life and death.

"Crazy Jane Talks with the Bishop" (1933)

Crazy Jane would have no patience at all with the youthful sentimentality of "Adam's Curse" or the hankering after abstract perfection and soul of "Sailing to Byzantium" and "Among Schoolchildren." She is rooted in nature, reality, humanity.

The Bishop embodies the values of orthodox religion, and he counsels Jane, now that she is old and her body dried up, to exchange the values of the flesh for those of the spirit and "Live in a heavenly mansion."

Jane argues back that the distinction between body and soul, mansion and sty, is not so easy to make: "'Fair and foul are near of kin,/And fair needs foul,' I cried." Jane proves her point with one of the basic ironies of the human condition: "But Love has pitched his mansion in/ The place of excrement." Our genital organs serve *both* our need to excrete bodily wastes and the need to express sexual love, a love which inspires some of our highest human aspirations and actually creates life.

The Bishop's "heavenly mansion," like Byzantium, is a house of the pure and the dead, and Jane cannot accept the Bishop's counsel because she is not dead yet. Moreover, she knows we build human triumphs out of and in spite of the inevitability of failure: "For nothing can be sole or whole/ That has not been rent." Crazy Jane rejects the split between body and soul, real and ideal, physical and spiritual that troubled Yeats in so many earlier poems. Yeats captures the informality and directness of his character by having her speak not in ottava rima or heroic couplets, but in short lines resembling nursery rhymes.

'The Circus Animals' Desertion" (1939)

Yeats himself seems to accept Jane's position in "The Circus Animals' Desertion," a self-reflective poem written in the year of his death. Poetry's idealism, Yeats will conclude in this poem, grows out of our fragmentary, desperate human condition.

Yeats begins the poem by complaining about the difficulty of writing. He argues that since he is now only a broken old man, perhaps he has to be satisfied with his heart, with himself; for the customary mythological Irish themes that have served him well all his life have recently lost their savor. He tries to minimize this loss by referring to them *merely* as his "circus animals"; but his disappointment and impotence are nonetheless clear as he goes on in Part II to enumerate them and comment on their insufficiency. His early themes, for instance, have become "Vain gaiety, vain battle, vain repose"; they now seem outdated and an outgrowth of his dissatisfied love life.

The next stanza alludes to Maud Gonne, for whom he wrote *The Countess Cathleen*, a political play, and to the political circumstances in Ireland that made it seem she would lose her soul in fanaticism and hatred. She did not, but Yeats had already concocted a dream that turned "all my thought and love" away from life's realities toward an ideal, unreal world. He mentions in the next stanza a number of dream-figures he wrote about and again accuses himself of being consumed by the dream rather than by what had inspired it: "Players and painted stage took all my love,/And not those things they were emblems of." This is not only an extraordinary honesty on Yeats's part, but an extraordinary, even heroic humility. He admits that all he had devoted himself to in order to fashion one of the great bodies of poetry in the English tradition is folly, failure, and insufficiency, offering him no satisfaction, pride of accomplishment, or relief from the pain of age and impotence.

"Those masterful images" became "complete," he says, because they "Grew in pure mind," where reality could not interfere in any way. But he realizes immediately that they grew in pure mind because they originally came from these facts of life:

> A mound of refuse or the sweepings of a street,
> Old kettles, old bottles, and a broken can,
> Old iron, old bones, old rage, that raving slut
> Who keeps the till.

And rather than accept these facts, Yeats created what he has elsewhere called "the whole phantasmagoria" of his old myths, new heroes, and the image of a united heroic Ireland. We might say that a terrible beauty has been born there but has not yet achieved its maturity or given any final comfort to the man who tried so hard to imagine it into being, and by that imagination to bring about an actual political reality. In other words, he believes he has failed. And to redeem that failure, he must simply begin himself, within himself, to devise a new poetry and construct another sense of transcendence and vision, to build a new ladder.

> Now that my ladder's gone,
> I must lie down where all the ladders start,
> In the foul rag-and-bone shop of the heart.

Artifice will no longer suffice: he must seek the origins of poems.

Yeats spent his entire life defining and redefining what art could and should provide. This late poem offers yet another possibility. As always in Yeats, though, there is no simple answer. If indeed his "ladder's gone," why is he still writing in ottava rima? If his circus animals have deserted him, why is he still writing about them?

Yeats one time summed up all his beliefs with this statement: "Man cannot know the truth, but he can embody it." His great poems record his struggle to reconcile oppositions, to ask troubling questions, to achieve visions that may help us lead our daily lives. The phrase "heroic humility" seems to describe Yeats, both as a poet and as a man. An **oxymoron**, like "cold fire," "terrible beauty," or "tall midget," "heroic humility" is a startling phrase in which the noun and its modifier seem to contradict or oppose each other. Yeats is *humble* in his constant admission of failure and in his refusal to be satisfied with his views, his style, or himself. He is *heroic* in his intense struggle to overcome human limitations, to strive for something ideal, to create affirmation out of failure. Yeats's poetry embodies and reveals a great man. We hope this introduction to a few of his poems will lead you to read the remaining poems in your anthology and then visit the library or bookstore for more.

BIBLIOGRAPHY

Bloom, Harold. *Yeats*. New York: Oxford University Press, 1970.

Jeffares, Alexander N. *A Commentary on the Collected Poems of W. B. Yeats*. Stanford, CA: Stanford University Press, 1968.

Tuohy, Frank. *Yeats*. New York: Macmillan, 1976.

Unterecker, John. *A Reader's Guide to William Butler Yeats*. New York: Noonday Press, 1959.

WRITTEN ASSIGNMENT 3

Complete all three parts of this assignment.

Part I

For each of the four passages below, a) identify the poem and b) write about one paragraph discussing its meaning.

a.   Consume my heart away; sick with desire
      And fastened to a dying animal

It knows not what it is; and gather me
Into the artifice of eternity.

b. Things fall apart; the centre cannot hold;
Mere anarchy is loosed upon the world,
The blood-dimmed tide is loosed, and everywhere
The ceremony of innocence is drowned;

c. "Those breasts are flat and fallen now,
Those veins must soon be dry;
Live in a heavenly mansion,
Not in some foul sty."

d. ... and yet when all is said
It was the dream itself enchanted me:
Character isolated by a deed
To engross the present and dominate memory.
Players and painted stage took all my love,
And not those things that they were emblems of.

Part II

Yeats constantly revised and remade his poetry, approaching the same themes from differing angles and perspectives. Choose any *two* of the following, and answer each in two-to-three pages.

a. Compare/contrast Yeats's approach to artistic vision and the escape from reality it offers in "Sailing to Byzantium" and "The Circus Animals' Desertion."

b. Compare/contrast Yeats's feelings about himself in "The Wild Swans at Coole" and "Among Schoolchildren."

c. Compare/contrast Yeats's approach to politics and his vision of the world's future in "Easter 1916" and "The Second Coming."

(The discussion in Audio Program 3 will help with this question.)

d. Compare/contrast Yeats's approach to women and love in "Adam's Curse" and "Crazy Jane Talks with the Bishop."

Part III

Answer either a or b.

a. [*Creative*] Yeats observes in "Adam's Curse" that one line of poetry may take hours of work. Underlying poems like "The Wild Swans at Coole" or "Sailing to Byzantium" is a skillful devotion to craft. Discover this yourself by writing *one stanza* of poetry using a style Yeats adopts in one of the nine assigned poems: heroic couplets, ottava rima, ballad stanza, etc. Try as closely as you can to imitate the meter and rhyme scheme of this form. You may write your stanza on any topic you choose. If you have trouble beginning, you may use the iambic pentameter line, "The student cried when asked to write in verse." After you finish your stanza, write one or two paragraphs discussing the problems you had when completing this exercise.

b. Some Yeats poems are memorable simply for their sheer beauty. Pick one poem read in Audio Program 3, and write about one page discussing the elements that create its beauty. Think about sound devices like rhythm, rhyme, and alliteration, and visual devices like color and imagery. Be as specific as you can. You may also wish to discuss your personal response to the poem, including the thoughts, moods, and images that come to your mind as you listen to it.

Unit 4

Virginia Woolf

READING

To the Lighthouse

LISTENING

Audio Program 4, with Professors Julie Rivkin and Christine Froula

OVERVIEW

Virginia Woolf's *To the Lighthouse* is an autobiographical novel, a "portrait of the artist as a young woman." The novel's stylistic, structural, and thematic features illustrate Woolf's achievements as a modernist and feminist.

VIRGINIA WOOLF (1882-1941): A BIOGRAPHICAL SKETCH

Virginia Woolf was born Virginia Stephen, daughter of Leslie and Julia Stephen, in London in 1882. Her family was an established presence in the intellectual circles of late Victorian upper-middle-class society. Leslie Stephen, an intellectual and man of letters, had written an important literary history of the eighteenth century, and in the year of his daughter Virginia's birth, was beginning the *Dictionary of National Biography*. (In *To the Lighthouse*, Mr. Ramsay's inability to reach "R," ostensibly a metaphor for a more abstractly defined form of intellectual achievement, reflects the alphabetical nature of Leslie Stephen's progress on the Dictionary: Stephen wrote 378 essays for the Dictionary, but he wasn't able to reach "R" before his energy gave out.) The Stephen household entertained literary visitors with some frequency, and writers like George Meredith and Henry James could be counted among Leslie Stephen's friends. And Leslie Stephen's library, to which his daughter Virginia had free access, was a literary world of its own. But the intellectual legacy bequeathed by her father was a mixed blessing: while his daughter might pour tea for Henry James or read unrestrictedly through his library, Leslie Stephen did not consider giving his daughters a formal education and sending them to the university. In a Victorian household, this privilege was restricted to sons. Virginia Woolf thus felt herself to be both undereducated and intellectually stimulated in her father's household, and this double sense of her own intellectual identity was one she would carry with her throughout her life.

In her earlier years, however, it was her mother rather than her father who was the more important presence, and given the portrait of Julia Stephen (Mrs. Ramsay) that emerges in *To the Lighthouse*, we can easily see the reasons for her centrality. She was a legendary beauty, a splendid mother, a selfless and attentive wife. She, like her husband, had been widowed by the death of an earlier spouse, and she and Leslie Stephen had found comfort for their griefs and new possibilities of love in this second marriage. Virginia was the third child of four born to Julia and Leslie Stephen, but with the children from the earlier marriages, she was part of an expanded family of eight. The childhood world that Virginia Stephen inhabited, shared with siblings and half-siblings, was filled with a joy associated above all with her mother. Happiest of all, according to Woolf's memoirs, were the summers spent in St. Ives, Cornwall, in the house that is the prototype for the one we encounter in *To the Lighthouse*. This world fell apart with the death of Julia Stephen in 1895, and for the young Virginia Stephen this death led to the first of a series of mental breakdowns that were to plague her the rest of her life. Moreover, the Stephen children were to suffer not only the death of their mother, but the transformation of their father into a morose egotist who demanded constant female sympathy and attention from his daughters.

Virginia Stephen lived in the rather gloomy family home in London--her father refused to return to the house in St. Ives after his wife's death--until her father's death in 1904. Then, at her sister Vanessa's urging, the two left Hyde Park and established their own household in the London neighborhood of Bloomsbury. The word itself has come to be associated with a certain literary and artistic circle, one that grew up in this neighborhood in these early years of the twentieth century. Although the Stephen daughters' household provided its earliest London gathering point, the circle actually was made up of the young men their brother Thoby had come to know in his years at Cambridge. The experience of dwelling in this circle was a liberation from the Victorian strictures that had bound the Stephen daughters, and they took pleasure in new unconventionalities and freedoms. It was from among the members of this circle that Vanessa met her husband Clive Bell and that Virginia came to know the man she was to marry, Leonard Woolf. In retrospect, cultural historians have attributed to Bloomsbury a more unified set of views and values that it actually possessed; for Virginia Woolf, it provided an intellectual environment that took her outside the Victorian intellectual world embodied by her father.

Virginia Woolf's literary career might be traced back to the writing projects of her childhood; even in their early years Virginia Stephen was determined to be a writer, just as her sister Vanessa was to be a painter. Woolf's adult career, however, actually began with her work as a reviewer and literary journalist, and the writing of essays and reviews always remained an important part of her literary production. (Her essays have been collected into a four-volume set.) She began writing her first novel at the age of twenty-five, and *The Voyage Out*, as it came to be called, traced the emergence of a young woman from a protective nineteenth-century upbringing into a world of more open conversation and society. The parallels with Virginia Woolf's own social emergence are actually less important than they might be; what is most striking is the appearance of a certain lyrical mode that characterizes Woolf's best fiction. Although in her next novel, *Night and Day*, Virginia Woolf was to retreat to a somewhat more conventional social fiction, the tremendously innovative lyrical mode would emerge again in the novels that followed. With the publication of her fourth and fifth novels, *Mrs. Dalloway* (1925) and *To the Lighthouse* (1927), Virginia Woolf's stature as a major novelist was established; these two, along with *The Waves* (1931) and *Between the Acts* (1941), are regarded as her most important fiction. In her work, Woolf questions and alters all the traditional categories of fiction--plot, character, point of view. Her novels change the very notion of what a novel is.

Any discussion of Woolf as a writer would be incomplete without a discussion of Woolf as a feminist. Her book-length essay *A Room of One's Own* (1929), from which two excerpts are read in Audio Program 4, marks a point of departure for twentieth-century-feminist thought, for in it she confronts directly the social and political forces that have made it so difficult--and at times impossible--for women to write. Her brief biography of a hypothetical "Judith" Shakespeare, sister of the bard, traces the sorry fate of literary genius which resides in a female form. Somewhat less well known, though no less important, is her later essay *Three Guineas* (1939). Written on the brink of the Second World War, it pursues the connections between the political repressiveness of fascism and the oppression of women under patriarchal society.

Virginia Woolf did not survive the war that was to occasion some of her most potent reflections. The mental illness against which Woolf periodically struggled returned in the winter of 1941, caused either by the bombings from the Battle of Britain or the depression that inevitably followed the completion of a novel. This time, she found the prospect of facing the illness unbearable, and in a final act not of madness but of rational resistance to madness, chose instead to take her own life.

TO THE LIGHTHOUSE

Virginia Woolf, in a diary she kept for such reflections, recorded her first thoughts on the work that was to become *To the Lighthouse*:

> But while I try to write, I am making up *To the Lighthouse*--the sea is to be heard all through it. I have an idea I will invent a new name for my books to supplant "novel." A new _____ by Virginia Woolf. But what? Elegy?

Virginia Woolf's sense that what she is writing does not conform to any traditional literary category places her in the company of other modernists. Like Ezra Pound, Woolf found that in order to write she must "make it new." But Virginia Woolf's need to remake the form of the novel reflects her position not only as a modern writer but as a woman writer; she is, in fact, more like her character Lily Briscoe than like Ezra Pound in the sense that what she is doing does not yet have a name.

One name that might be given *To the Lighthouse* is autobiography, and the name is useful as a point of departure. The Ramsay family is based on the Stephen family. Mr. Ramsay is, like his prototype, a famous intellectual and a penetrating thinker, a great patriarchal authority--and a tyrant to his wife and children. And Mrs. Ramsay is drawn from Woolf's memories of her mother, a great beauty and an ideal Victorian wife and mother, generous and self-sacrificing. But Woolf moves this work out of the realm of a straightforward family memoir by including the figure of Lily Briscoe--which is to say the figure of the woman artist. In working out the relation between Lily Briscoe and the Ramsays, Woolf is able to explore the problems a traditional Victorian family poses to the woman artist. Lily's attempt to paint her vision runs counter to the example of both Mrs. Ramsay, who insists that women must marry and have children, and Mr. Ramsay, who restricts the creative and intellectual sphere to his male colleagues and disciples. As compelling as each figure is, to remain under either influence would have silenced or erased the attempts of the woman artist.

A diary entry from 1928 is explicit about the danger posed by the Victorian patriarch Leslie Stephen:

> Father's birthday. He would have been 96, 96, yes, today; and could have been 96, like other people one has known; but was not. His life would have entirely ended mine. What would have happened? No writing, no books--inconceivable.

The threat posed by Leslie Stephen to his daughter Virginia Woolf is mirrored in the third part of the *Lighthouse* where Lily Briscoe finds it impossible to paint in the presence of Mr. Ramsay. Only when Mr. Ramsay turns away from her canvas does Lily Briscoe find her way back to it, back to the vision that she has been attempting to capture.

If the threat presented with Mr. Ramsay may be more overt, no less potent is the danger associated with Julia Stephen/Mrs. Ramsay. In an essay entitled "Professions for Women," Virginia Woolf describes a figure called "the angel in the house." This "intensely sympathetic," "immensely charming" and "utterly unselfish" creature--and her resemblance to Mrs. Ramsay should be noted--is deadly to the woman writer because this is the advice she tenders: "You are writing about a book that has been written by a man. Be sympathetic; be tender; flatter; deceive; use all the arts and wiles of our sex. Never let anybody guess you have a mind of your own. Above all, be pure." Just as the Victorian patriarch would be fatal to the woman writer, so too is the Victorian matriarch. Virginia Woolf must kill the "angel in the house" to survive as a writer.

This emphasis on resistance and struggles to the death may seem odd in a book that is also and so overtly about love. In fact, the first section of the novel could be described as a kind of family idyll, centering on the beloved figure of Mrs. Ramsay. Surrounded by children, guests, admirers, and the difficult figure of her husband, Mrs. Ramsay sits knitting not only a stocking but the entire fabric of a human community. If Mrs. Ramsay tends home and hearth, making the garden grow, worrying about the cost of the greenhouse roof, draping her green shawl over an animal skull, insisting that people must marry, she is able to do so because Mr. Ramsay stands at the periphery, guarding the shore like the lighthouse itself. For Mrs. Ramsay, her husband's stance is the support of male civilization, those "cubes and square roots . . . this iron fabric of the masculine intelligence" that supports and upholds the world to her. The centerpiece of the Ramsay family life--and of Mrs. Ramsay's creative force in particular--is the dinner party scene, where she is to turn an oddly assorted collection of individuals into a whole and a community. Outside there is a world of darkness and fluidity, erosion and death; but for its moment the world of warmth and unity created by Mrs. Ramsay is able to prevail.

In the second section of the novel, the most experimental, this world of warmth and love is exposed in all its fragility. The second section is like the dark interval between the flashes of light emitted by the lighthouse; it is a night between days of summer, a winter between seasons of bounty. In this section, what we think of as the background--the natural setting, the empty house--becomes the foreground. Human events--the death of Mrs. Ramsay, the death of Prue in childbirth, the death of Andrew in the First World War-- become parenthetic. In fact, there is nothing as shocking in the entire book as the death of Mrs. Ramsay reported in parentheses. How could she--in her centrality, her vitality, her mystery--be discarded with so little ceremony? It is important to remember that as much as Mrs. Ramsay is associated with creation and nurturance, she recognized the forces of time and dissolution against which she was working. The image of her green shawl wrapped around the animal skull is significant: the fabric she creates can only conceal death temporarily, not make it disappear. And now, in the second section, Mrs. Ramsay's green shawl unravels to expose the animal skull; there is no human will to resist a natural process of dissolution--or even growth indifferent to human presence. But at the end of this section the house is saved from destruction through the humble efforts of Mrs. McNab and Mrs. Bast, whose task of housekeeping may represent the creative activity of women. Also we might note that it is Lily Briscoe, the woman artist, who wakes at the end of this section ("*The Lighthouse*") and completes the unfinished painting from the first section of the novel. In each of these actions--but particularly in that of Lily Briscoe's painting--there is an image of Virginia Woolf's own writing of this novel, the success of what she referred to in the initial diary entry as her "elegy." The term **elegy**, discussed in Audio Program 4 and in the Glossary, refers to a form that mourns the past but also provides a kind of consolation. In the final section of the novel we feel both the mourning and the consolation: like her character Lily Briscoe,

Virginia Woolf cannot literally bring back the dead, but she can represent her vision of the past, and thus test the ability of her art to make a kind of life. After completing the novel, Virginia Woolf wrote in her diary:

> I used to think of him and mother daily; but writing the *Lighthouse* laid them in my mind. And now he comes back sometimes, but differently. (I believe this to be true --that I was obsessed by them both, unhealthily; and writing of them was a necessary act.)

To the Lighthouse is, of course, not a literal autobiography, but a transformation of her own past into a new fictional turn. Just as Lily Briscoe finds a way of capturing Mrs. Ramsay in the brilliant colors and forms she paints on her canvas, Virginia Woolf develops the new narrative strategies that will allow her to represent her vision. In reading--or rereading--the novel, try to determine what is most distinctive about Woolf's style and form. Notice, for example, what she does with **point of view**; the narrative shifts from one character's perspective to another's, often within a single sentence. What is the effect of this kind of narrative mobility? Why do you think Woolf would need to represent the world from so many characters' points of view? Look also at the ways in which she handles transitions, from one scene to another, one topic of thought to another, one event to another. Look at her sentence structure. What is the purpose of those long sentences? (Woolf had an idea that there was a difference between men's and women's sentence structure.) See how she uses **stream of consciousness** in her narrative. (A "stream of consciousness" narrative represents the unbroken flow of thoughts and associations in someone's mind.) This close study of Virginia Woolf's style and form should allow you to see not only how she translated autobiographical material into fiction, but also how she transformed fiction itself into something extraordinary and new.

BIBLIOGRAPHY

Beja, Morris, ed. *Critical Essays on Virginia Woolf*. Boston: G. K. Hall & Co., 1985.

DiBattista, Maria. *Virginia Woolf's Major Novels: The Fables of Anon*. New Haven: Yale University Press, 1973.

Naremore, James. *The World Without a Self: Virginia Woolf and the Novel*. New Haven: Yale University Press, 1973.

Rose, Phyllis. *Woman of Letters: A Life of Virginia Woolf*. New York: Oxford University Press, 1978.

Virginia Woolf

WRITTEN ASSIGNMENT 4

Write about two pages each for *three* of the following questions.

1. Mrs. Ramsay appears to be extraordinarily preoccupied with marriage. Minta Doyle and Paul Rayley seem to get engaged under her influence. Seeing Lily Briscoe with William Bankes, Mrs. Ramsay is determined that they marry. Why is Mrs. Ramsay so focused on marriage? What do you think the institution represents to her? Do the fates of the various marriages in the novel offer any comment about her conviction? Pay special attention to how Lily Briscoe views Mrs. Ramsay's attitude toward marriage.

2. Examine and comment on the unusual three-part structure of the novel. What is the relationship between the first section and the third? In the second part, which presents a world largely without characters, why does Woolf try to tell the story of an empty house? How does the division into sections emphasize the novel's main ideas?

3. The novel *To the Lighthouse* takes its title from a proposed journey--a journey, of course, to the lighthouse. What is the significance of this journey? Explain why the lighthouse is an important destination. Contrast how different characters see the lighthouse. Is the title related to other ideas in the novel?

4. Analyze the use of color **imagery** in the novel *or* analyze Woolf's use of one recurring pattern of imagery (e.g., trees, flowers, birds, windows, doors, knitting, the sea). How does Woolf use the imagery to develop the novel's themes?

5. Listen carefully to the discussion of women and art in Audio Program 4, including the excerpts from Woolf's *A Room of One's Own*. Analyze Lily's painting. What does Woolf use it to illustrate about the woman artist?

54

Unit 5

Robert Frost

READING

"Mending Wall, "After Apple-Picking," "The Road Not Taken," "Birches," "Stopping by Woods on a Snowy Evening," "Acquainted with the Night," "Desert Places," "Design," in *Modern Poems*; "'Out,Out--'" in Study Guide Anthology

LISTENING

Audio Program 5, with Professors Jay Clayton and David Field

OVERVIEW

Frost became immensely popular for his soothing verse, old-fashioned values, and unmistakably American poetic voice. Yet there is far more to Frost's poetry than simple, homespun wisdom and pleasing rhythms. Frost uses a blend of familiar speech and haunting imagery to capture the painful and confusing divisions, conflicts, and oppositions of modern life.

ROBERT FROST (1874-1963): A BIOGRAPHICAL SKETCH

Robert Frost, the great poet of New England, was born in San Francisco, where he lived until he was eleven years old. His father had moved to the west coast because of his anger at what he viewed as the stubborn orneriness of the New Hampshire country where he had been raised. For the same reason, the poet was named Robert Lee Frost, after the famous Southern general of the Civil War, Robert E. Lee.

Frost's father died in 1885, and the family moved back to New England. There Frost's mother, a cultivated woman who had introduced her son to the poetry of Wordsworth and Emerson, taught school in Massachusetts and New Hampshire. Frost went to Dartmouth, and later, Harvard, where he studied with William James, the founder of the most important philosophical movement that America has yet produced: pragmatism. James's pragmatism, which held that truth is to be measured by practical standards according to what we use it for, played a critical role in shaping Frost's skeptical approach to ultimate values and his commonsense attitude toward unknowable mysteries.

After college, Frost moved to a small farm in New Hampshire, which his grandfather had given him. Here, for ten years, he raised chickens, supplementing his small income by occasionally teaching high school. All the time, however, he was reading voraciously and writing poetry, none of which he could publish. This period was one of frustration not only for Frost but also for his wife, whom he had married shortly after graduating from high school, and their four children. His lack of success weighed heavily on his mind, leading him at times to intense rages and to thoughts of suicide. But this period also made Frost intimate with nature and with the simple hardships and joys of rural life.

In 1912, nearly forty years of age, Frost left New Hampshire and traveled to England. There he met Ezra Pound, one of the expatriate American writers who played such a prominent role in the literature of the early part of the twentieth century. Through Pound, Frost began to achieve some of the success that he had been denied in his native country. It is a sad irony that the most American of all modern poets should have had to go to England to publish his first books. With Pound's assistance, Frost was able to publish two books of poetry, including many of the poems that he had written during the ten frustrating years on his farm in New Hampshire. *A Boy's Will* (1913) and *North of Boston* (1914) contain many of his finest works and made him well known back in America, the country that had formerly spurned his poetry.

Unlike Ezra Pound, T. S. Eliot, Gertrude Stein, and other expatriates, Frost remained fiercely American in his attitudes and loyalties. His growing Americanism was spurred by an article in the *Encyclopedia Brittanica* in 1913 that denounced the American university system for not teaching American literature. Such public advocacy of a position Frost himself had long espoused encouraged the poet to stick to his principles and hope that his native country would one day change. Frost loved the literature of his birthplace, particularly the works of three great nineteenth-century New England authors: Ralph Waldo Emerson, Henry David Thoreau, and Emily Dickinson. The attentive reader can find many signs of their influence in Frost's poetry.

When Frost returned to the United States in 1915, he chose to live once again on a farm in New Hampshire. This choice represented a conscious allegiance to the New England heritage that his father had rejected, a heritage that extended not only to literature but to a distinctive style of life. New Hampshire was the least populous, most backward of all New England States, and many of its farms had been abandoned, turning back into the wilderness from which they had been claimed. The people who survived there were likely to be strong-willed, resilient, independent types--or so Frost portrayed them in his poetry. And Frost attempted to reflect the values of this region, both in the subject matter and in the level-headed simplicity of his style.

He continued to write prolifically and with great success. He increasingly seemed to be a literary conservative, writing traditional verse about old-fashioned values. Perhaps because he was perceived as rejecting the experimentalism and arcane subject matter of much modernist literature, he achieved a wider popular audience than any other twentieth-century poet. He won four Pulitzer prizes; he was invited to teach college at Amherst and Harvard; he was commissioned to read a poem for the inauguration of John F. Kennedy, an honor unprecedented for an American poet in the twentieth century; he became regarded by the public at large as the greatest American poet in our history. Although most of his best work was written before his mid-fifties, Frost lived until he was nearly ninety, churning out poems like butter.

Despite his public success, some critics failed to admire his work, viewing it as technically reactionary and philosophically naive. These critics characterized him as an escapist, who responded to complex problems with simple, homespun wisdom. Frost himself did much to create this image of himself, an image that we have now learned to be utterly false. The poet loved to pose as the cracker barrel philosopher, speaking his homely wisdom to his farmer friends gathered around a potbellied wood stove in a country store. His admirers, too, did much to foster a false image of the poet, emphasizing his sentimental, optimistic, folksy side and ignoring the dark undercurrents that ran through his works.

At Frost's eightieth birthday party in New York City in 1954, a well-known critic, Lionel Trilling, shocked and offended Frost's friends by saying that "Frost was a terrifying poet" and that the "universe Frost conceives is a terrifying universe." Trilling, however, was paying Frost a high compliment. He was saying that Frost was not superficial, that the poet's affirmations of life came in the face of his knowledge of the darkness at the center of the human condition. Frost believed that there was a dark and threatening mystery at the heart of reality, that ultimately we could not comprehend the world. Hence, to get by in life, we must have a faith that can rise above this terror, not ignore it. Poetry, for Frost, was one of our few means of holding back the darkness. A good poem served, in Frost's memorable phrase, as "a momentary stay against confusion." Thus, the poet's choice of a rustic life and the old virtues was not a nostalgic retreat to a Christmas card vision of America, but a grim acknowledgment that the good life is a matter of self-discipline and moral character, that we need one another in order to face the hardships and disappointments of life.

And Frost knew many disappointments in his personal life. Fatherless at the age of eleven, he was unable to find himself until he was nearly forty years old. Throughout his life, he suffered bouts of depression, inner turbulence, and rage, which resulted in occasional cruelty to his wife and family. His first child died at the age of four. His sister, a mentally unstable woman, was arrested in Portland, Maine, by police whom she thought were white slavers; she was placed in a mental institution, which she never left. Frost's daughter died of tuberculosis in her twenties, and a son committed suicide. Frost and his wife had constant fights, many of which he transmuted into some of his most soothing and reassuring poems. Part of his genius was his ability to transform his bitter personal experiences into life-affirming works, which for all their positive strength do not ignore the darkness at their core. At the time of his death, Frost was the most celebrated poet of the twentieth century.

SELECTED POETRY

At first reading, Frost's poems can seem comforting and homey. After all, they give us peaceful rural images--snowy woods, flowers, apple trees--and values from an earlier time. Frost, who remarked that free verse was like playing tennis without a net, uses traditional forms of meter and rhyme that do not shock or grate. Unlike Eliot and Yeats, Frost rarely alludes to the literary tradition, mythology, or world events, choosing instead to focus on the everyday lives and scenes of his fellow New Englanders.

Yet as Professors Jay Clayton and David Field observe in Audio Program 5, there is also a dark, disturbing side of Frost's poetry and a depth of meaning. Because Frost knew pain, frustration, loss, fear, madness, loneliness, and anxiety, he created poems that do not suggest life is easy or simple or without consequences. Images of darkness, night, mystery, tangled undergrowth, death, and longing fill his poetry and provide a contrast to images of neighbors, oaken buckets, apples, horse rides, and children playing.

Audio Program 5 focuses on three of the assigned poems: "The Road Not Taken," "Mending Wall," and "Birches." These three poems reveal Frost's interest in division, whether it occurs between two paths, between two sides of a stone fence, or between life and death. Frost recognized that making choices creates a terrible tension or splitting within us. If we choose one path in a forked road, we cannot go down another. If we build a fence to preserve our privacy and state our boundaries, we shut out fellowship and freedom. If we climb toward heaven and the escape it offers, we may lose sight of earth and its beauties. The nine assigned poems reveal both the familiar, rustic side of Robert Frost and the darker side as well. Frost captures in his work the conflict between the safe, comfortable pleasures of home and the magical allure of the strange, the unfamiliar. Frost associates home with the real, with ordinary, substantial existence, with all that is traditional, ordered, controlled, and bounded. This world can be tolerant of our weaknesses, loving, even embracing, but it also can seem dull and restrictive. In contrast, the alternative to home is not so easy to describe: it is something unreal, dreamy, beyond the ordinary, insubstantial yet strangely appealing. It might be a path less trodden, as in "The Road Not Taken," or the "heaven" described in "Birches" as an escape from the familiar, or the dark, snowy woods described in "Stopping by Woods on a Snowy Evening."

The following brief comments and questions cover the six assigned poems not discussed on the audio program.

"After Apple-Picking"

In this poem, Frost presents a dream world as an alternative to home. This marvelous, mysterious poem is about work and rest, waking and sleeping, reality and dreams. But the categories, as so often in his poetry, cannot be kept distinct. Waking and sleeping merge in this poem: the real is seen as a dream, and dreams are seen as a greater, more mysterious reality. The poet has looked through a pane of ice that he skimmed from the drinking trough early in the morning before going out to work. All through the day he "cannot rub the strangeness from [his] sight" that he got from peering through this distorting glass. Even as he works, he feels as if he is still sleeping, and the wonderfully evocative description of his day's labor, apple picking, takes on the mysterious quality of a dream. By the end of the poem, this sleep of his, "whatever sleep it is," has become a rich metaphor. Sleep, rest, is the reward of work well-done. But the poem refuses to say whether this reward is the final peace that ends all our labors--death--or a briefer respite, a sleep that we shall wake from to work again.

The poem also seems to be about excess: "For I have had too much/Of apple-picking." As when we take too great a helping on our plate and suddenly feel full, the speaker recognizes "I am overtired/Of the harvest I so desired." Overwhelmed by the "ten thousand thousand fruit"--or the great abundance of earth--he feels tempted into a sleep as deep as the woodchuck's hibernation. The autumn harvest time and the speaker's recognition that the picked apples will wind up on the cider-apple heap suggests an awareness of fruition, decay, death.

This awareness is introduced in the very first lines of the poem with such images as heaven, a partially filled barrel, and "winter sleep." The precise meaning of these images is never clarified. Frost creates a dreamy, magical quality by intermingling states like fantasy, sleep, and death that we usually consider sharply defined. Yet Frost's poems are always grounded in concrete reality. What literal explanations are offered for the speaker's confusion?

"Out, Out--"

This poem leads us from its familiar, everyday beginning--the sound of the buzz saw, a boy longing for a break from work, the sister appearing in her apron to announce supper--to a world of pain, terror, and death. Reading the poem is like falling off a cliff, hurtling from familiar, stable ground into a frightening unknown.

Frost uses **personification** to describe the saw, which seems to possess a force or life of its own:

> His sister stood beside them in her apron
> To tell them 'Supper.' At the word, the saw,
> As if to prove saws know what supper is,

60

Leaped out at the boy's hand, or seemed to leap--. . .
Neither refused the meeting.

The poem moves from the homey image of the aproned sister announcing supper to a cannibalistic saw making a meal of the young boy's hand. The "dark of ether" the doctor administers foreshadows the darkness of death soon to follow.

Most frightening of all in the poem is not the accident itself but the coldness of the adult world. Though the boy possesses "a child's heart," he has been given a man's work and denied even "the half hour/ That a boy counts so much when saved from work." Once dead, the boy holds no interest for others:

No more to build on. And they, since they
Were not the one dead, turned to their affairs.

At the beginning of the poem, the boy's "lifted eyes" see the mountain ranges and sunset "far into Vermont," suggesting a world beyond daily drudgery, repetition ("snarled and rattled, snarled and rattled"), and "affairs." Has a part of him been cut off even before the saw takes off his hand? Is the adult world responsible for his death?

The poem's simplicity is deceptive. Frost uses **allusions** differently than Eliot or Yeats, and one can understand this poem without recognizing the source of its title. What do you think it adds to your reading of the poem to know that the title alludes to the brevity of life described in the "Out, out brief candle!/ Life's but a walking shadow . . ." speech from the last act of Shakespeare's *Macbeth*? What is the effect of Frost's shift in imagery from detailed descriptions of the wood and sawdust to bare statements like ". . . that ended it"? How do words like "snarled," "rattled," and "puffed" (defined in your Glossary as examples of **onomatopoeia**) intensify our involvement in the scene Frost describes?

"Stopping by Woods on a Snowy Evening"

This poem is so well-known that the reader's task today is to try to recover the original power that made it famous. At first it can seem just a peaceful, soothing poem about a pretty winter scene, but when read along with other Frost poems it again suggests his fascination with tensions and oppositions: the lure of the lovely, deep woods on "the darkest evening of the year" versus the demands of "promises to keep."

Frost chooses a highly traditional and regular **rhyme** and **meter** in this poem, one similar to nursery rhymes and songs. The rhyming (three rhymed lines in every four line stanza) increases in the last stanza, creating an almost hypnotic effect:

> The woods are lovely, dark and deep
> But I have promises to keep,
> And miles to go before I sleep,
> And miles to go before I sleep.

One one level, Frost captures the desire to stop--to be silent and still in a world of darkness. Yet he also raises questions about life and death, about responsibility and the kind of freedom he describes in his poem "Birches." Do the imagery, almost sing-song rhythm, obvious rhymes, and repeated final lines of "Stopping by Woods on a Snowy Evening" suggest a figurative as well as literal meaning to the poem? How does the sound of the poem draw us into the enchantment of the scene Frost describes?

"Acquainted with the Night"

This time we again follow Frost away from society to something beyond. We move not from village to the countryside, as we did in "Stopping by Woods on a Snowy Evening," but from the city to its dark outskirts.

Frost has known the night, has "outwalked the farthest city light" and the "saddest city lane" to a region that is "unearthly" and "luminary." Like Prufrock, who feels he cannot share his vision with others, Frost stands alone in this poem, unwilling or unable to express himself to another man who is acquainted with the night not for its mystery but for his job:

> I have passed by the watchman on his beat
> And dropped my eyes, unwilling to explain.

The sounds of other human beings--feet, cries--only remind him of his separateness, his aloneness: the sounds "are not to call me back or say good-by." The luminary clock he reaches does not provide either shining light or illumination: it merely "Proclaims the time was neither wrong nor right."

Both the meter and form Frost chooses for this poem heighten its power. The meter is so pronounced and regular that one can almost hear a faint drumbeat accompanying the words. Frost adapts the form of a **sonnet**, a fourteen-line poem traditionally used to express love and generally moving toward a conclusion in the final two lines, or couplet. But just as Prufrock's "Love Song" is neither a song nor a poem about love, so Frost's sonnet describes not love but aloneness, and it builds not to a tidy conclusion but to a sense of void. Frost divides the sonnet into small parts, accentuating the feeling of fragmentation.

"Desert Places"

The poem's title is a metaphor expressing such deep loneliness that only dead weeds and leafless winter trees interrupt the barrenness. The feeling of isolation intensifies as the poem develops. Until halfway through the poem, the sense of loneliness is too vague even to articulate. Yet the featureless landscape will become increasingly empty: ". . . that loneliness/ Will be more lonely ere it will be less." Frost would obviously welcome any representative of the animal world, yet all are hiding from the snow "with no expression."

The last stanza seems deliberately ambiguous. Exactly who are "they"? Despite the bleak surroundings, the speaker indicates that the loneliness comes from within. Does the poem conclude that the painfulness of life makes death a welcome friend? Or is there a hint that familiarity with loneliness strengthens the speaker enough to regard the empty universe without fear? How does Frost use rhyme, meter, and imagery in "Desert Places"? What kind of feeling do the sounds of the poem seem to create? Note the effect of introducing the "stars." Is there a contradiction in the poet's ability to express something beautiful about a landscape with "nothing to express"?

"Design"

In this poem, Frost again chooses the highly traditional form of a sonnet, but uses it here to convey his feelings about both the beauty and the terror of nature.

The first stanza (lines 1-8) describes the scene: a white spider on a heal-all plant holding a dead moth it has caught in its web. Frost sees these three living things as "assorted figures of death and blight"-- like ingredients in a ghoulish witches' brew--but he also uses his poetic powers to see them as forming a beautiful, artistic design: the moth "like a piece of white satin cloth" and its wings "like paper kites"; the spider like "snow-drop"; the flower "like froth."

The last stanza turns away from the objects themselves to questioning their meaning. What has brought them all together? The final couplet answers the question--or does it?

> What but design of darkness to appall?--
> If design govern in a thing so small.

Have the objects "designed," or intended, to form an alliance of white in order to "appall" ("to make pale") the forces of darkness? Or is there any design governing the natural world? Note the many instances of irony, from the "dimpled spider" to the white creatures of death to the "witches' broth" for starting the day "right." The title itself suggests both evil purpose and careful planning to create an artful final product. How do these ironies contribute to the poem's ambiguity? Is design only a product of the poetic imagination, the human mind that can turn a scene of death into an intricate sonnet like this one? Unlike Wordsworth, who sensed a "blessed power" and "divine presence" in "kindly Mother Nature," Frost is never sure what lies behind the natural objects he observes.

Frost remarked, "It's for the world to decide whether you're a poet or not." The world has decided--with four Pulitzer Prizes and many other honors--that he was indeed a poet, perhaps the most popular American poet of the twentieth century. The appeal of Frost's poetry comes not only from its simplicity, ease, and gracefulness, but also from its exploration of life's conflicts, mysteries, and complexities. As Frost noted in his essay "The Figure a Poem Makes," a poem "begins in delight and ends in wisdom."

BIBLIOGRAPHY

Brower, Reuben A. *The Poetry of Robert Frost: Constellations of Intention*. New York: Oxford University Press, 1963.

Cox, James, ed. *Robert Frost: Twentieth Century Views*. New York: Prentice-Hall, 1962.

Poirer, Richard. *Robert Frost: The Work of Knowing*. Oxford: Oxford University Press, 1977.

Trilling, Lionel. "A Speech on Robert Frost: A Cultural Episode." *Partisan Review* 26 (1959): 445-52.

WRITTEN ASSIGNMENT 5

Part I

Identify all of the following passages. For each, write a few sentences explaining what Frost is describing.

a.   He moves in darkness as it seems to me
Not of woods only and the shade of trees.

b.   What brought the kindred spider to that height,
     Then steered the white moth thither in the night?

c.   Were he not gone,
     The woodchuck could say if it's like his
     Long sleep, as I describe it coming on,
     Or just some human sleep.

d.   They cannot scare me with their empty spaces
     Between stars--on stars where no human race is.

e.   Earth's the right place for love:
     I don't know where it's likely to go better.

f.   Then the boy saw all--
     Since he was old enough to know, big boy
     Doing a man's work, though a child at heart--

g.   Oh, I kept the first for another day!
     Yet knowing how way leads on to way,
     I doubted if I should ever come back.

h.   He gives his harness bells a shake
     To ask if there is some mistake.

i.   I have walked out in rain--and back in rain.
     I have outwalked the furthest city light.

Part II

Pick *two* of the following questions and answer each in approximately two pages.

1.   Pick one of the following images--night, trees, snow, ice, sun, boys--and show how Frost uses it in two or more poems.

2.   Listen to the discussion on "The Road Not Taken," "Mending Wall," and "Birches" in the audio program. Pick one of these poems to analyze, commenting on both theme and style. Be specific: look closely at individual words and images.

3.   We learn in the audio program that Professor Jay Clayton was expelled from his high school English class for insisting that T. S. Eliot was a greater poet than the "simple" Robert Frost. Write an essay comparing/contrasting "The Love Song of J. Alfred Prufrock" with a Frost poem [pick one you have not already analyzed for Part II]. What similarities in theme and style do you observe? what important differences? How does your own response to the two poems and poets differ?

UNIT
6

WILLIAM
FAULKNER

READING

William Faulkner, "The Bear," sections 1, 2, 3, and 5

LISTENING

Audio Program 6, with William Andrews and Fred Hobson

OVERVIEW

Faulkner's "The Bear" is an initiation story about a young boy coming of age as the wilderness declines. The novelette illustrates Faulkner's ambivalent attitudes toward modernity and his native South, his skill as a storyteller, and his experimentation with sentence structure to capture the workings of the mind.

WILLIAM FAULKNER (1897-1962): A BIOGRAPHICAL SKETCH

Faulkner grew up in Oxford, Mississippi, a location he later would make the setting of most of his fiction. His family had been prosperous and prominent in the political leadership of his state in the nineteenth century, but by the time Faulkner was born (in 1897) his father's fortune and social influence had been considerably reduced.

The theme of "decline and fall," which is so pronounced in much of his Yoknapatawpha fiction (including "The Bear"), stems partly from Faulkner's knowledge of his own family's experience. In a larger sense, however, by virtue of his growing up a southerner, Faulkner learned to identify with a society that, since Reconstruction, had felt a sense of irretrievable loss, a need to forestall change, and a reverence for traditional values associated with a rural farm culture. That Faulkner identified himself with the South does not mean that he tried to write as a defender of all things southern, however. Those who read "The Bear" in its entirety (including the lengthy and challenging section 4) will discover something of Faulkner's sense of the South's tragic heritage of racial injustice. Sections 1, 2, 3, and 5 of "The Bear," which Faulkner wrote as a coherent, self-contained unit, reveal how Faulkner's modern perspective on a traditional southern hero, Isaac McCaslin, illustrates his ambivalence about the consequences of change in the twentieth-century South.

Faulkner's great theme, as he put it in his own words, is "the problems of the human heart in conflict with itself." Faulkner spent much of his youth grappling with conflicting ambitions and an apparent aimlessness born of an inability to settle on a fulfilling vocation. Bookish as a boy, he quit high school in 1917 before receiving his diploma, hoping to enter World War I as a pilot in the Royal Canadian Flying Corps. When the war ended before he could get overseas, he returned to Oxford and enrolled in the state university, but he completed only a little more than a year of course work. During the 1920s he tried his hand at poetry, with slight success, and worked at several unsatisfying jobs (from postmaster of his hometown to whiskey smuggler in New Orleans) before settling down to write novels. With his third published novel, *Sartoris* (1929), based on the life of his great-grandfather, he "discovered," as he wrote later, "that my own little postage stamp of native soil was worth writing about and that I would never live long enough to exhaust it." Soon Yoknapatawpha novels like *The Sound and the Fury* (1929), *As I Lay Dying* (1930), *Sanctuary* (1931), and *Light in August* (1932) proved not only that Faulkner had an astonishing wealth of southern material to work with, but also that he had an extraordinary capacity to infuse into that material the glory and the pathos of the human condition.

Unfortunately, only rarely did his novels achieve commercial success. Beginning in 1932, under financial pressure, Faulkner made the first of several trips to Hollywood to work as a scriptwriter. During the 1930s and early 1940s, he also cultivated a readership through the writing of short stories for popular magazines. In 1942 "The Bear" first appeared in the *Saturday Evening Post* as essentially a hunting story. Later that year a revised version of "The Bear," lengthened considerably by the insertion of a fourth section, was published in *Go Down, Moses*, a short story collection that Faulkner intended to be read as a novel. Although stories like "The Bear" would eventually add much to his international reputation, in the 1940s Faulkner considered them less important than the novels to which he wanted to devote his sustained attention. But it was only after the prominent critic Malcom Cowley published *The Portable Faulkner* (1946), a one-volume anthology of his work, that the author finally begin to enjoy real public and critical acclaim. In 1947, only three of his novels were in print; three years later Faulkner was awarded the Nobel Prize for Literature. He continued to publish novels in the 1950s, though these are generally not regarded as highly as his earlier work. He died in 1962, barely a month after his novel *The Reivers* closed his career on a comic note. Many consider him to have been America's greatest fiction writer.

"THE BEAR"

"The Bear" takes place in northern Mississippi during the early 1880s in a mythical region Faulkner called Yoknapatawpha County. Yoknapatawapha is a world of immense human variety and deep historical roots. The story of its people and their history dominates more than a dozen of Faulkner's greatest novels, as well as at least a score of his best short stories. The county seat of Yoknapatawpha is a town called Jefferson, which Faulkner patterned after the Mississippi city of Oxford, where he grew up and lived most of his adult life.

The two great themes of "The Bear"--the initiation of a young man and the despoliation of an ancient wilderness--take the reader deeply into some of Faulkner's most characteristic concerns. As a southerner keenly ambivalent about the mixed heritage of the past and the uncertain promise of the future, Faulkner persistently probed the moral and social impact of changes associated with modernity on a people grounded in tradition, the people of Yoknapatawpha. Faulkner summed up his conflicting attitudes toward change during an interview at the University of Virginia. His aim as a student of southern change, he said, was "not to choose sides at all--just to compassionate the good splendid things which change must destroy, the splendid fine things which are part of man's past too, but [which] were obsolete and had to go, [since] no matter how fine anything seems, it can't endure, because once it stops, abandons motion, it is dead."

In "The Bear" we see both sides of Faulkner's attitude toward change. The death of Old Ben, the near-mythic bear, is both right and necessary to the initiation of Isaac McCaslin into a mature awareness of the ways of Nature. By contrast, the violation of the bear's habitat, "the big woods," the beginning of which we witness through McCaslin's eyes at the end of the story, is neither necessary nor justifiable. At the end of "The Bear," Faulkner suggests that because the triumph of modern technology inevitably leads to a collapse of traditional values, we lose our ties to the land and thus our understanding of humanity as part of Nature.

And yet we oversimplify Faulkner's message in "The Bear" if we think that he is just attacking modernization and idealizing the conservation of tradition. In the second paragraph of the story we find that it has been a "fatuous" claim of white and red men for generations to buy and sell "the wilderness," to divide it and bequeath it to their heirs as though it could ever be possessed and controlled by transient people. At the beginning and at the end of "The Bear," Faulkner ridicules this traditional assumption that people can control Nature and transfer it according to their acquisitive whims. Boon Hogganbeck's pathetic warning to Ike in the last scene, "'Don't touch a one of them! They're mine!'" registers the pathetic futility of our claim to ownership of Nature, whether it be an entire wilderness or only a tree full of squirrels. Clearly, as the last section of "The Bear" indicates, modern humanity can lay waste to the land in its insatiable pursuit of profit. The owners of the Memphis lumber company, whose railroads carve a serpentine path through the once-untouched wilderness, understand nothing of the reverence for and humility before Nature that Ike McCaslin learns through his initiation. Nevertheless, although McCaslin can see that the big woods is "doomed" and that his days as a woodsman are numbered, he does not give in to the despair of the uprooted modern individual. As his visionary moment in section 5 of the story demonstrates, McCaslin's faith in the land transcends all the losses he has suffered at the hands of death.

Some students of Faulkner believe that he is most at home in the novel, where his natural inclination seems to take him toward a certain repetitiousness of words and situations, rather than in the short story, where concentration of effect is at a premium. "The Bear" shows that Faulkner can be an effective storyteller in the short form despite his willingness to construct sentences and paragraphs of astounding and sometimes bewildering complexity. What Faulkner's characters do and say do not usually puzzle his readers; it is what the characters think, or rather, *how* they think, that makes them, and Faulkner's intentions in creating them, sometimes difficult to understand. While Faulkner may seem to be a critic of much that modernity signified in the early twentieth century, he was very much a modernist in his interest in human consciousness and in the ways he tried to represent the workings of consciousness in fiction. Because he was a literary modernist, he wanted to be the kind of storyteller who takes his reader inside the minds of his major characters--in this case, Ike McCaslin--so that his reader can experience the story as McCaslin experiences it, processes it, and tries to make sense of it. Faulkner's style takes on a twisted, sprawling quality when his narrator or Ike McCaslin wrestles with feelings and ideas that are themselves difficult to put directly and succinctly in a simple sentence or paragraph. Words, we sometimes feel when we read Faulkner, are as much a barrier to expression as a medium of it.

The most important things he wants to depict in his fiction turn out to be very difficult to sum up; the more Faulkner tries to sum up, the more additional words are needed to represent the thought or feeling completely in all its dynamic complexity. Thus readers who look for something in a Faulkner story that states the message or makes the final point of the story are likely to be frustrated. To read Faulkner in the right spirit, we must recognize that his storytelling takes us deeply into the human predicament, but it does not offer us an escape from it. When we grapple with Faulkner's difficult style, we are confronted with the same type of problem that his greatest characters, like Ike McCaslin, must grapple with in their lives--how to make sense of the apparent chaos of life and our shifting, often contradictory feelings about it. In his storytelling Faulkner tries out many ways of making sense of experience. He challenges his reader to participate in the process of making meaning. What we can learn from his way of telling a story is, if nothing else, how to "compassionate" (in his words) the endless, humbling, but heroic effort of the artist to embody in language the truth of the human experience.

BIBLIOGRAPHY

Blotner, Joseph. *Faulkner: A Biography*. New York: Random House, 1984.

Brooks, Cleanth. *William Faulkner: The Yoknapatawpha Country*. New Haven, CT: Yale University Press, 1963.

Cowley, Malcolm, ed. *The Portable Faulkner*, rev. ed. New York: Viking, 1967.

Millgate, Michael. *The Achievement of William Faulkner*. New York: Random House, 1966.

Minter, David. *William Faulkner: His Life and Work*. Baltimore: Johns Hopkins University Press, 1980.

Taylor, Walter F., Jr. *Faulkner's Search for a South*. Champaign: University of Illinois Press, 1983.

WRITTEN ASSIGNMENT 6

Write two pages on *three* of the following questions.

1. Trace the stages of Ike McCaslin's initiation as a woodsman and a hunter. What does he learn at each stage? What does he have to unlearn? Is his development similar to anything Nick experiences in Hemingway's *In Our Time*?

2. What does the trip that Ike makes to Memphis with Boon Hogganbeck illustrate about Ike's character?

3. The modern world is often described as one that has lost its center, that feels itself fragmented with little sense of purpose for the future or connection with the past. Unlike the nineteenth century, the twentieth century is often depicted in modern literature as having lost its faith in God and Nature as sources of transcendent knowledge. The importance and value of the individual, a cardinal virtue in nineteenth-century thought, becomes extremely doubtful in the twentieth century. Given this context in which Faulkner is writing, why do you think he sets "The Bear" in 1883 instead of in the modern era? How is this related to whatever point or theme you feel Faulkner tries to communicate in this story?

4. Listen to the discussion of Faulkner's style in Audio Program 6, and read the definition of **cumulative sentence** in the Glossary. Find one example of Faulkner's giant cumulative sentences in "The Bear." Quote the sentence (citing the page number in parentheses) and then analyze it carefully. What effect does Faulkner achieve through his use of complex sentence structure?

PART II

1945-Present

Part II: 1945-Present

Enough time has elapsed since the early decades of the twentieth century (1900-1945) to identify the most important literary figures, those whose writing has had a profound and lasting impact on literary history and on the modern world. Eliot, Frost, and Yeats changed poetry; Hemingway, Woolf, and Faulkner changed fiction. Along with James Joyce (not included in this introductory course because his most important works require such extensive study), the six writers included in Part I are undisputably major figures of the literary tradition. Their works form an accepted **canon** of literature taught in colleges and universities throughout the country.

In the second half of the twentieth century, however, the dust has not yet settled. The century is not over, nor can we see clearly which writers and works and stylistic movements will endure. We believe the writers we selected--Eudora Welty, Peter Taylor, Alice Walker, Malcolm X, Nadine Gordimer, Elizabeth Bishop, Toni Morrison, Philip Roth--have made or are continuing to make important contributions to literature, expanding or enriching it through their unique voices. We believe that their works have a relevance not only for our time but for later eras as well. Of course, the history of the arts is filled with examples of geniuses who go unrecognized by their contemporaries or minor figures who attain an unwarranted and fleeting popularity. We can only speculate on what an introductory twentieth-century literature course like this one might include in the twenty-first century, when the turbulent decades of the 1940s, '50s, '60s, '70s, and '80s will be seen at a greater and clearer distance.

The most striking feature of these last four or five decades appears to be diversity. In politics, minorities have demanded and received greater political rights: a widespread civil rights movement has led to gains by American blacks; Native Americans have rejected the label of "American Indian" and demanded a fairer writing of history; women (not a minority but treated as one) have made inroads in almost every profession; gays and lesbians have sought acceptance in a heterosexual society; third world countries have attempted to recapture a cultural identity lost under colonial rule; Jews have transformed Israel into a major power and have fought against an anti-Semitism that did not end with World War II; Asian-Americans have struggled against stereotyping and prejudice.

English and American literature reflects this growing awareness of race, gender, sexual orientation, nationality, religion, and ethnic background. Some of the most powerful writing of the last few decades has come from those men and women who speak for a special group of people, capturing both their uniqueness and universality in such a way that all of us are enriched.

One cannot read Malcolm X without considering his position as a black man in white America, nor can Nadine Gordimer be understood except as a white South African novelist attacking apartheid. Nadine Gordimer, Eudora Welty, Alice Walker, Toni Morrison, and Elizabeth Bishop all seek to capture the thoughts and exeriences of women in their fiction, prose, or poetry. Eudora Welty and Alice Walker, along with Peter Taylor, write with an acute awareness of their southern heritage, while Elizabeth Bishop adopts the perspective of a northeastern American who often saw her country through third-world eyes. Toni Morrison and Alice Walker create fiction that reveals the lives of black women in a white patriarchal society. Philip Roth not only writes but *obsesses* about his position as a Jewish-American writer living in a post-Holocaust world. Any discussion of contemporary literature would be incomplete without an awareness of political and social movements and trends.

Recent writers have reacted against the modernists in a variety of ways: some by returning to traditional storytelling forms and linear plots; others by deliberately choosing more direct, less "difficult" language; others by experimenting with even more cryptic and fantastic approaches than their predecessors; and others by finding humor the only means for coping with a chaotic world. Like the modernists before them, contemporary writers have often rebelled against the "establishment," both literary and political, by breaking down barriers in style and theme. A poet today can write in any conceivable style, from traditional forms to avant-garde free verse to haiku poetry borrowed from non-Western worlds to personal confessions to mystical, symbolic musings. No subject or style is off limits to writers of English and American fiction, and the autobiography and essay are now hailed as imaginative genres with tremendous potential for expression and persuasion. Creators of literature can speak in voices as varied as their backgrounds. Perhaps to a greater extent than ever before, the field of literature stands wide open.

CHRONOLOGY

FOR

PART II

Part II
CHRONOLOGY 1945-1990

	COURSE LITERATURE	THE OTHER ARTS	SCIENCE & TECHNOLOGY	WORLD HISTORY
1945	Welty, "Petrified Man" (1941) Bishop, "Man-Moth"; "The Fish" Taylor, "A Wife of Nashville"	Britten, *Peter Grimes* Matisse, *Dahlias & Pomegranates* Picasso, *Reclining Nude* Pollock, drip painting Snow White film Cage, *Sonatas & Interludes for Prepared Piano*	Jet planes and rockets First computers First supersonic flight First "long-playing" record	Surrender of Germany U.S. atomic bombing of Nagasaki & Hiroshima; Japan surrenders FDR inaugurated for 4th term Death of Roosevelt; Truman Administration (1945-53) Committee on Un-American Activities hunts for Communists Formal U.S. recognition of Israel
1950		Leger's *Still-Life with Knife* Modern Jazz Quartet Theatre of the Absurde Goeritz, *Steel Structure* Safdie, *Habitat*	First hydrogen bomb explosion Beginning of jetliner service Nautilus becomes first atomic submarine	Beginning of Korean War Eisenhower Presidency Segregated education declared unconstitutional McCarthy's list of 205 alleged Communists Malenkov suceeds Stalin in Russia
1955	Bishop, "Over 2,000 Illustrations"; "At the Fishhouses"	Chagall's *The Circus Rider* Elvis Presley Hindemith, *World Harmony* Bernstein, *West Side Story* Wright, Guggenheim Museum	Salk anti-polio vaccine U.S. launches earth satellite; launch of Sputnik I St. Lawrence Seaway opened Antarctica designated scientific preserve	Merger of AFL-CIO Alaska & Hawaii become states Racial crisis at Little Rock, AR Civil rights demonstrations and bus boycotts Khrushchev Premier of USSR
1960		Movies: *Citizen Kane; The Birds* Beatles; Bob Dylan Penderecki, *Lament for the Victims of Hiroshima* "Art of Assemblage" show at Museum of Modern Art	First U.S. manned sub-orbital space flight (John Glenn) Telstar, first private communications satellite China becomes fifth nation with nuclear power Watson & Crick win Nobel Prize for DNA studies	John F. Kennedy elected; assassinated (1963) Peace Corps created Soviet arming of Cuba causes Bay of Pigs crisis Civil rights demonstrations; Martin Luther King receives Nobel Peace Prize U.S. troops in Vietnam Berlin Wall erected

	Literature	Arts	Science	History
1965	*The Autobiography of Malcolm X* Bishop, "Arrival at Santos"; "Sestina"; "First Death in Nova Scotia"; "Questions of Travel" Walker, "Strong Horse Tea"	Lincoln Center (N.Y.) world's largest opera house Warhol's Pop Art The Rolling Stones Movies: *Funny Girl, The Graduate, 2001: A Space Odyssey* Ligeti, *Requiem*; musical minimalism	Moon walk by Neil Armstrong Lasers First heart transplant Astrophysics	U.S. bombing of North Vietnam; anti-war protests Assassination of Malcolm X, Martin Luther King, Robert Kennedy Israeli-Arab Six-Day War Nixon presidency Racial riots in Watts
1970	Walker, "In Search of Our Mothers' Gardens"	Britten, *The Burning Fiery Furnace* Carole King; Stevie Wonder; rock opera *Tommy* Movies: *Fiddler on the Roof, Cabaret, M*A*S*H* Bernstein, *Mass* Babbitt, *Reflections for Piano & Tape*	Preparation for nuclear power plants Ecology movement; growing awareness of pollution problems Atomic Energy Commission prepares nuclear power plants	Indo-Pakistan war Killing of 4 Kent State students by National Guardsman during anti-war protest Watergate hearings lead to resignation of Nixon Ford Presidency War between Israel, Syria, Egypt U.W. Supreme Court legalizes abortion
1975	Toni Morrison, *Song of Solomon* Bishop, "One Art"; "In the Waiting Room"	Movies: *Star Wars, Annie Hall, Apocalypse Now* 4-part TV series, *The Holocaust* Liberman, junk metal sculpture	Legionnaires Disease bacterium identified Nuclear power plant accident at Three Mile Island Mars landings by Viking space probes Gene cloning Louise Brown first "test tube baby" (*in vitro* fertilization)	Carter Presidency Israel & Egypt sign Framework for Peace Formation of Sandinista government in Nicaragua

	COURSE LITERATURE	THE OTHER ARTS	SCIENCE & TECHNOLOGY	WORLD HISTORY
1980	Nadine Gordimer, *July's People* Philip Roth, *The Ghost Writer*	Reggae; New Wave Stockhausen, operas for each day of the week (*Thursday*, 1982; *Saturday*, 1984) Lutoslavski, *Symphony 3*	Photographs of Saturn by Voyager I Sally Ride first female U.S. astronaut AIDS cases reported	Reagan Presidency Drought/famine in Africa Iran-Iraq War
1985		Chagall exhibit in Russia Movies: *The Color Purple* *Amadeus, Rain Man* Perrin's song, "Don't Worry, Be Happy" wins most Grammys (1984) "Elliot Erwitt: Personal Exposure," NY photo-journalism exhibit Elliott Carter, *Enchanted Preludes* John Adams' opera *Nixon in China*	Chernobyl nuclear accident First infant heart implant Extensive research on AIDS virus to combat epidemic	Emergency state declared in South Africa Death of 7 astronauts in Challenger explosion Gorbachev introduces "glasnost" Iran-contra scandal Bush Presidency Exxon Oil Spill in Alaska

Unit 7
Contemporary Southern Writers

Eudora Welty, Peter Taylor, Alice Walker

READING

Eudora Welty, "Petrified Man"; Peter Taylor, "A Wife of Nashville"; Alice Walker, "Strong Horse Tea" and "In Search of Our Mothers' Gardens"

LISTENING

Audio Program 7, with William Andrews

OVERVIEW

Eudora Welty, Peter Taylor, and Alice Walker have continued Faulkner's fascination with the unique characteristics of the American South, especially its oral storytelling tradition and its history of racial injustice. Welty's "Petrified Man," Taylor's "A Wife of Nashville," and Walker's "Strong Horse Tea" and "In Search of Our Mothers' Gardens" focus on the consciousness and condition of women in the contemporary South.

BIOGRAPHICAL SKETCHES AND GENERAL BACKGROUND: EUDORA WELTY (1909-); PETER TAYLOR (1917-); ALICE WALKER (1944-)

In "The Bear," as we have seen, Faulkner foresees the demise of the Mississippi wilderness and the men who live by its timeless rhythms and laws, both the victims of a region rapidly undergoing modernization. The fear of change, in particular, the resistance to the mechanization of southern life and the substitution of materialism for more traditional values, can be found in the work of many of Faulkner's contemporaries in southern literature between the two world wars. After 1945, when the work of a new generation of southern writers matured and gained well-deserved respect, figures like Eudora Welty, Peter Taylor, and Alice Walker continued their predecessors' analysis of the impact, now full-blown, of modernism on southern consciousness.

Eudora Welty was born and raised in Jackson, Mississippi, and has continued to live there virtually all of her adult life. She earned a bachelor's degree from the University of Wisconsin in 1929, but soon thereafter she returned to her native state to work as a journalist and photographer while developing her literary career. She began publishing her short stories in the late 1930s, placing many of them in *The Southern Review*, the most prestigious literary magazine in the South. In 1941 her first collection of stories, *A Curtain of Green* (in which "Petrified Man" appears), was published to much acclaim. In 1942 and 1943 she won the O. Henry Memorial prize for the best short story of the year. Since then she has received many awards and prizes, including the Pulitzer Prize for her novel *The Optimist's Daughter* (1972).

From her perspective as a lifelong resident of Jackson, Welty could see an acceleration of change in the small-town South, the locale of most of her fiction, after World War II, despite what seemed to be a return to normality. While their ways of talking and living seem, at least on the surface, to have little in common with modern, urban life, the people of Welty's fiction are revealed to have suffered a profound erosion of faith in the traditional southern world view. Welty's sharp sense of humor distances her reader from the anxieties of her characters and allows her to treat them satirically at times. Her eye and ear for southern distinctiveness sometimes focuses on the zany, the unexpected, and the grotesque in her fictional world, yet she does not simply play over the surface of her characters. She makes every nuance of their language and behavior mean something, at times something very profound, about the modern predicaments of her characters.

In contrast to Welty, **Peter Taylor** has lived mostly in academic communities in and outside of the South, where he has taught literature and creative writing for the past forty years. Since 1948 he has published a half-dozen volumes of short fiction and two novels, the most recent of which, *A Summons to Memphis* (1986), has won the Ritz-Hemingway Prize. "A Wife of Nashville" (first published in the *New Yorker* in 1949) is typical of Taylor's work in its focus on the domestic crises of the emerging southern middle class in the postwar era. In some ways similar to Welty, Taylor has found in the middle class a deep-seated anxiety about their identity as southerners and their sense of purpose in the modern world. Taylor's humor is generally more restrained than Welty's, and his characters are less often grotesque in appearance or manner than hers, as one might expect given the class of people and the focus on family life that his fiction is usually concerned with. Yet both Welty's and Taylor's characters share a sense of anxiety about their inability to accept comfortably the social roles and mores that have traditionally governed southern lives, although Taylor's characters are usually more sophisticated in the ways in which they rationalize or adjust to change. In the work of both writers, characters typically struggle with a sense of rootlessness and isolation that comes of their loss of faith in or ambivalence about their situation as modern people who are not at home in the new order but who cannot go back to the old order of things either.

As one might expect, black authors who write about contemporary southern life consider the modernization of the region both necessary and long overdue in many respects, particularly with regard to racial justice. Two generations younger than Taylor, **Alice Walker** was born to sharecropper parents in Eatonton, Georgia. As a student at Sarah Lawrence College in the mid-1960s, she began to write poetry and won a writing fellowship to Africa, which she turned down to work as a caseworker in the New York City welfare department and a voter registration activist in Mississippi. In the 1970s her poems, short stories, and novels earned her increasing recognition. Walker's novel *The Color Purple* (1982) made her both famous and wealthy: it won an American Book Award and a Pulitzer Prize (1983) and was made into a successful film in 1985. Despite her personal success, Walker remains conscious of her origins and the many generations of oppressed black women who came before her. She captures her sense of the past in her essay "In Search of Our Mothers' Gardens."

Walker's fiction is notable for the richness of the southern black vernacular that its characters speak and for the depth of character that Walker communicates through that medium. When Walker takes up the question of the impact of change on the southern black community, she, like Welty and Taylor, depicts a people caught up in the throes of a modern crisis of identity. Walker recognizes, with her white predecessors, that black as well as white southerners have an investment in change as a potential liberation from traditional restraints and barriers. Yet that same change can divest black people of their faith and their sense of identity with a community and a set of values that has sustained blacks through the worst of their oppression in the South.

SELECTED WORKS BY WELTY, TAYLOR, AND WALKER

Eudora Welty, Peter Taylor, and Alice Walker share a concern with the benefits and the costs of a new, modernized South to the traditional southern sense of identity, community, and purpose. Each of these writers endows her or his characters with what appears to be a recognizably "southern" identity, evidenced especially in the way they talk. But the more these characters express themselves, the more their speech betrays their lack of certainty about who they are, what they want, and what they believe. It is important to notice this tension between what characters say and the way they say it in the fiction of Welty, Taylor, and Walker, for this serves not only as an index to the southernness but also the modernness of these writers.

The language, the rhythms, the accents and tones of southern speech have always fascinated outsiders, just as they have southern writers, who consistently seek to capture that peculiar essence in their narratives. Traditionally the South has been an oral culture with a particular fondness for rhetoric. In the South books and book learning have not always been treated with the same respect as the spoken word uttered by someone at home in the southern style of talk. In the nineteenth and early twentieth centuries, white southerners accorded hero's status to their military men and their orators, not their business leaders or their writers. Since the end of slavery, a love of the spoken word embellished with emotional power and rhetorical skill has made ministers and politicians the leading public figures among black southerners as well. The two dominant folk cultures of the South, the Scotch-Irish and the Afro-American, brought with them richly developed oral traditions. Their intermingling and mutual influence in the last two hundred years have made the South, until recently a predominantly rural region, the last stronghold of oral storytelling in America.

In "Petrified Man," (1941) "A Wife of Nashville," (1949) and "Strong Horse Tea," (1968) the importance of talk, not simply ordinary chitchat, but real self-expression in language, is doubly important to the central characters. First of all, the **protagonist** of each story is a southerner who as part of an oral culture must depend on speech as her main way of making contact with the rest of the world. Secondly, as a southern woman, the protagonist of each story is even more dependent on her powers of self-expression, since her restricted status as a woman in a male-dominated society bars her from most other ways of influencing the world around her. Thus for Leota in "Petrified Man," telling her story, even to as unsympathetic an ear as Mrs. Fletcher, is necessary to expressing her sense of powerlessness and outrage in a world in which the scheming Mrs. Pikes seem to get all the breaks. For Helen Ruth Lovell at the end of "A Wife of Nashville," it is imperative to find a way to articulate to her all-male family the "loneliness" and consequent despair that women feel, white as well as black, when too much is assumed and not enough is spoken. In "Strong Horse Tea," the written words of the advertisement of the white merchants have deceived Rannie Toomer. She must replace her illusory belief in the power of prescriptions from a white doctor with the real presence of her black neighbor, Sarah, who prescribes home remedies that embody the only power that Rannie Toomer has left. Rannie's uneducated vernacular speech ("I don't believe in none of your swamp magic." "Please God, make him git bitter.") reveals an honesty and directness lacking in the deceptive white world.

Ultimately, in all three stories, we find southern women reaching out to form some kind of community that cannot be recovered or established with men. Leota's problems with her husband Fred, along with the revelations of the hidden violence in Mr. Petrie, so disturb her that she cannot help but confide her anxieties in Mrs. Fletcher, even though these two women needle each other incessantly. Leota does not establish a genuine friendship with any woman in "Petrified Man," but despite her crassness and self-centeredness, she seems to long for someone and something to entrust with her most personal needs and fears. Similarly, Helen Ruth Lovell does not find in the women who belong to her social class the real understanding of her situation and her needs. However, she does discover some genuine appreciation and sympathy in the words and actions of some of her black maids. Thus by the end of the story, she can defend Jess McGehee's charade out of a deep sense of empathy with her situation as a woman, despite their racial and class differences. For Rannie Toomer black men are not present to help her in her plight, and the white mailman whom she appeals to is indifferent. Her only hope is to have faith in the black female community represented by Sarah. At the end of the story, we know that Snooks will not be saved, but the image of Rannie Toomer resolutely reaching for the horse tea, despite the filth, humiliation, and misery of the entire situation, is indicative of the complex attitude that each of these stories takes toward female community. These three authors do not suggest that such community is a safe haven for the women who have found themselves caught up in the dilemmas and anxieties of modern living. But they imply in these stories that in a world of alienation, loneliness, and confusion, women have no alternative but to turn to each other as emotional resources and bases of faith.

BIBLIOGRAPHY

Bradley, David "Novelist Alice Walker: Telling the Black Woman's Story." *New York Times Magazine*, 8 January, 1984.

Griffith, Albert J. *Peter Taylor*. New York: Twayne, 1970.

Tate, Claudia. *Black Women Writers at Work*. New York: Continuum, 1983.

Vande Kieft, Ruth M. *Eudora Welty*, rev. ed. New York: Twayne, 1987.

Welty, Eudora. *One Writer's Beginnings*. Cambridge: Harvard University Press, 1984.

WRITTEN ASSIGNMENT 7

Answer *four* of the following questions in one or two pages each. If possible, try to write at least once on each of the four assigned works.

1. Leota in "Petrified Man" seems to be a woman who has few traditional beliefs and cares little for traditional institutions (notice her cynicism about marriage, for instance). What *does* she seem to believe in? Why is she so attracted to and impressed by Lady Evangeline?

2. Discuss in detail the relationship that Helen Ruth Lovell has with one of her maids in "A Wife of Nashville." Do you find, as suggested in the audio program, that the maid (like all the maids in the story) reflects back to Helen Ruth something important about herself or her marriage?

3. Analyze the character of Rannie Toomer in "Strong Horse Tea" in terms of Walker's essay "In Search of Our Mothers' Gardens."

How does Rannie illustrate Walker's ideas about black women and their unique plight? Is Rannie one of the "mules of the earth," as Walker describes some black women in her essay? At the end of the story, do you see Rannie as noble or pathetic?

4. Which of these stories sounds the most like an orally told story? Why? What is gained by making the story sound this way? What is lost?

5. Discuss the setting of one of the three stories. How does the author describe the place or region where the events occur? What is the importance of the southern setting to the story's themes?

6. Discuss the issue of *racism* or *sexism* in any two of the four assigned works. To what extent do the works expose or attack oppression of blacks or of women? Compare/contrast the attitudes presented, and give specific details to illustrate your ideas.

Unit
8

Malcolm X
and the
Autobiography Genre

READING

The Autobiography of Malcolm X

LISTENING

Audio Program 8, with William Andrews, Houston Baker, and Nellie McKay

OVERVIEW

The Autobiography of Malcolm X is an influential twentieth-century work with both literary and political importance. Malcolm X helped establish the autobiography genre as a powerful form of self-expression and persuasion by using skillful rhetoric and by turning his life into a lesson. Careful study of *The Autobiography of Malcolm X* reveals a complex, reflective side of this controversial public figure.

MALCOLM X (1925-1965): BACKGROUND

Because Malcolm X provides such a detailed account of his life in his *Autobiography*, it is unnecessary to add a biographical sketch to this chapter. However, background information about Malcolm X and his relationship to the broader civil rights movement will help place his work in context. Rather than writing accounts of fictional characters--like Alice Walker's story of Rannie Mae Toomer--Malcolm X found the most eloquent illustration of racism and oppression to be the story of his own life.

On May 17, 1954, the Supreme Court of the United States ruled in the case of *Brown v. Board of Education of Topeka, Kansas*, that "in the field of public education, the doctrine of 'separate but equal' has no place." It was a momentous decision not only for the education of white and black children throughout the United States, but also for the future of American political institutions and cultural traditions. Spurred by the Supreme Court's emphatic rejection of segregation in schooling, the Civil Rights Movement burst onto the national scene in 1955. Led by a young Baptist minister named Martin Luther King, Jr., blacks in Montgomery, Alabama, organized a boycott of the city bus company that forced it to end its racially discriminatory policies. King went on to found and lead the Southern Christian Leadership Conference, which along with other civil rights organizations touched the conscience of the nation by staging massive nonviolent demonstrations against segregation. King stimulated the idealism of many young whites and blacks of the1960s with his dream of a racially integrated society founded on the principles of the equality and brotherhood of all mankind.

In the early 1960s, when King's star was at its zenith, his dream and his method of achieving it came to be increasingly challenged by younger "militant" blacks. Their pride of race and their outrage over the slow pace of change in America on the racial front found a spokesman in a man whom the media depicted as the antithesis of King, the stoical, peaceful, Christian integrationist. Malcolm X, formerly Malcolm Little, was unknown outside of small segments of the urban black community until late 1959, when he and the religious sect of which he was a minister, the Nation of Islam, were introduced to the American television audience in a program provocatively entitled "The Hate That Hate Produced." Founded in Detroit during the Depression, The Nation of Islam, or Black Muslims as they were popularly known, denounced the white man as inherently evil and stubbornly opposed to justice for people of color. Through their leader Elijah Muhammad, they advocated black separatism in political, social, economic, and religious life so as not to be confused and tainted by white ideas. Disgusted by the poverty, disease, and exploitative practices that dominated the black ghettos of big-city America, the Black Muslims tried to regenerate their people through a straight-laced moral code, an emphasis on the importance of African traditions and the beauty of blackness, and a belief in self-help, self-defense, and the ultimate triumph of black people over their adversaries on the world scene. Malcolm X, who rose from Assistant Minister of the Detroit Temple in 1953 to the major national organizer and spokesman for the Black Muslims by the end of the decade, became the symbol of a new kind of black leader in the 1960s--controversial, uncompromising, charismatic, and utterly unafraid to "tell it like it is."

As the 1960s unfolded, the style and message of Malcolm X won more literary adherents among the new generation of black writers than did that of Martin Luther King, Jr. Worsening conditions in the urban ghettos and a sense of the urgency of recovering their true "black" identity from the strangulation of white cultural norms caused young black writers like Sonia Sanchez and Etheridge Knight to celebrate Malcolm X in their poems. He was to them the quintessential black man who understood his blackness and gloried in it and who showed his people through act and word their own potential greatness. In Knight's image, he was a kind of savior, "the Sun" who came "after all the night years . . . spitting fire from his lips." This view of Malcolm was enhanced when he was assassinated in New York City on February 21, 1965, while speaking to a gathering of his followers. Perhaps because he predicted this end, he spent a great deal of time during the last months of his life working on his life story, which was published nine months after his death. During the late 1960s and early 1970s, *The Autobiography of Malcolm X* became a kind of Bible for young black militants who never heard the martyred minister preach and for young white radicals and liberals in search of a hero in an era that had lost its faith in heroism.

The Autobiography of Malcolm X is considered by many the high-water mark of Afro-American autobiography since World War II, certainly the most influential first-person narrative in black literature since Richard Wright's *Black Boy* (1945). Though a preoccupation with racial difference pervades the book, more than one critic has looked beyond Malcolm's racial concerns to place him in a Western literary tradition as old as the *Confessions* of St. Augustine. Like the fifteen hundred-year-old autobiography of the Christian saint from North Africa, Malcolm's story is a testament, an apology for past sins and a painfully honest assessment of moral failure as a prelude to an account of eventual salvation. Yet what makes *The Autobiography of Malcolm X* such a powerfully contemporary story is its refusal merely to titillate the reader with a sordid story or to praise God for delivering the sinner from the depths of his private hell. Malcolm X leads his reader into his "sordid past" with a certain kind of confidence in his own blamelessness. While denouncing his errors, he saves the full force of his scorn for the devil that he could not overcome until he learned the truth of Islam. That devil is white Western civilization, and the portrait that Malcolm provides of modern America as viewed from the underside by a street-wise black man is incisive and devastatingly realistic. Though twentieth-century American literature is full of attacks on mass culture and consumer society, no other analyst of the United States in the post-World War II era has had greater impact on America's smug assumptions of superiority than Malcolm X.

Yet Malcolm X was not merely a prophet protesting a corrupt America. He was also a man of his time who always lived *in* the world of his enemies, though he tried not to be *of* that world. He shows just how much of a product of his era he was in the almost frenetic pace of his life and his virtually total absorption in his vocation. *The Autobiography*, according to the critic Albert Stone, is unsurpassed in its expression of "the experience of living at breakneck speed in twentieth-century urban America." Alex Haley, Malcolm's collaborator on *The Autobiography*, notes in his "Epilogue" that Malcolm X had "an almost fanatical obsession about time." There are many good reasons for this, among them Malcolm's almost fatalistic assumption that he would die young and violently. Yet aside from this, Malcolm X seems to have regarded life as almost inherently too brief to allow a man like him the luxury of developing at a less than urgent pace. "No man is given but so much time to accomplish whatever is his life's work," he states. "My life in particular never has stayed fixed in one position for very long."

Even a brief listing of the "positions" Malcolm held in his life-- numbers runner, dope dealer, burglar, preacher, public speaker, political organizer--testifies to the astonishing self-transformative power of this man. In a sense, Malcolm X remained throughout his life a young man in a hurry, a kind of intellectual hustler, whose "life's work" (in ways quite typical of other postwar American culture-heroes) was always himself. Rootless and restless, Malcolm seems always in transit, while the pattern of his life seems almost deliberately to contradict the American norm. The prescription for American success has been traditionally, "Go West, young man, go West!" Yet Malcolm Little journeys not from East to West but from Michigan to Boston and New York and ultimately from the New World to the Old World, to Mecca and Africa by the end of his book. As he travels he tries out various identities along the way, testing his capacity to survive and adapt to the ever-changing circumstances of the modern world. His story ends, like Benjamin Franklin's, abruptly and without final resolution, as if defying the idea that a man so protean, or variable, could ever be confined between the covers of a book.

It is appropriate that *The Autobiography of Malcolm X* breaks off with its hero caught in a kind of freeze-frame, in the process of refashioning himself once again for the next stage on which he must play. Moving from the ghetto to the prison, the pulpit, and eventually the national and international rostrum, Malcolm X sought and found a constantly wider sphere in which to identify himself. If he seems not to have reconciled all his self-contradictions by the time of his death, he comes to the end of his story with one crucially liberating realization: he will no longer be an actor in the scripts of others, even Elijah Muhammad's. He will now write his own script and thus dictate *to* the media, rather than remaining a creature *of* it. In an age in which media heroes are made and unmade in a day, Malcolm X, one of the earliest national media figures in black America, shows us the power and the pitfalls that come of being identified as a public man. In its highly personal tone and self-revealing candor, the *Autobiography* registers Malcolm's determination to create his own monument to himself in his own words, rather than in the celluloid images of the white media which he both served and manipulated in all-too-familiar ways.

The Autobiography of Malcolm X is truly a classic American success story--"whatever I have done since [leaving school in the eighth grade], I have driven myself to become a success at it"--except that Malcolm's concept of success runs deliberately in opposition to mainstream notions of success in his time. It is clear that to this black man, success had little to do with amassing individual trophies and status symbols. A successful man, as his life story suggests, is one who seeks and speaks the truth in an effort to liberate himself and his people from ignorance and despair. To Malcolm X, whose youth was defined by many forms of physical and spiritual slavery, success meant becoming a free man, a man with a future of possibility, a man who not only knew himself but who knew how to articulate the path to self-knowledge for others. The *Autobiography* pictures Malcolm's ultimate conversion and dedication to the ministry as a natural progression since, next to mental illumination through private study, he "always loved verbal battle, and challenge" the most.

"You *never* have to worry about me biting my tongue if something I know as truth is on my mind," Malcolm warns his reader. "Raw, naked truth exchanged between the black man and the white man is what a whole lot more of is needed in this country--to clear the air of the racial mirages, clichés, and lies that this country's very atmosphere has been filled with for four hundred years." The black man as unwelcome truth teller, as a battler with words who shows no mercy and gives no quarter--this is the image of Malcolm as angry black spokesman that was both a blessing and burden to him as an autobiographer. His book is filled with examples of his sharp-edged argumentative style. He makes calculated use of the sweeping statement (The *Brown v. Board of Education* Supreme Court decision was "one of the greatest magical feats ever performed in America"). He denies conventional pieties ("Christianity is the white man's religion"). Finally, he uses verbal shock tactics ("did I feel *any* white men had ever done anything for the black man in America. I told him, 'Yes, I can think of two. Hitler, and Stalin. The black man in America couldn't get a decent factory job until Hitler put so much pressure on the white man. And then Stalin kept up the pressure--'"). This is Malcolm X the public man, the scary black man whom white America loved to hate.

Yet the *Autobiography* takes us inside this image to show us, first, the *method* behind Malcolm's seeming madness in making such outrageous statements and baiting white America in such apparently counterproductive ways. Second, because the *Autobiography* shows us Malcolm X reexamining himself and reinventing his own philosophy by the end of his story, the book reveals to us just how earnestly and successfully Malcolm finally resisted becoming merely Elijah Muhammad's mouthpiece. The last two chapters of the *Autobiography* read differently in style and tone because they reflect a new Malcolm X, no less angry at injustice, but a great deal less willing to attack it with the verbal weaponry of his past. After the break with Elijah Muhammad, Malcolm states that "I became able finally to muster the nerve, and the strength, to start facing the facts, to think for myself." Thinking for himself, El-Hajj Malik El-Shabazz returns to America after his soul-searching trip to Mecca in 1964 and begins to stake out political positions that allow him the freedom to change and to grow. Significantly, on the New York freeway, he encounters a white man who asks if he, Malcolm X, would mind "shaking hands with a white man." "I told him, 'I don't mind shaking hands with human beings. Are you one?'" In recognizing the white man's humanity, El-Hazz Malik El-Shabazz affirms his own by the end of his story, thus liberating himself from the public caricature that is in part his own creation. This is a crucial mark of Malcolm X's success as a man and an autobiographer. Because he comes to this pass in the end, many readers of Malcolm X's story regard it as a commentary on and even an affirmation of American ideals. It celebrates the human spirit, rejects all the forces in the modern world that alienate and dehumanize people, and affirms the traditional American faith in the capacity of every person to overcome.

BIBLIOGRAPHY

Butterfield, Stephen. *Black Autobiography in America*. Amherst: University of Massachusetts Press, 1974.

Clarke, J. H., ed. *Malcolm X: The Man and His Times*. New York: Macmillan, 1969.

Cooke, Michael G. "Modern Black Autobiography in the Tradition," in *Romanticism, Vistas, Instances, Continuities*. David Thornburn and Geoffrey Hartman, eds. Ithaca, NY: Cornell University Press, 1973, pp. 255-280.

Stone, Albert E. *Autobiographical Occasions and Original Acts*. Philadelphia: University of Pennsylvania Press, 1982.

WRITTEN ASSIGNMENT 8

Answer *four* of the following in one-to-two pages each.

1. Although Malcolm X was often accused of being a hate-spewing revolutionary, William Andrews suggests in the audio program that he also adhered to traditional American social, economic, and religious values. Can you make a case for this traditionalism in Malcolm X? What examples do you find in *The Autobiography* of his conservative or traditional ideas or practices?

2. Aside from Elijah Muhammad, who do you think was the single most important influence on Malcolm X's development? Was the effect more positive than negative? Why?

3. Discuss Malcolm X's life as a member of the criminal underworld in cities like Detroit and Boston. Why do you think he spent so much time in *The Autobiography* describing this stage of his life? How did his experiences as an inner city criminal influence his later thinking and development?

4. Discuss the final stage in Malcolm X's life. How does his position at the end of *The Autobiography* represent a change in his development? Can you project the direction in which his thinking might have gone had he lived into the 1980s and '90s?

5. Select an excerpt from one of Malcolm X's public speeches--one read in the audio program or contained within the text of *The Autobiography*. After studying the discussion of **rhetoric** in the Glossary, analyze the passage in detail. What rhetorical techniques does Malcolm X use? What makes the passage

effective or persuasive? controversial? How would you have responded to the speech if you were in the audience, and why?

Unit 9

Nadine Gordimer

READING

July's People

LISTENING

Audio Program 9, with Julie Rivkin, Sheila Roberts, and Moses Nkondo

OVERVIEW

Nadine Gordimer's *July's People* illustrates the intimate relationship between contemporary literature and politics. As a political novelist, Gordimer writes in the context of South Africa and its **apartheid** system. Personal relationships in the novel--those between masters and servants, whites and blacks, European colonialists and African tribalists, men and women--reveal broader political struggles and dilemmas.

NADINE GORDIMER (1923-): A BIOGRAPHICAL SKETCH

Nadine Gordimer was born in Springs, South Africa, a small town in a gold mining region near Johannesburg. Even though it seemed to her one of the more boring and remote places in existence, she later came to realize that it presented her with a sharp picture of political relations in South Africa. In her childhood she saw black Africans used as beasts of burden to bring forth the gold out of their land, while a small white European population gleaned the wealth and imposed their cultural expectations on this alien landscape. The color-bar was so absolute that it seemed to mark a separation less between peoples than between species. Gordimer's own family background was directly European: her father was a Jewish watchmaker who had emigrated from a Baltic town, while her mother had been born in England. Gordimer grew up living what she called a "second-hand" version of genteel European ways. In *July's People*, her character Maureen Smales, who grew up in a mining town and took ballet lessons instead of learning *fanagalo* (the language spoken by the African mine workers), might have been drawn from Gordimer's own childhood.

Gordimer traces her emergence from the racial attitudes of this colonial existence as due in part to her reading. Encountering worlds beyond her own enabled her to see her own world differently. Rather than remaining a colonialist, clinging to European gentility and repressing an entire African cultural context, she began to see the richness and excitement of a life taking place among a variety of colors and cultures. This new vision of her existence seemed at first a purely personal one; only with time did it grow into a strong political conviction, an opposition to apartheid, the system of racial separation that rules South Africa.

Gordimer's move from her suburban life in Springs to university life in Johannesburg clearly had something to do with this wider sense of existence. She attended the University of Witwatersrand, and these years of study and of city life led her to a social and cultural expansion of her vision. During this period she also began reading some of the writers who were most important to her own development as a writer. She credits D. H. Lawrence with influencing her way of looking at the natural world, Henry James with giving her a consciousness of form in fiction, and Hemingway with teaching her about the workings of dialogue.

Gordimer began writing early, beginning with a number of short stories. Her stories appeared in American magazines like *The New*

Yorker and *Harper's*; later they were collected in two volumes called *Face to Face* (1949) and *The Soft Voice of the Serpent* (1952). These stories would be followed by a number of novels, beginning with *The Lying Days*, and including *A World of Strangers* (1958), *The Late Bourgeois World* (1966), *A Guest of Honor* (1970), *The Conservationist* (1975), *Burger's Daughter* (1980), *July's People* (1981), and most recently *A Sport of Nature* (1987). She has also continued to write short fiction and has published several other story collections, including *Six Feet of the Country* (1956) and *A Soldier's Embrace* (1980).

What Gordimer's work makes absolutely clear is that the situation of literature cannot be separated from the situation of politics. This connection is not unique to the South African writer; it is simply more urgently and explicitly present in South Africa than in many other parts of the world. In exploring the ties that bind literature to politics, Gordimer focuses inevitably on the racial laws of apartheid. The color-bar so marks every dimension of experience in her country that it would be impossible to write about a realm of private life not influenced by the politics of race. For the writer, one way to speak of this racial barrier is as a barrier to the literary imagination. Because it is as impossible for whites to enter and participate in the world inhabited by blacks, there is no writer who could write an inclusive work about South African experience. That barrier is, of course, less visible than the one we are more familiar with: that of censorship. Banning books marks a recognition on the part of the government in South Africa that literature not only reflects political conditions but constitutes a form of political action. Some of Gordimer's books have been banned in her own country, even as they have reached a wide audience around the world.

Gordimer continues to live in Johannesburg and remains a critic of her government's policies from within. Her audience is an international one, though, and she travels widely, lecturing and teaching in universities abroad. Indeed, her fiction provides the international community a form of access to life in South Africa that reaches places untouched by the journalist or documentary filmmaker. Gordimer records with a quiet intensity the textures and tensions that characterize South African experience today.

JULY'S PEOPLE

Nadine Gordimer sets *July's People* in a South Africa of the future, a South Africa during a war of revolution. Rather than focusing directly on the revolution, though, Gordimer explores the changing relations between a particular family of white masters and their black servant. In their personal relations, we see an image of the larger political struggle. We also see an image of the necessary distortions and disruptions that result from apartheid.

The novel takes as its epigraph the following passage from Antonio Gramsci's *Prison Notebooks*: "The old is dying and the new cannot be born; in this interregnum there arises a great diversity of morbid symptoms." *July's People* takes place during this period of "interregnum" (or period between reigns): the old world inhabited by the Smales and their servant July, a world Maureen refers to as "back there," no longer exists, while the new world that will replace it has not yet emerged. Instead, this period of transition exhibits the "great diversity of morbid symptoms," symptoms that range from the disrupted relations of husband and wife to the power struggle taking place between Maureen Smales and her former servant.

In exploring a political struggle through a series of personal relationships, this novel typifies Gordimer's fiction. While overtly what has been altered is the relation between master and servant, actually we find the change runs through all the relations in the novel, putting into question the notions of marriage, family structure, and even personal identity.

We might note that Gordimer, in detailing these changing relations, pays an enormous amount of attention to the details of the bourgeois life left behind--the master bedroom suite, the seven room house, the ballet lessons, the recreational vehicle or bakkie. But who are the Smales without the trappings of bourgeois life? The events of the novel strip them of not only their middle class possessions, but also their middle class identities. Who is Bamford Smales if he is not in "Smales, Caprano and Partners, Architects"? Who is Maureen (Hetherington) Smales if not the wife of a successful architect? They bring the framework of their old middle class life expectations to this new world, seeing the mud hut that now shelters them through their memories of camping trips. The bakkie that served as their escape vehicle still retains its old associations with recreation from a leisure life of the past. But as they use up their tinned food and are left with mealie pap like the rest of the villagers, as their precious supply of toilet paper dwindles, they can no longer base their sense of who they are on bourgeois possessions or associations.

Bamford Smales' response to this new life in hiding is in some ways the most straightforward. He takes on various "male" tasks: building and hunting. He constructs a water tank and he shoots game to feed his family and the others. But just as Bam's identity is associated with (and sustained by) the use of various tools, it is threatened by the loss of those tools. Without the bakkie, the gun, and the radio, Bam suddenly seems lost. As the contours of the white male "master" grow indistinct, we sense that Gordimer is exposing the arbitrariness of how gender as well as race gets used to define an identity.

Maureen's response is both more complex and more fully recorded than her husband's; the novel stays close to her point of view and traces her reflections at length. Her marriage to Bam--indeed Bam himself--comes to seem increasingly unreal to her, as if "the Smales" could not exist without the bourgeois context in which that life took place. If Bam seems not to exist for her, July comes to seem increasingly important; her disorientation manifests itself in part as a need to fix July in a determinate place. It is this need, in fact, which propels the novel to its climax. The mounting tension between Maureen and July reaches its high point when she accuses him of stealing and he begins speaking to her in his own language. Suddenly she realizes that she doesn't know the least thing about him--and we remember that she didn't even know his name--not July at all, but Mwatwate. Earlier Maureen had thought that she understood July, while her husband didn't. Now that small smugness is shown as completely inappropriate--and her whole concept of life "back there" is exploded. "Theft" as she understands it doesn't apply here; it is part of the bourgeois world that she left behind. It is in that sense like "adultery," another bourgeois notion that doesn't fit African experience. Maureen comes to realize that what she had called her "humane creed," her set of values based on the rights and privileges of personal relationships, is not absolute or universal, but based instead on one's place in the economic structure.

The Smales children's response interestingly differs from that of their parents and provides the novel's largest measure of hope for the future. Although at the beginning they ask for the expected things from their old life--movies or cokes or batteries for their racing car-- they soon get incorporated into the children's life of the village. Gina's friendship with Nyiko takes her into huts her parents have never entered. She begins to speak the language, and Victor, by the novel's end, receives a gift from July with a gesture indistinguishable from that of any of the African children: "Victor is seen to clap his hands, sticky with mealie-pap, softly, gravely together and bob obeisance, receiving the gift with cupped palms."

The novel, of course, hinges on July as much as on the Smales, and yet July remains in many ways a mystery to us. After all, we see July largely from the point of view of characters who do not understand him. But this inaccessibility is in itself significant; as Gordimer noted, the apartheid system makes it impossible for writers to write with authenticity about those on the other side of the color line. July's story is not fully told; instead what we have are guesses and glimpses. One way to see him is as a man among women--a man in a matriarchy--balancing between his wife, his mother, his town-woman, and Maureen. However, these relations never get fully explored; one untold story suggested by the novel's circumstances is that of a man's return to a wife that he does not know, and to a way of life that he has ceased to live.

While Gordimer's novel can be read as prophecy or warning, it also should be seen as a portrait of the present. The future she envisions is only a heightened form of the current situation, of those omnipresent tensions and contradictions between two forms of existence--urban European and tribal African--in a terribly divided country. Indeed, the "interregnum" to which Gordimer refers in the epigraph is no mysterious future state or condition; it is South Africa in the twentieth century. And while Gordimer cannot pretend to cure her country's ills, she can provide an account of its "morbid symptoms." The prognosis may not be cheerful, but it is only through this kind of exacting observation that a political analysis can proceed.

BIBLIOGRAPHY

Clingman, Stephen R. *The Novels of Nadine Gordimer: History in the Making.* London: Allen and Unwin, Ltd, 1986.

Cooke, John. *The Novels of Nadine Gordimer: Private Lives/Public Landscapes.* Baton Rouge: Louisiana State University Press, 1985.

Haugh, Robert F. *Nadine Gordimer.* New York: Twayne, 1974.

Heywood, Christopher, *Aspects of South African Literature*. New York: Africana Publishing Company, 1976. Contains an important essay by Nadine Gordimer entitled "English-Language Literature in Politics in South Africa."

WRITTEN ASSIGNMENT 9

Answer *three* of the following in approximately two pages each.

1. *Propaganda* (a term coming from the Vatican's *Congregatio de Propaganda Fide*, or Congregation for the Propagation of the Faith) refers to a form of communication that consciously or deliberately manipulates group attitudes; all other concerns are secondary. In contrast, *literature* may have important political ideas to communicate, but these are combined with other attributes and presented in a less blatantly one-sided way.

   Write an argument in which you demonstrate that *July's People*, though highly political, is literature rather than propaganda. Be specific in providing examples of its literary qualities.

2. We have seen in other works (e.g., "The Love Song of J. Alfred Prufrock") examples of the modern **anti-hero**. In *July's People*, is Maureen Smales an **anti-heroine**? To what extent do we admire her? pity her? How does she change in the course of the novel, and to what extent is this change positive or negative? Do you read the ending of the novel--Maureen's act of running (read and discussed in the audio program)--as an act of heroism or cowardice?

3. The professors in the audio program suggest that the children may be the only sign of hope in the novel. Analyze Gordimer's portrayal of the Smales children. What kinds of changes do you witness? Are there differences among the children and their responses to their displacement? What might we infer about the future from Gordimer's depiction of the children?

4. The novel focuses on the Smales' response to life in a tribal village and does not give a fully balanced sense of what the Smales might look like from the African point of view. From what the novel does tell you, though, see whether you can construct some version of this novel's untold story. What impact does the Smales' arrival have on village life? How might the Smales be regarded? Does your attempt to tell this other story change your reading of the novel?

5. Racial relationships are at the center of the novel. Yet Gordimer also explores the dynamics of male-female relationships, particularly the eroding marriage of Bam and Maureen Smales. Analyze this marriage and how it changes in the course of the novel. To what extent do you think Gordimer challenges traditional assumptions of male and female roles within a marriage?

6. Analyze the climax (see **plot**) of *July's People*--the confrontation between July and Maureen, leading to July's outburst in his own language. What does the scene reveal about both characters and about apartheid? How does Gordimer use setting and imagery to add to the effect of this scene? Be specific.

Unit 10

Elizabeth Bishop

READING

"The Fish," "The Man-Moth," in *Modern Poems*; "Over 2000 Illustrations and a Complete Concordance," "At the Fishhouses," "Arrival at Santos," "Questions of Travel," "Sestina," "First Death in Nova Scotia," "In the Waiting Room," and "One Art," in the Study Guide Anthology

LISTENING

Audio Program 10, with Julie Rivkin and James Merrill

OVERVIEW

Elizabeth Bishop's poetry contrasts home with foreign lands, imagined visions with real observations. Bishop makes ordinary events seem extraordinary by viewing them figuratively, poetically; she makes strange scenes familiar by capturing them in minute detail. Ten selected poems reveal Bishop's experimentation with both traditional and nontraditional forms of verse, her use of travel as a metaphor, and her gift for moving from concrete description to philosophical illumination.

104

ELIZABETH BISHOP (1911-1979): A BIOGRAPHICAL SKETCH

Elizabeth Bishop was born in Worcester, Massachusetts, in 1911. Her father died when she was eight months old; her mother, who suffered from mental illness, was put in an institution when Bishop was four years old. Elizabeth Bishop was raised by her maternal grandparents in Nova Scotia up to the age of sixteen, when she left to attend first a boarding school near Boston and then Vassar College. This world of Bishop's childhood appears in a number of poems including "Sestina" and "In the Waiting Room," and in her prose piece "In the Village," in which her mother's mental breakdown is represented in the form of a scream that hangs over the village. However, the influence of Bishop's childhood may be felt not only in her subject matter, but also in her poetic stance. Her early experiences of uprootedness, like her later experiences of travel, led her to write from the perspective of the outsider or wanderer, one who did not take her place in the world for granted.

Bishop's literary career began at Vassar, where her fellow students included Mary McCarthy, Eleanor Clark, and Muriel Rukeyser, all of whom would become important poets and fiction writers. Mary McCarthy was a particular friend of Bishop's, and the two worked together on publishing a small magazine. However, the most influential literary friendship that Bishop made during these years was not with any of her fellow students, but with the poet Marianne Moore, whom Bishop met through the college librarian. This introduction marked the beginning of a friendship that would last forty years, and that would provide an important poetic influence on Bishop's own development.

After college, Bishop began the travels that were to constitute such a central part of her experience and a central subject for her poetry. She spent time in Europe and North Africa, before settling for a while in Key West. During this period she began to publish her poems in periodicals but did not bring out her first collection until 1946, when she was thirty-five. Entitled *North and South*, this volume drew heavily on her experience of travel, and as its title suggests, registers a movement from nordic to tropical realms. The book (which includes "Man-Moth" and "The Fish") met with immediate success, receiving an award from its publisher and high praise from the reviewers. The poems in this volume mark not simply different geographical directions, but also different poetic directions, with a poem like "The Man-Moth" exploring a kind of surrealism and others written more in the vein of irony and wit.

After the publication of *North and South* Elizabeth Bishop's renown as a poet grew, and she began to receive fellowships and other honors. This next phase of her literary career would also be marked by a change in locale; after an exploratory journey around South America, she came to settle in Brazil. Brazil was to remain her home for some twenty years and to provide the material for much of her poetry. However, her periodic return visits to Nova Scotia also left their mark, and in a poem like "At the Fishhouses" we find her moving back from "South" to "North." In 1956 Bishop published her second volume of poetry; entitled *A Cold Spring*, it included the poems "Over 2,000 Illustrations," and "At the Fishhouses."

Bishop's life in Brazil and her growing connection with the Portuguese language led her into a new series of literary ventures; she began translating the writers of Brazil in order to introduce them to a North American audience. Her first project was the diary kept by a Brazilian girl in the 1890s, a book that had become a kind of classic in Brazil. Bishop then moved from prose to poetry, translating works by a number of Brazil's important poets. Her translations of Carlos Drummond de Andrade are particularly remarkable, and are included in her *Complete Poems* (1969).

Bishop's own poems about Brazil are contained in her third collection, *Questions of Travel*, with the title poem reflecting on some of the central questions of her own itinerant existence. (Audio Program 10 opens and closes with this poem.) The poems in this volume are divided between those about Brazil such as "Arrival at Santos," and those she subtitles "Elsewhere," including "Sestina" and "First Death in Nova Scotia."

After the publication of this volume, Bishop took a series of academic positions in the United States, beginning with the University of Washington and then later Harvard. She continued to live part of the year in Brazil, even buying and restoring a ruined colonial house there; it was not until 1974, after the death of her woman companion in Brazil, that she returned to the United States and settled in Boston. During this period she also published her *Complete Poems*, which received the National Book Award. The title was, however, something of a misnomer, since she went on to publish another volume-- *Geography III*--in 1976. The book takes its title from a children's geography text, and in certain ways represents a continuation of her earlier interests in exploring different parts of the world. However, the poems in this volume (including "One Art" and "In the Waiting Room") have both a looser, more prosaic quality and also a more personal voice, making for some of her strongest work.

Elizabeth Bishop died suddenly in 1979. One final volume, *The Complete Poems: 1927-1979*, was published that same year and is now considered a major contribution to American poetry.

SELECTED POEMS

In a letter to a friend, Elizabeth Bishop described the experience of reading Charles Darwin: "Reading Darwin one admires the beautiful solid case being built up out of his endless, heroic observations, almost unconscious or automatic--and then comes a sudden relaxation, a forgetful phrase, and one feels the strangeness of the undertaking, sees the lonely young man, his eyes fixed on facts and minute details, sinking or sliding giddily off into the unknown." What Bishop admires in Darwin, we might also admire in Bishop; she too has a genius for "heroic observations." In her poems, written between 1927 and 1979, we also see how the observation of minute details can "giddily slide off" into the unknown. Her poems, characteristically understated and matter-of-fact in tone, have the power to present the surreal in everyday life. Bishop herself apparently liked to say her poems were "just description," but this modest claim is deceptive. The ten assigned poems illustrate that for Bishop, description becomes the occasion for reflections and revelations about herself and her relation to the outside world.

"The Fish"

"The Fish" transforms a common occurrence--catching a fish--into an inspirational, visionary event. Audio Program 10 includes a complete reading and detailed discussion of this wonderful poem. As you read "The Fish" on your own, look closely at how Bishop moves from literal description (objective reporting) to a more poetic, figurative vision of the fish. What is the "victory" that "filled up/the little rented boat"? What transforms the location into one where "everything was rainbow, rainbow, rainbow!"? Why does the speaker let the fish go? Do we identify with the fish in any way and feel glad of its liberation?

"Man-Moth"

If in a poem like "The Fish" Bishop takes the ordinary and discovers in it something marvelous and rare, she also has poems that begin with the extraordinary and discovers in them something surprisingly familiar. "The Man-Moth," a creature born out of a newspaper misprint for "mammoth," is reminiscent of the surreal human/cockroach and other nightmarish creations of the German writer Franz Kafka. He is mothlike in his nocturnal existence and in his dangerous attraction to the light. Yet what finally characterizes him is a uniquely human feature: his tear.

> Then from the lids,
> one tear, his only possession, like the bee's sting,
> slips.

> Slyly he palms it, and if you're not paying attention
> he'll swallow it. However, if you watch, he'll hand
>   it over,
> cool as from underground springs and pure enough
>   to drink.

The concealed tears--emotional pain contained--mark Bishop's "Man-moth" not as some strange, dreamlike creature, but as an emotional being very like herself. In what ways do we feel ourselves kin to this Man-Moth? Like Bishop's imagined figure, do we have recurrent dreams? do we feel we are riding backwards? do we live in homes like "pale subways of cement" and exist in fear? Do we live in darkness but search for glimpses of light?

As in "The Fish" and many other poems, Bishop chooses a free verse style in "Man-Moth" without a fixed meter or rhyme (see **free verse** in your Glossary). The sense of order in the poem comes from the poet's accumulation of observations, her unfolding of thoughts, and her precise attention to individual words and images.

"Over 2,000 Illustrations and a Complete Concordance"

In this poem, as in many Bishop poems, travel appears as a theme and metaphor. Bishop takes the title from the description of an illustrated King James Bible. She contrasts the imaginative "travel" one does when looking at pictures in this gilt-edged book (Stanza 1) with the literal travel one does as a tourist visiting foreign lands (Stanza 2). The final stanza measures the value of both. If we open the book, we are "pollinated," stimulated by the vision of the created world as a divine art work ("God's spreading fingerprint" like a "burin," or engraver's tool). In contrast, the tourist's visits to Rome, Mexico, Morocco, and other countries lead only to random scenes, with "everything connected only by 'and' and 'and.'" No cosmic vision or divine presence underlies the traveler's experiences.

The last lines bring the two modes of traveling together as Bishop asks, a bit impudently, why did the tourist not include the Nativity as one of her travel stops?

> Why couldn't we have seen
> this old Nativity while we were at it?
> --the dark ajar, the rocks breaking with light,
> an undisturbed, unbreathing flame,
> colorless, sparkless, freely fed on straw,
> and, lulled within, a family with pets,
> --and looked and looked our infant sight away.

Bishop boldly describes the Nativity scene as "a family with pets," domesticating this mystical event and making it suddenly human, like the Man-Moth's tear. What does her poetic description of the Nativity demonstrate about her ability to achieve visions? In this poem, what does travel represent? How is it connected with the poet going beyond "infant sight" to a more mature, profound consideration of what she can see or imagine?

"At the Fishhouses"

Just as in "Over 2,000 Illustrations and a Complete Concordance" Bishop takes a religious scene and familiarizes it, so in "At the Fishhouses" she takes Christianity down from the pulpit and out of the church, singing Baptist hymns and "A Mighty Fortress is Our God" to a seal. This powerful poem illustrates the way Bishop moves from concrete observation to philosophical reflection.

The lengthy first stanza (again written in a free verse style much like conversation) sets the scene: the fishhouses where an old man smokes a Lucky Strike while waiting for a herring boat to come in. The short second stanza leads us away from the buildings, lobster pots, and fish tubs to the water's edge, where we begin to descend into something intangible, mysterious, unknowable.

The water is "cold dark deep and absolutely clear," Bishop tells us twice in the third stanza, an "element bearable to no mortal." Like the seal that disappears into the water, Bishop believes in "total immersion" into this water that is paradoxically "above the stones and then the world." Like the "heaven" of Frost's "Birches" or the dark woods of his "Stopping by Woods on a Snowy Evening," the "clear gray icy water" of Bishop's poem lies tempting, alluring, and somewhat frightening in its power.

> If you should dip your hand in,
> your wrist would ache immediately,
> your bones would begin to ache and your hand
>   would burn
> as if the water were a transmutation of fire
> that feeds on stones and burns with a dark gray
>   flame.

To Bishop, the water is like "a transmutation of fire"; the word "transmutation"--or change from one form to another--seems to apply to the whole poem as well, which moves from prosaic reality to a realm human beings can only imagine. Water takes on symbolic importance in the last lines, where it becomes "like what we imagine knowledge to be: dark, salt, clear, moving, utterly free," drawn from the depths of the world yet transcending time and space, "forever, flowing . . . and flown."

As you read this poem, look for connections to Eliot, Yeats and Frost. How is the water like the waves Prufrock gazes at or the "silent seas" to which he wishes to retreat? How is it like Yeats's Innisfree? Frost's dark woods? Is Bishop's relationship to the music-loving seal like the one she feels with the fish in "The Fish"? What significance is there to the religious references in the poem--the hymns she sings; the "million Christmas trees" that are around even before Christmas? What connotations are associated with the color "silver," used here to describe the sea, the benches, the lobster pots, the masts, and the rocks? Words like "irridescent," "opaque," and "translucent" appear in the poem: to what extent is the poem about sight, obstacles to sight, and vision? Finally, what is the effect of the sounds Bishop combines in the poem's closing lines?

"Arrival at Santos"

This poem is the first of many Bishop poems about Brazil, where she went to live for many years. Travel would seem to bring her in contact with the exotic, the strange, yet what she finds often mocks that desire for something new. The tourist in the poem sets off for the port of Santos with "immodest demands for a different world,/ and a better life, and complete comprehension/ of both at last, and immediately," grand aims that can only lead to disappointment when the country turns out to have a flag, coins, and other mundane signs of civilization.

"Arrival at Santos" illustrates Bishop's comic wit. As James Merrill observes in Audio Program 10, even the clinking rhymes-- unusual for Bishop--become part of the joke, helping to characterize the naive tourist and her fellow passenger, Miss Breen. Although the poem mocks the tourist's hopes for a new world, the last line ("We are driving to the interior") suggests that perhaps the traveler willing to go beyond the surface may realize some of those dreams about what travel can offer.

As you read the poem, note the two very different voices: one the poet who can cynically and patronizingly ask, "Oh, tourist, is this how this country is going to answer you . . .?"; the other the tourist herself who describes her experiences in naive exclamations ("Please, boy, do be more careful with that boat hook!").

In addition to having fun with rhymes, Bishop experiments with syntax and punctuation and spacing here. Why do you think she divides up the name "Glens Falls," starting a line with "s"? Does she perhaps want to emphasize the word "fall" contained within it? In what sense is the port like postage stamps or soap, both small, mundane objects? Have you ever felt like the tourist in this poem who discovers the foreign land is not as exotic as she expected?

"Questions of Travel"

This poem is included along with "Arrival at Santos" in a collection Bishop entitled *Questions of Travel*. Here Bishop questions the impulse that brings people to make great journeys, to "rush to see the sun the other way around." Do we travel out of "childishness" or a desire to "dream our dreams/and have them, too"? Is it "right" to watch strangers? "Should we have stayed at home and thought of here," content with what our imagination can create?

Why do you think the poem begins by emphasizing "too many waterfalls"? The poem switches from condemning travel to praising its value. Bishop expresses a series of potential regrets for what she would have missed if this journey had not been taken: "But surely it would have been a pity/not to have seen the trees along this road . . ." But as her list continues, we begin to sense that it is not the sights she would miss but rather the stimulation they provide to her imagination. The trees are "like noble pantomimists, robed in pink," and the rain is "like politicians' speeches." We watch her transform objects into images and then search for connections between them: "what connection can exist for centuries" between the wooden clogs she hears and the song of "the fat brown bird"? What conclusion does she reach about missing the chance to see, hear, and ponder the wonderful, minute details of the world?

The poem ends by returning to its beginning question: should we travel or stay at home?

> *Is it lack of imagination that makes us come*
> *to imagined places, not just stay at home?*
> *Or could Pascal have been not entirely right*
> *about just sitting quietly in one's room?*

The traveler questions the convictions of the philosopher-monk Pascal who praised thought and isolation. One needs a world outside one's own mind for observations one could never imagine, observations it would be a "pity" never to have known. The poet comes to know this world through "heroic observations," an amassing of detail that allows glimpses into something strange and significant. At the poem's conclusion Bishop is still asking, "Should we have stayed at home,/wherever that may be?" Along the way, however, she poses, rather than solves, the questions that the title promises. What is the individual's relationship to the world? Do we trust philosophers, or our own observations and feelings? Why is travel "never free"? In the end, she convinces us that travel can be both literal and metaphorical, real and imagined, unnecessary and important.

"Sestina"

"Sestina" and "First Death in Nova Scotia" are both included in *Questions of Travel* in a section labeled "Elsewhere," to indicate they are not about Brazil. In "Sestina" we discover a Bishop who can turn away from exotic landscapes and philosophical questions to a poignant description of a sad, domestic scene. Our knowledge of Bishop's own childhood--living among grandparents in Nova Scotia after her father's death and mother's breakdown--sheds light on this poem.

The title of the poem calls attention to its form. Unlike many other free-verse Bishop poems, "Sestina" follows the strict requirements of a traditional verse form (see **sestina** in the Glossary). The rhyme scheme requires a repetition of six words: house, grandmother, child, stove, almanac, and tears. These are domestic words; the only one that does not seem to fit is "tears," which (as in "Man-Moth") startles us with its intrusion of pain. The grandmother attempts to hide her tears, but they come out everywhere, in the rain, the drops of water from the kettle, the tea itself, even the buttons in the child's drawing. The scene seems to be so cozy--especially with that Little Marvel Stove--and yet sorrow spills onto everything. From this scene the child gets her sense of the domestic, and she keeps on drawing rigid houses, inscrutable houses. Bishop takes us from the familiar, the domestic, into a strange, "inscrutable" realm. The sestina form emphasizes recurrence and transformation: words reappear, but with different meanings. This form allows Bishop to illustrate how a childhood sorrow keeps resurfacing in her adult life. Pain can be temporarily submerged or transformed but never obliterated.

"First Death at Nova Scotia"

Like "Sestina," "First Death at Nova Scotia" focuses on a child-- one we come to see as young Elizabeth Bishop--in a sad domestic setting. As Julie Rivkin observes in the audio program, this poem presents a child's perspective on death. The joy of this poem comes from its successful rendering of a child's point of view and from its haunting images of coldness, aloofness, rigidity, and death. The adult world is not malicious, as it was in Frost's "'Out,Out--,'" but simply incapable of providing answers to satisfy the questioning child who encounters death for the first time.

As you read the poem, think about whether there is any significance to the location (Nova Scotia). How does Bishop use imagery of coldness to unify the poem? What **similes** and **metaphors** does the child use to describe the scene? How does the child personify inanimate things, like the chromographs, loon, and frost? Does this suggest her imagination will be able to "animate"--i.e., give life to--her dead cousin as well? Is the view of death presented in this poem similar to that in "Sestina"?

"One Art"

This poem, read in its entirety in the audio program, illustrates how Bishop moves from a small, everyday event (lost keys) to something much larger and uncontained (the loss--perhaps death--of a loved one). As with "Sestina," Bishop chooses in "One Art" to adopt a traditional form, this time a **villanelle**. She integrates style and theme, making use of the villanelle's repetition and refrain to explore many different kinds of losses.

Bishop's wit--or "art"--in this poem resides in treating the loss of one's home or place in the world as if it were simply a larger version of losing keys and watches. Like the word "design" in the Frost poem of that title, the word "art" has several meanings. How do these different meanings contribute to the main idea of "One Art"? First the speaker loses keys and plans, then memories and houses, then a continent. How does the progression emphasize the significance of "losing you"? How does Bishop's tone change from the beginning to the end of the poem, and does this change intensify the impact of the final lines? Does Bishop convince us that we can indeed "master" this type of loss, or does she only communicate how disastrous such pain would be? How do Bishop's references to geography reflect the uprootedness we discover in many of her poems?

"In the Waiting Room"

This poem, along with "One Art," comes from Bishop's collection entitled *Geography III*. Poems in this volume have a more personal voice and seem more self-revealing than her earlier, more studiedly "cool" poems. She actually refers to herself by name--"you are an *I*,/you are an *Elizabeth*." "In the Waiting Room" records an experience of dislocation that begins in her childhood but also feels emblematic of much of her adult experience. In the moment of her aunt's small exclamation of pain, Bishop suddenly loses her sense of a differentiated self. The cry seems to have come from within--within herself as much as within the dentist's office. Though she tries to keep her place--in the family, in the waiting room, in the *National Geographic* she is reading, in the universe itself--she feels herself falling:

> I said to myself: three days
> and you'll be seven years old.
> I was saying it to stop
> the sensation of falling off
> the round, turning world
> into cold, blue-black space.

Her sense of who she is becomes absolutely precarious: "Why should I be my aunt,/or me, or anyone?" she wonders. There is no language for the child's sense of uncertainty: "How--I didn't know any/ word for it-- how 'unlikely' . . ."

The child asks "what similarities . . . held us all together"--what connections link her both to her aunt and to the strange people in the *National Geographic* from other lands? Can you see a resemblance between "the cry of pain" and the Man-Moth's "tear"? What is the significance of the date and the events of the outside world?

> The War was on. Outside,
> In Worcester, Massachusetts,
> were night and slush and cold,
> and it was still the fifth
> of February, 1918.

Is the "big black wave" that seven-year-old Elizabeth feels somehow related to a global darkness? Like "First Death in Nova Scotia," "In the Waiting Room" is written in short lines (five to seven syllables each). Does this form help portray the voice and perspective of a child?

Bishop's poetry captures moments when the familiar world suddenly becomes strange and unknown, as when the child of "In the Waiting Room" reaches toward a mystery, and senses "that nothing stranger could ever happen." Her poems record experiences of discovery, moments when, to return to her own comment on Darwin, observation seems to "giddily slide off" into the unknown.

In her other poems, Bishop uses geography and travel as metaphors to represent her own acts of describing, exploring, and questioning the world. But her focus is always on moments--moments of vision and discovery when alien scenes suddenly become familiar or significant. Bishop's gift is her ability to move from observation--both of real and imagined worlds--to startling revelations about our human condition.

BIBLIOGRAPHY

Bishop, Elizabeth. *The Complete Poems: 1927-1979*. New York: Farrar, Straus & Giroux, 1979.

Ivask, Ivar, ed. "Homage to Elizabeth Bishop, Our 1979 Laureate." *World Literature Today*, Winter 1977.

Kalstone, David. *Five Temperaments*. New York: Oxford University Press, 1977.

Schwartz, Lloyd, and Sybil P. Estess. *Elizabeth Bishop and Her Art*. Ann Arbor: University of Michigan Press, 1983.

WRITTEN ASSIGNMENT 10

Part I. Identification

For each passage, a) identify title; b) write one paragraph discussing its meaning and/or significance to the poem as a whole.

a.　I was saying it to stop
　　the sensation of falling off
　　the round, turning world
　　into cold, blue-black space.

b.　I thought of the coarse white flesh
　　packed in like feathers,
　　the big bones and the little bones,
　　the dramatic reds and blacks
　　of his shiny entrails,
　　and the pink swim-bladder
　　like a big peony.

c.　Oh, must we dream our dreams
　　and have them, too?
　　And have we room
　　for one more folded sunset, still quite warm?

d.　But how could Arthur go,
　　clutching his tiny lily,
　　with his eyes shut up so tight
　　and the roads deep in snow?

e.　*It's time for tea now;* but the child
　　is watching the teakettle's small hard tears

dance like mad on the hot black stove,
the way the rain must dance on the house.

Part II. Essay

Answer *three* of the following questions in approximately two pages each.

1. Bishop's poems often begin with observation but end with a sense of wonder or mystery. Pick *one* of the following poems and trace the shift from careful observation to commentary on the world: "The Fish," "At the Fishhouses," "First Death in Nova Scotia," "Man-Moth" "In the Waiting Room." How does Bishop use details to convey something more than just description? When in the poem do we sense this shift? What words and images in the poem enable her to reveal as well as describe?

2. Travel is central as both subject and metaphor in Bishop's poems. Select *one* of the following poems and explain how she uses travel to express her feelings about the world: "Questions of Travel," "Arrival at Santos," "Over 2,000 Illustrations and a Complete Concordance." Why is the setting she chooses for each poem important? What does travel represent to her? Explain why her journeys do or do not seem to arrive at destinations.

3. Bishop wrote her poems in a number of different forms, from a kind of controlled free verse to structures as fixed as the **sestina** and the **villanelle** (discussed in detail in the Glossary). Select *either* "Sestina" or "One Art," and try to determine why Bishop picked either the sestina or villanelle form for this poem. Pay special attention to the ending. What relationship can you detect between the form Bishop chooses and the ideas she expresses? Explain.

4. Which is your favorite Bishop poem, and why? Analyze *one* poem in detail (choose a different poem than you analyzed for Questions 1, 2, or 3.). What images and ideas stand out for you? To what extent do you identify with the speaker of the poem, or find yourself able to relate the poem to your own life?

5. (*Creative*) Using a free verse style, write a short poem in which geography or setting is vitally important. Choose a location you live in or have visited. After writing your poem, write a few paragraphs analyzing it. How is it like or unlike the travel poems of Elizabeth Bishop? Which specific details and images help describe the scene? Have you used geography as a metaphor, moving from observation to revelation?

Unit
11

Toni
Morrison

READING

Toni Morrison, *Song of Solomon*

LISTENING

Audio Program 12, with Jay Clayton and Theodore Mason

OVERVIEW

Song of Solomon focuses on a young black man's self-discovery and his search for understanding of his familial and racial heritage. Morrison weaves history, folklore, and myth into her fiction to suggest that individuals are part of a larger cultural community.

TONI MORRISON (1931-): A BIOGRAPHICAL SKETCH

Toni Morrison, whose humble origins reflect an experience common to many black Americans, is one of the most celebrated novelists of our age. Morrison was born in Lorain, Ohio, a small town on the edge of Lake Erie, but her family on both sides came from the South. Her father grew up in Georgia, where his first-hand observation of racial violence convinced him that white people were "in some way fundamentally, genetically corrupt." Her grandparents on her mother's side moved north from Alabama, looking for an escape from poverty and racism. They stopped for awhile in Kentucky, where her grandfather worked in the coal mines, but eventually moved on in search of a better education for their children.

Toni Morrison was born Chloe Anthony Wofford in 1931. Her father had to maintain up to three jobs simultaneously in order to support his family. But his children inhabited a world that was rich in the myths, rituals, and music of black culture. Morrison remembers both of her parents as wonderful storytellers who could spin out the most terrifying ghost stories. Morrison's grandmother kept a dream book in which she sought portents to help her play the numbers. Morrison's girlhood was haunted by signs and visions. "We were intimate with the supernatural," she told one interviewer. She was an excellent student, and on her own, read the great nineteenth-century Russian novelists, as well as Jane Austen's works and Gustave Flaubert's *Madame Bovary*.

She graduated from high school with honors and then attended Howard University, an all black institution in Washington, D.C. Her mother took what Morrison once called "humiliating jobs" in order to help her to stay in college. There she studied literature and participated in student theater. After receiving her bachelor of arts degree in 1953, she attended Cornell University, from which she earned a master's degree in English in 1955. Her thesis was on the theme of suicide in William Faulkner and Virginia Woolf. For the next nine years, she pursued a career in teaching, working first at Texas Southern University and then at her alma mater, Howard University. It was during her time in Washington that she married Harold Morrison, a Jamaican architect, and had two children, Harold Ford and Slade.

It was also during this period that she began to write. She became a member of a writer's group at Howard, and she forced herself to write a story so that she would not be too embarrassed to attend. The story was about a little black girl who wanted blue eyes--and it was eventually to become the basis of her first novel. In 1964 she separated from her husband and moved to Syracuse, New York, where she started working for a division of Random House. She did not cease to work on her short story, however, which gradually expanded to novel length. In 1970 Holt, Rinehart, and Winston published *The Bluest Eye*, a haunting, experimental book that received high praise from reviewers. In 1968 she moved to New York City, where she became a senior editor for Random House. Since then, she has done the work of three women, dividing her time between writing fiction, editing, teaching creative writing at a number of different universities, and raising two sons. Despite this seemingly impossible load, she has continued to produce important novels at regular intervals.

Her second novel *Sula* appeared in 1973. The story of the lifelong relationship of two black women, it was set in a small town in northern Ohio, as was *The Bluest Eye*. *Song of Solomon* (1977) also began in the same part of the country, but it ranged over a larger geographical territory and marked the author's first foray into the historical past. Much longer than either of her previous works, this novel immediately strikes the reader as a more ambitious effort, although it inevitably sacrifices some of the poetic compression of her first books. It was awarded the National Book Critics Circle Award for fiction in 1978. *Tar Baby*, which appeared in 1981, represented something of a departure. Set primarily on a Caribbean island, it was the first of her novels to concentrate on the relations between blacks and whites rather than on the black community. It also featured characters from a higher social class than any of her earlier fiction. But, like all her work, it still remained close to a level of myth and ritual that is unusual in contemporary fiction. A recent work was *Beloved* (1987), Morrison's historical novel about an ex-slave. A powerful, even harrowing tale about a mother driven to take the life of her own child, it was awarded the Pulitzer Prize for fiction in 1988.

SONG OF SOLOMON

Toni Morrison is one of the most important of a new group of black women novelists who have achieved extraordinary recognition in the seventies and eighties. Along with Alice Walker and Gloria Naylor, Morrison has written a distinguished body of fiction that focuses as much on problems of being a woman as of being black. Before the emergence of these novelists, the black experience in America had been represented primarily by male authors: Richard Wright, Ralph Ellison, and James Baldwin being the most famous. Like Alice Walker, Morrison has complained that these male novelists tended to forget the situation of black women in their passionate analyses of American race relations.

Song of Solomon is unique among Morrison's novels in taking for its central character a young black male. She has been praised for this decision as demonstrating her willingness to expand her imagination to encompass experience foreign to her. But *Song of Solomon* does not neglect gender questions entirely. Pilate and her matriarchal family group stand as a provocative alternative and challenge to the way families are traditionally organized. Milkman's treatment of his two older sisters as well as his brutally insensitive behavior toward his lover Hagar also serve as reminders of the inequity of relations between the sexes today. Nonetheless, the novel's primary focus is on Milkman's journey of self-discovery and on his consequent discovery of his familial and racial heritage.

Song of Solomon can be divided into two parts. The first deals with Milkman's childhood, his family, and his difficulty growing up. It is a personal story, the tale of one boy's attempt to discover his identity. This section of the novel is organized by the contrast between the two family groups. On the one hand there is the stifling family in which Milkman grew up. Milkman's father, a self-made man who has married the daughter of the richest and most respected black in the town, hungers for wealth, status, and the respect of the white business community. This household is an arid, loveless place, obsessed with appearances but barely containing violent tensions. Milkman wakes up one day to discover that his conception, birth, and upbringing have been the occasions of a sordid and incestuous drama involving his mother, father, and maternal grandfather.

This discovery marks the beginning of his efforts to find out who he is and to reexamine some of the assumptions that have governed his youth. This process inevitably leads him into closer contact with the other family group, Pilate's household.

Pilate's family consists of three generations of nonconformist women, including Pilate herself, her daughter Reba, and her granddaughter Hagar. This family is as poetic, nurturing, and mysterious as Milkman's family is prosaic, alienated, and conventional. They stand as a refreshing contrast not only to the style of life that he is used to but also to the values that he has inherited. Further, they serve as a repository of a rich heritage of black songs and customs, a heritage that Milkman's father has conscientiously suppressed in his effort to become a successful businessman in the white world. We are introduced to this treasure store on the first pages of the novel where we see Pilate singing the children's rhyme that will ultimately hold the key to the novel's mystery. We see its power to enchant even Macon Dead at the end of the first chapter, when he stops outside Pilate's window to listen and to watch the women sing. Even as a boy, Milkman is fascinated by this group of women; as a teenager he becomes romantically involved with the youngest of them; but he has no conception of what his true relationship to them should be until his journey in the second half of the novel has taught him a sense of responsibility.

The second part of the novel follows Milkman on his quest, a journey initially undertaken to find a mere sack of gold but later pursued to discover the truth about his family's past. This section becomes less a personal story than an attempt to come to terms with the experience of a whole group of people. His quest to discover his roots leads the novel into the realms of history, folklore, and myth, the realms that had played such a small role in his protected, suburban childhood. This section teaches what may be the novel's most important lesson: before Milkman can understand anything about himself he must recognize that he is a part of a larger cultural community.

If Milkman's discovery of his parents' unhappy past forces him to begin to reexamine his self, his discovery that his best friend Guitar is part of a terrorist organization called the Seven Days forces Milkman to begin thinking about social issues larger than his own personal concerns. For the first time, he realizes that he has never had a goal in his life, never had any purpose other than finding the next party. Initially he hopes that looking for the gold will provide him with a goal, but in the course of his journey he discovers something more valuable than gold, the joy of being part of a larger group. By the end of the novel he has learned that he is bound to his family, to his race, to his cultural heritage, and most of all, to the woman who represents all three of these things, Pilate--bound by ties that are stronger and more important than those that bind him to life itself.

Song of Solomon contains much that is violent and shocking, but it ends on a note of affirmation and promise. Its vision of the possibilities of genuine change is a hopeful one, a vision of what we all could become were we to surrender ourselves to the best in our heritage.

BIBLIOGRAPHY

Christian, Barbara. "Community and Nature: The Novels of Toni Morrison." In *Black Feminist Criticism*. New York: Pergamon Press, 1985, 47-64.

Mason, Theodore. "*On Song of Solomon*." *Contemporary Literature* 29 (1988).

McKay, Nellie. "An Interview with Toni Morrison." *Contemporary Literature* 24, 1983, 413-430.

Willis, Susan. "Eruptions of Funk: Historicizing Toni Morrison." In *Specifying: Black Women Writing the American Experience.* Madison: University of Wisconsin Press, 1987, 83-109.

WRITTEN ASSIGNMENT 11

Answer *three* of the following questions in approximately two pages each.

1. "Reasonable? You can't get no pot of gold being reasonable." So Guitar comments in *Song of Solomon*. Why does Guitar think that a person must take great risks to find fulfillment in life? If he is right, then a certain amount of violence may be an inevitable part of one's search for meaning. Discuss the need (or lack of need) for risk, violence, and total commitment to a cause as illustrated in Morrison's novel.

2. Why does singing play such an important role in Morrison's novel? Trace the singing motif throughout the novel. What does singing seem to represent? Discuss a few of the instances or passages that led you to your conclusion.

3. According to Morrison, in the black community people's names take on a special meaning. This certainly appears to be the case in *Song of Solomon*. Analyze the significance of three personal names in this novel. What do the names reveal about the individual characters and the black community as a whole?

4. Discuss the ending of *Song of Solomon*. What kind of resolution does Morrison provide for the novel? Do you find it a satisfying or unsatisfying conclusion? Explain.

Unit 12

Philip Roth

READING

The Ghost Writer

LISTENING

Audio Program 12, with Terrence Doody and Rosellen Brown

OVERVIEW

The Ghost Writer illustrates the ethnic orientation of contemporary fiction. Roth uses humor, dialogue, and fantasy to explore history and imagination, the family and the self, from the special perspective of the Jewish-American writer. *The Ghost Writer* also provides an example of **metafiction**, or literature that analyzes the nature and purpose of fiction itself.

PHILIP ROTH (1933-): A BIOGRAPHICAL SKETCH

Just as Malcolm X's shocking political rhetoric generated controversy, so Philip Roth's fiction has elicited intense, often angry response from readers. Roth is often known as the "bad boy" of Jewish-American literature, a label acknowledging his outrageous

123

Philip Roth

humor, sexual candor, and deliberate exploitation of his Jewish background for fictional purposes.

Philip Milton Roth was born in Newark, New Jersey, in 1933. He has observed of his childhood, "I was by and large a good, responsible, well-behaved boy, controlled (rather willingly) by the social regulations of the self-conscious and orderly lower-middle-class neighborhood where I had been raised, and mildly constrained still by the taboos that had filtered down to me . . . from the religious orthodoxy of my immigrant grandparents." The tensions between religious restrictions and natural impulses, between control and abandon, between a minority culture and the mainstream, between self and family, form the basis of much of Roth's fiction.

Roth's first collection of short stories, *Goodbye Columbus* (1959), won the National Book Award. *Goodbye Columbus*, *Letting Go*, and *When She Was Good* established Roth as a Jewish-American writer who used wit, satire, and candor to describe his background. His third and most famous novel, *Portnoy's Complaint* (1969), brought him condemnation as well as praise: its explicit account of a young Jewish man's family problems and sexual experimentation outraged many people, particularly Jewish readers who saw Roth as perpetuating prejudices and ignorance toward Jews. Later novels such as *The Breast* (in which a man turns into a giant female breast), *My Life as a Man*, *The Professor of Desire*, and others furthered Roth's reputation as a writer whose ethnic humor often went beyond the bounds of good taste.

Roth's recent novels, including *The Ghost Writer*, are increasingly self-reflective, focusing on a Jewish-American writer named Nathan Zuckerman who often resembles Roth himself. *The Ghost Writer* is the first installment in what has now become a tetrology, or four-part series. *Zuckerman Unbound*, the second, is a study of the mixed blessings of literary success. *The Anatomy Lesson* tells of Zuckerman's writer's block and psychosomatic illness. These second and third novels are straightforward and realistic in their method--and funny and outrageous and compelling. The fourth novel, *The Counterlife*, is, like *The Ghost Writer*, a story about making stories. Roth seems to delight in creating fiction about characters who create fiction. He challenges the reader to keep clear the differences between truth and fiction, art and life.

THE GHOST WRITER (1982)

Philip Roth's *The Ghost Writer* is a small book that asks many large, important, and often unanswerable questions. What does it

124

mean to be a Jew? What does it mean to be an American? What does it mean to be a writer or artist? What does it mean to be a Jewish American writer? Does the Jew's special relationship to history--as an outsider and victim of persecutions that culminated in Hitler's attempt to eradicate the Jewish race entirely--still affect an American Jewish writer who has never been so disastrously threatened or victimized--who has, more or less, been assimilated into American society?

Roth does not even try to answer all these questions. He raises them, considers them in all their complexity, and dramatizes the personal difficulty Nathan Zuckerman has in trying to work out conclusions of his own.

We do not, or perhaps we should not, ask literature for answers. We read to have honest questions raised and to see the consequences of this kind of questioning in the lives of people we can imagine ourselves to be. For even if we are not Jewish, we can imagine ourselves in familial and historical circumstances that are similar, or analogous, or even virtually identical. The nineteenth-century poet Percy Shelley has said this kind of imagination is absolutely essential to our moral lives, when he said in his "Defense of Poetry":

> The great secret of morals is Love; or a going out of our own nature, and an identification of ourselves with the beautiful which exists in thought, action, or person, not our own. A man to be greatly good, must imagine intensely and comprehensively; he must put himself in the place of another and of many others; the pains and pleasures of his species must become his own.

Section I

Nathan Zuckerman, the young writer who is the hero and narrator of *The Ghost Writer*, summarizes his situation when he says:

> For I had come, you see, to submit myself for candidacy as nothing less than E. I. Lonoff's spiritual son, to petition for his moral sponsorship and to win, if I could, the magical protection of his advocacy and his love. Of course, I had a loving father of my own, whom I could ask the world of any day of the week, but my father was a foot doctor and not an artist, and lately we had been having serious trouble in the family because of a new story of mine. He was so bewildered by what I had written that he had gone running to *his* moral mentor, a certain Judge Leopold Wapter, to get the judge to get his son to see the light. As a result, after two decades of a more or less unbroken amiable conversation, we had not been speaking for nearly five weeks now, and I was off and away seeking patriarchal validation elsewhere.

Zuckerman not only thinks of Lonoff as the "Maestro," the master, he admires Lonoff's style of life--his dedication to nothing but writing, his patient perfectionism, his demands on himself in the name of art.

But what Zuckerman learns is that Lonoff is also impossibly demanding of those around him, especially his wife Hope. At dinner, an argument suddenly erupts when Hope can take no more of Lonoff's "moral fiber," his harshness and superiority.

> With that, she rose to begin to clear the dishes for dessert, and all at once a wineglass struck the wall. Hope had thrown it. "Chuck me out," she cried, "I want you to chuck me out. Don't tell me you can't, because you must! I want you to! I'll finish the dishes, then chuck me out, tonight! I beg of you--I'd rather live and die alone, I'd rather endure that than another moment of your bravery! I cannot take any more moral fiber in the face of life's disappointments! Not yours and not mine! I cannot bear having a loyal, dignified husband who has no illusions about himself *one second more!*"

As shocking as Zuckerman finds this, he is even more astonished when Hope says:

> "Take her, Manny. If you want her, take her," she cried, "and then you won't be so miserable, and everything in the world won't be so bleak. She's not a student any more--she's a woman! You are *entitled* to her--you rescued her from oblivion, you are more than entitled: It's the only thing that makes sense! Tell her to accept that job, tell her to stay! She should! And I'll move away! Because I cannot live another moment as your jailer! Your nobility is eating away the last thing that is left! You are a monument and can take it and take it--but I'm down to nothing, darling, and I can't. Chuck me out! Please, now, before your goodness and your wisdom kill us both!"

Hope is referring to Amy Bellette, the beautiful and mysterious young woman Zuckerman has seen working on Lonoff's papers and manuscripts in order to prepare them for donation to a library. Hope clearly implies Lonoff is having an affair with Amy, whose full name is a pun on the French words for "friend" and "literature." (Belles-lettres literally means beautiful letters. An English derivation of the phrase, "belletristic," usually connotes writing that is overly refined and effete, which would be an insult to Lonoff and a belittlement of his "heroic" work.)

When Hope leaves the room and things settle down, the two writers discuss Lonoff's relationship to two great European Jews, Isaac

Babel and Franz Kafka. Zuckerman intends to flatter Lonoff by mentioning these literary masters. This then leads to a mention of Felix Abravanel, who is Lonoff's contemporary competition, but who is a flashy, volcanic, public man altogether unlike Lonoff in every important way. Though Zuckerman has met Abravanel and admires his power and success, he clearly prefers Lonoff not only for the style of his work but also for the way of life he has chosen--removed, ascetic, even "priestly" in its concentration on art.

Section II

After Lonoff invites Nathan to spend the night and goes off to bed himself, Zuckerman is left alone in Lonoff's study. In a flashback he explains the difficulty he has been having with his father. His latest story, "Higher Education," has grown out of an episode in his family's history. Zuckerman clearly intends to show the sacrifices Jewish parents have made in order to ensure their children's education and, therefore, their upward mobility. But the story also contains some unsavory elements, which are in a way scandalous, yet also poignant and funny. Zuckerman's father fears these elements will not only shame the family but allow anti-Semitic Gentiles to think the worst of all Jews. For Zuckerman's father, art has an immediate impact on life; this "story" is, paradoxically, *real* and will bring about real effects. Most artists would like to think their work has this effect but know their stories, poems, and novels simply do not change the world for better or for worse. So Zuckerman's dilemma is this: is he first of all an artist responsible for imagining and telling the "truth"? Or is his first responsibility to his father and his family's Jewish heritage? The problem is a basic one and has this additional irony: Zuckerman's father has more belief in the power of art than his son the artist does. Yet the son would nevertheless be violating himself and his vision if he were to withdraw the story from publication in order to remain the faithful child.

The title of this section is "Nathan Dedalus," which is both an appropriate allusion to the hero of James Joyce's classical novel *A Portrait of the Artist as a Young Man*, Stephen Dedalus, and a little bit of bragging on Zuckerman's part. Stephen Dedalus decides that in order to have the freedom necessary to achieve his artistic ambitions he must repudiate his family, the narrow culture of Ireland, and the oppressive authority of the Roman Catholic Church. He is even willing to risk the loss of his soul, and *A Portrait of the Artist* ends as Stephen adopts a mythical father, Dedalus himself, and vows to flee Ireland for Europe. (The original Dedalus is famous for having built the labyrinth on the island of Crete. He was later imprisoned in it, and to escape, fashioned wings of feathers and wax for himself and his own son,

Icarus. But Icarus, symbolizing the artist whose ambition is self-destructive, flew too close to the sun; the wax in his wings melted, and he plunged to his death in the sea.)

Joyce is not the only artist Zuckerman enlists in this section as a role model and example of the artist's plight; there is also Henry James and his story "The Middle Years." James, like Joyce (and Lonoff, for that matter), is another artist absolutely devoted to his art. As Joyce left Ireland to gain the freedom he needed, so James left America to live in Europe and England where, shortly before his death, he became a British citizen to protest America's entrance into World War I. James's story is an ironic study of art's power as the young Dr. Hugh gives up his inheritance because he cares too much for the man who wrote his favorite literature. But the artist Dencombe thinks Hugh is a fool and takes no personal satisfaction or comfort in Hugh's renunciation of the fortune he could have had. Renunciation is a constant and important theme in all of James's work; renunciation has also characterized Lonoff's life; and renunciation--or what exactly to renounce, his art or his father--is the problem Zuckerman faces.

Despite the essential seriousness of all these concerns, Roth is nonetheless a very funny writer, and his great gift allows him to see the humor in situations that are also painful, extreme, and absurd.

As you read *The Ghost Writer*, look for examples of comic moments, exaggerated statements, and ridiculous posturing. What makes Roth funny? When does the humor become offensive or disturbing? The conversations between Nathan and his father Nathan and his mother (dramatized in the audio program) capture the tensions and manipulation within the family.

The letter Zuckerman's father elicits from Judge Wapter is astonishing for its presumption and unctuous hypocrisy. With an exaggerated flourish, Wapter moves from an attack on Nathan to mention of Nazi war criminals, and Zuckerman's response is suitably outraged:

> "The Big Three, Mama! Streicher, Goebbels, and your son! What about the *judge's* humility? Where's *his* modesty?"

> "He only meant that what happened to the Jews--"

> "In Europe--not in Newark! We are not the wretched of Belsen! We were not the victims of that crime!"

> "But we *could* be--in their place we *would* be. Nathan, violence is nothing new to Jews, you *know* that!"

"Ma, you want to see physical violence done to the Jews of Newark, go to the office of the plastic surgeon where the girls get their noses fixed. That's where the Jewish blood flows in Essex County, that's where the blow is delivered--with a mallet! To their bones--and to their pride!"

Newark is not Belsen; Germany is not the United States. Nothing Zuckerman could ever say in his stories about Jews and Jewish experience could affect lives the way the Nazi war criminals did.

These issues are not the only thing on Zuckerman's mind, however. He has also been thinking all night of Amy Bellette and fantasizing about her as he masturbates in Lonoff's study--which he admits is a terribly unJamesian vulgarity. But funnier still is the way he "uses" James to "understand" Lonoff: that is, he stands on the volume of James's stories to bring his ear closer to the ceiling so he can eavesdrop on Lonoff's conversation with Amy. And what he hears astonishes him. Amy and Lonoff are sexually involved, and Amy wants him to repudiate Hope and run away with her. Lonoff's renunciation is in refusing Amy, however, not his wife; and Zuckerman realizes that he is still a very young man who knows much less about life than he thought he did. His response in the final words of this second section is, perhaps, the most important passage in the novel:

> I collapsed. My astonishment at what I'd overheard, my shame at the unpardonable breach of his trust, my relief at having escaped undiscovered--all that turned out to be nothing, really, beside the frustration I soon began to feel over the thinness of my imagination and what that promised for the future. Dad-da, Florence, the great Durante; her babyishness and desire, his mad, heroic restraint--Oh, if only I could have imagined the scene I'd overheard! If only I could invent as presumptuously as real life! If one day I could just approach the originality and excitement of what actually goes on! But if I ever did, what then would they think of me, my father and his judge? How would my elders hold up against that? And if they couldn't, if the blow to their sentiments was finally too wounding, just how well would I hold up against being hated and reviled and disowned?

All of Zuckerman's problems as both a man and an artist are right here.

Section III

"Femme Fatale," the title of the third section, is a phrase that is usually understood to mean something like a woman who leads men to their destruction. But Amy Bellette, in Zuckerman's account, is fated in another way--fated to sacrifice her life for her art. Roth never lets go of this theme. As we can see already, he brilliantly questions art's effect on life, and life's on art. He considers this from every angle, embedding one version of the story in another again and again.

Amy, we are told, is really Anne Frank, the Dutch Jewish girl who kept a diary of the period when she and her family were forced to live for months in a hidden attic in order to escape being captured and put to death by the Nazis, simply for being Jewish. And what Anne Frank herself thinks about this kind of murderous intolerance is important, for she realizes her family are not even very Jewish Jews. They are, first of all, Europeans, and their culture and the books they read are not even exclusively Dutch.

Much more poignant and ironic, however, is her realization after she has supposedly survived that she can never again get in touch with her father. She has to renounce him, as it were, because the diary of the *dead* Anne Frank, the girl murdered by the Nazis, is a much more powerful document if she is seen as a martyr rather than as a survivor. Jews and Gentiles, Europeans and Americans, find it easier to imagine the enormity of the Holocaust when they can identify with a teenager and her family hidden in an attic instead of the millions of "faceless" Jews who died in the concentration camp gas chambers. So in order for her book to have its powerful effect, she must remain her own ghost, be "The Ghost Writer."

Anne Frank's story is more powerful than anything Zuckerman could ever write. Anne's supposed need for Lonoff as a foster-father and a lover is a need much deeper than either the real Amy Bellette's or Zuckerman's; and Anne's cruelty to her own father, by refusing to acknowledge even his existence, is harsher than anything Zuckerman could ever imagine doing to his father, the foot doctor. For these reasons, Zuckerman imagines marrying Anne and bringing her back home to his parents, so that he could say: "Look! I *am* a good son. I am marrying a nice Jewish girl as you always wanted me to. And you know what? She is the greatest Jewish writer in history! Anne Frank! So there!" Nathan's fantasy about Anne Frank raises questions about Jewish-American writers and their link to the European past, art and life, art and the power of the imagination.

Section IV

Section four, "Married to Tolstoy," begins quietly as Amy prepares to leave for Cambridge. It is here that Zuckerman reveals that all of section three has been a story he has made up.

But I could not really think of her as Amy any longer. Instead I was continually drawn back into the fiction I had evolved about her and the Lonoffs while I lay in the dark study, transported by his praise and throbbing with resentment of my disapproving father-- and, of course, overcome by what had passed between my idol and the marvelous young woman before he had manfully gone back to bed with his wife.

Throughout breakfast, my father, my mother, the judge, and Mrs. Wapter were never out of my thoughts. I'd gone the whole night without sleep, and now I couldn't think straight about them or myself, or about Amy, as she was called. I kept seeing myself coming back to New Jersey and saying to my family, "I met a marvelous young woman while I was up in New England. I love her and she loves me. We are going to be married." "Married?" "But so fast? Nathan, is she Jewish?" "Yes, she is." "But who is she?" "Anne Frank."

This is a brilliant coup on Zuckerman's part. If we reread section three, we can see in retrospect that Roth has given us clues that the story of the "Femme Fatale" is *very* hard to believe. Most of us swallowed Zuckerman's explanation of who Amy Bellette "really" is because it is such a wonderful story of heroism and escape, sacrifice and transformation. It is a story that allows us to hope, to believe in the possibilities of the future. We can acknowledge that the kind of edifying art that Judge Wapter and his wife wholly appreciate (like *The Diary of Anne Frank*, which has been made into a play and a movie) actually does have a powerful effect for the good on our moral life and understanding.

Roth never cancels this effect, but he does make it more complicated, and he makes Zuckerman's triumph more ambiguous. For Zuckerman's story has been a triumph. Zuckerman has proved himself to be a daring writer, one bold enough to challenge history and even "re-write" it with nothing but the strength of his own imagination. He has also, in a way, "stolen" Lonoff's girl for himself because, in his imagination, he makes Amy his own bride rather than Lonoff's lover; and in doing all of this, he has also pleased his father and been reconciled. But because it is only a story, Zuckerman realizes: "No, the loving father who must be relinquished for the sake of his child's art was not hers; he was mine." In real life, Zuckerman cannot have it both ways: his desire for artistic integrity and his wish for a reconciliation with his parents are not compatible.

And, in a sense, he must even relinquish his symbolic father, Lonoff, who can do no more for him as a role model or example of behavior. Lonoff's own life is a mess. His success as an artist has not guaranteed his success as a man. Though a great writer, he is a cruel, insensitive, lousy husband. As he pursues Hope down the driveway, as she is apparently leaving him, he remarks to Zuckerman, "It's like being married to Tolstoy." This suggests that *he* is the *victim*, as Tolstoy's real wife was, of the "madness of art." The saddest moment in the whole novel is the last, when we and Zuckerman realize that Lonoff's admirable devotion to his work has ruined his life as a man and that we know this better than Lonoff himself does. How terrible for Zuckerman to see that his hero has a soul of clay.

There are two more important observations about *The Ghost Writer*. First, it is a representative work of American literature after World War II because it is so specifically ethnic and has as one of its basic themes an account of how minorities and minority writers enter the mainstream of the dominant culture. Roth, of course, is not alone in dramatizing this. In the generation before him, Bernard Malamud (who resembles Lonoff to a certain extent) and Saul Bellow (who resembles Abravanel) broke important ground; *The Ghost Writer* is Roth's homage to them as it is Zuckerman's homage to Lonoff. But the history of assimilation is not exclusively a Jewish phenomenon. Southern writers, blacks, and contemporary feminists are each a minority who have made their entrance in the post-war literary culture and dramatized the problems of self-definition and acceptance that we have seen in Zuckerman. This assimilation of new groups of people and their specific experience has always been one of the most important social and political functions of the realistic novel since its "invention" in the late seventeenth or early eighteenth century, and the novel has always been one of our most effective agents of understanding, tolerance, and sympathy. So, in the novel and through it, we can now begin to look for more newly recognized minorities to have their own say.

Secondly, *The Ghost Writer* is a **metafiction**, a novel that self-consciously examines what fiction is, how it works, the ways in which it creates the meaning that it has. Since the nineteenth century, artist-figures have been a common type of the hero--characters important not so much for what they do as for how they think, for their consciousness. But lately, there have been a great many novels popular with the general public--such as *The World According to Garp* --that make the making of fiction their subject matter. At first, this may sound involuted and narcissistic, but it is part of a recurring need in every art to examine its own assumptions and methods. *Don*

Quixote, which is universally acknowledged as the first novel, or the first major novel, is a book about reading books and what effect they can have on a reader as ardent as the Don himself. Many of Picasso's works are paintings about painting. And all the plays and movies about producing plays and making movies--the backstage life of Show Biz--are "metafictional" in this sense. Shelley, the British romantic poet, said we must try to imagine history over again in other ways. Important recent literary works like Garcia Marquez's *One Hundred Years of Solitude*, Thomas Pynchon's *Gravity's Rainbow*, and now Philip Roth's *The Ghost Writer* try to do this.

History as it is written is a fiction, too. History as the Soviet Union has written and rewritten it officially is not necessarily the truth, *but politically useful*, a story that justifies the values of the state and rarely admits its mistakes. The pogroms in Russia under Stalin were as murderous and devastating as Hitler's attempts to eradicate European Jews. And no presidential administration ever tells the full truth about itself in its press releases and official memoirs. We need literature to help us get to the truth. Literature will explain the consequences institutions have on individuals and will help us to understand why stories are told, why there are different stories of the same events, and why this difference is important.

We do not have Lonoff's account of Zuckerman's visit because Roth has not chosen to write it. What was so crucial to Zuckerman may not have been as crucial to Lonoff. Maybe he has had other student-mistresses. Maybe he and Hope have this fight all the time. Who knows? Only Roth, of course, since he made it all up along with his other novels about Nathan Zuckerman.

Picasso once said that art is a lie that tells the truth. This is the best description we can get of the motives and effects of Zuckerman's story "Femme Fatale." It also recognizes all the complexities in Philip Roth's novel *The Ghost Writer*. In this extraordinary book Roth explores the sometimes terrible conflicts between potential future and real past, self and family, ambition and responsibility. He also looks at the humor and tragedy of daily life, and how and why we talk about ourselves in the slippery, self-serving, and often outlandish ways we do in trying to make some sense. Every one of us has invented another version of the "Amy Bellette" in our lives. She is our parent, our spouse, our friend, our child, our hope, whomever we love. That she may not really exist is really no matter. We are, in a way, all of us, ghost writers of our lives.

BIBLIOGRAPHY

Pinsker, Sanford, ed. *Critical Essays on Philip Roth*. Boston: G. K. Hall, 1982.

Lee, Hermoine. *Philip Roth*. London; New York: Methuen, 1982.

Bloom, Harold, ed. *Philip Roth*. New York: Chelsea House, 1986.

Rodgers, Bernard, Jr. *Philip Roth: A Bibliography*. Metuchen, NJ: Scarecrow Press, 1984.

Roth, Philip. *The Facts: A Novelist's Autobiography*. New York: Farrar, Straus & Giroux, 1988.

WRITTEN ASSIGNMENT 12

Choose *four* of the following questions and write one to three pages on each.

1. Discuss Nathan's search for a "father." Why does he go in quest of a someone other than his biological father? What does Lonoff, his "adopted" father, have to offer him?

2. Discuss Roth's humor. What examples do you find in the novel of funny passages, phrases, or ideas? What makes them funny? Does Roth use humor to entertain, to shock, to teach--or all of these things? Do you find the humor offensive? Explain why or why not.

3. Analyze the "Femme Fatale" section (section III) of *The Ghost Writer* in detail. What is the importance of this section to the novel as a whole? What does it add to Roth's exploration of the Jewish writer?

4. Novels often lead characters toward self-discovery. By the end of *The Ghost Writer*, what has Nathan Zuckerman learned about himself? What events have taught him important lessons?

5. (*Creative*) Write a dialogue in which you imagine a conversation between Philip Roth and Judge Wapter. Debate the merits of *The Ghost Writer* as a piece of Jewish-American fiction. Is it negative in its portrayal of Jews and Jewish culture? Should it have been written?

or

Extend Nathan's fantasy in Section III even further. Imagine that he has indeed brought home Anne Frank to meet his mother and father. Write a scene in which Nathan proudly introduces his fiancée to his astonished parents.

Conclusion

In 1950 when William Faulkner delivered his acceptance speech for the Nobel Prize in Literature, he commented on the extraordinary difficulty facing writers in the twentieth century. "There are no longer problems of the spirit," he remarked. "There is only the question: When will I be blown up?" Never before in history has the threat of destruction been so global and ever-present; pollution so widespread; beliefs, whether religious, political, economic, social, or philosophical, so uncertain and fragmented.

Not surprisingly, twentieth-century literature often conveys a sense of gloom and pessimism. Nineteenth-century writers like Jane Austen, Charles Dickens, and Charlotte Brontë concluded their novels by having characters marry, find happiness, or at least grow in self-knowledge. In contrast, characters at the end of twentieth-century works often commit suicide, feel overwhelmed by depression and impotence, fail to communicate with others, or realize the futility of searching for answers or enlightenment.

Perhaps you sensed this pessimism in the poems, fiction, and nonfiction included in this course. "The Love Song of J. Alfred Prufrock" has hardly a cheerful ending, as Prufrock gazes at the sea in sad realization that he is growing old, the mermaids will not sing to him, and human life is a sort of death. Hemingway's *In Our Time* implies that "our time" is one of loneliness, war, suppressed emotions, and severed relationships. Yeats's poetry possesses an exquisite beauty, but running throughout his verse are moods of sadness ("now my heart is sore"), impotence ("my ladder's gone"), despair with the present ("Things fall apart"), and an ominous foreboding about the future ("What rough beast . . . /Slouches toward Bethlehem to be born?") Virginia Woolf, who herself committed suicide, creates a world where characters come and go almost like the waves of the sea, never fully connecting with each other or stopping the onslaught of time. Frost's poetry, however pleasing in sound, exposes a world of painful choices and regrets ("The Road Not Taken"), solitude and barrenness ("Desert Places";"Acquainted with the Night"), longings ("Birches"; "After Apple-Picking"), divisions ("Mending Wall") and senseless deaths ("'Out,Out--'"). In Faulkner's novelette, the bear of the title dies and the wilderness is increasingly threatened by ugliness and corruption.

Gloom continues in the works of Part II. Eudora Welty's "Petrified Man" presents petty or paralyzed characters unable to transcend their narrow vision of the world. The main character in Peter Taylor's "Wife of Nashville" feels lonely, trapped, and unable to find understanding. Alice Walker's "Strong Horse Tea" ends with its central character performing a pathetically futile act: ignorant Rannie Mae Toomer collects horse urine to "cure" a baby who has already died. Malcolm X's *Autobiography* shows an America polarized by bigotry, hate, and economic injustice. Nadine Gordimer's *July's People* imagines a future where racism tears apart the very fabric of society. Elizabeth Bishop's poetry is tinged with a sadness as pervasive as the tears that keep spilling everywhere in "Sestina"; she conveys a fragile sense of home and implies that travel may never lead anywhere. Toni Morrison's *Song of Solomon* sings of racial injustice, incest, hatred, madness, and despair. *Song of Solomon* and *July's People* both end ambiguously: when Milkman Dead leaps and Maureen Smales runs, are they heading toward liberation or death? In Roth's *The Ghost Writer*, Nathan Zuckerman discovers that the distinguished writer he has admired is just an ordinary, flawed man whose artistic vocation has spoiled his personal life; Zuckerman also discovers that as a Jewish-American writer he can never break free from the past, from his family, or from the Jewish community.

Although Faulkner lamented our daily awareness that we may blow up our world, he also remarked in his acceptance speech, "I decline to accept the end of man." Despite the overwhelming chaos and corruption of modern life, Faulkner found reason for optimism:

> I believe that man will not merely endure: he will prevail. He is immortal, not because he alone among creatures has an inexhaustible voice, but because he has a soul, a spirit capable of compassion and sacrifice and endurance. The poet's, the writer's, duty is to write about these things. It is his privilege to help man endure by lifting his heart, by reminding him of the courage and honor and hope and pride and compassion and pity and sacrifice which have been the glory of the past. The poet's voice need not merely be the record of man, it can be one of the props, the pillars to help him endure and prevail.

Modern man (and modern woman too, no longer content to be contained within the generic term "man") possesses a new heroic status. We are heroic because we survive, learn from the past, and create art works that transcend our mortality. We are heroic because of our *effort*, our creative attempts to understand ourselves and our confusing world.

Viewed in this way, the works you have read in this course can seem uplifting and inspiring, occasions for optimism and celebration. We can appreciate the artistry of Eliot, Yeats, and Frost in creating insightful, evocative poems about our modern predicament. Prufrock may not reach understanding, but we sense that Eliot has, and perhaps has helped us see life differently, too. Yeats may lament that his "ladder's gone," but we as readers of his ottava rima poems know otherwise and admire his constant growth as an artist and man. Frost acknowledges life's dark places and tensions, but he also captures its beauty and allure, its moments of vision. Despite the obstacles they face, Hemingway's Nick Adams and Faulkner's Ike McCaslin both come of age and find in the wilderness and in bonds with other men a certain strength, wisdom, and dignity. Lily Briscoe, though alone at the end of Woolf's *To the Lighthouse* and aware of time's passage, finally has her vision and completes her painting. Pain seems to lead to maturation.

Even when characters do not grow, readers may sense their stagnation and find new illumination or understanding. While we may deplore the shallowness of Leota and her clients at the beauty parlor, we admire the keen-sighted vision of Eudora Welty and the way she captures the southern experience. Ruth Lowell and Rannie Mae Toomer are in some ways heroic in their ability to feel and to struggle. Reading past the chapters of hate-filled invective and monomaniacal thinking to the end of Malcolm X's *Autobiography*, we meet a man who has just turned a corner, recognizing the common humanity of all people and affirming his devotion to furthering fellowship and peace. *July's People* makes us marvel at the courage and convictions of a white South African woman who can write so sympathetically about both genders and about races kept apart by her country's rigid political structure. Elizabeth Bishop's poetry enables us to appreciate *both* home and not-home, imagined visions and real sights. Toni Morrison's *Song of Solomon* is in many ways a song of celebration--celebration of the rich oral tradition of black America, of the ways we can discover and use our past to grow, and of our capacity to create art that gives permanent form to fleeting events. With *The Ghost Writer* we discover the saving power of humor: If we can laugh at our predicament, then we may have found a way to come to terms with it.

Works of the second half of the course illustrate the glory of diversity. Alone, we experience only one gender, race, ethnic background, nationality, and religion. Through books, however, we suddenly enter other worlds and cultures, enlarging our definition of what it means to be human. The literary works included in this introductory course enable readers temporarily to become an aging man worrying about his bald spot, a young boy watching his father perform a Caesarean on an Indian woman, an Irishman viewing his country's struggle for independence, a Victorian woman trying to bring people together at a dinner party, a tourist arriving at Brazil, a white South African woman discovering her husband is a stranger, a Jewish man fantasizing about Anne Frank, and many other people in many other places and times. As Emily Dickinson wrote:

> There is no Frigate like a Book
> To take us Lands away
> Nor any Coursers like a Page
> Of prancing Poetry--

Frigate is a fast ship; *coursers* are race horses. Literature expands not only our vocabulary but our minds: it can transport us out of our own narrow world into a larger sphere.

This course has only scratched the surface of twentieth-century literature. Although we have looked at many representative trends and movements, other developments in modern literature have occurred and are occurring right now that have not been touched on here. To encourage continued reading of contemporary literature, the following pages offer a list of selected poems, short stories, and novels written after 1975. At the end an optional written assignment asks you to compare and contrast this new material with earlier works from the course.

The heroine of Jane Austen's *Emma* makes extensive reading lists, alphabetizes them, and proudly shows them to friends, but she never gets around to actually reading the books she so carefully lists. Like Emma, many of us are better at planning to read than in finding the time to carry out our intentions. We hope, though, that this course will inspire you to read more literature--more works by the fourteen writers included in the Units 1-12, works by writers included in the selected reading list that follows, and works from additional writers you encounter on your own.

Contemporary novelist Tom Robbins remarked in an interview (in *Alive and Writing*, 1987), "Reading is one of the most marvelous experiences a human being can enjoy. Being alone in a room with a book is so intimate, so individualistic, so kaleidoscopically imaginative." Literature can indeed enrich lives and increase vision.

139

Suggestions for Additional Reading

Selected Reading List: Works After 1975

The brief and highly selective list below provides suggestions for additional reading in contemporary poetry, short fiction, and novels. To encourage diversity of reading, we have not included recent works by the fourteen writers featured in Units 1-12 (e.g., Toni Morrison's novel *Beloved*; Philip Roth's *Counterlife*) unless their work is in a different genre.

Although excluded from both the course and the reading list, drama is another highly important literary genre, worthy of a separate course of its own. Reading and attending plays can augment your knowledge of modern literature.

To locate the texts listed below, consult local bookstores and libraries. Extensive interlibrary loan systems should make it possible to obtain most of this material.

POETRY

The poets listed below have published volumes of poetry after 1975; most are continuing to write today.

Ammons, A. R.

Ashbery, John

Berry, Wendell

Brooks, Gwendolyn

Broumas, Olga

Corn, Alfred

Davie, Donald

Dickey, James

Forché, Carolyn

Giovanni, Nikki

Graham, Jorie

Gunn, Thom

Hecht, Anthony

Hirsch, Edward

Hollander, John

Howard, Richard

Kinnell, Galway

Kumin, Maxine

Levertov, Denise

Lorde, Audre

Matthews, William

Merrill, James

Merwin, W.S.

Olds, Sharon

Piercy, Marge

Plumly, Stanley

Rich, Adrienne

Shange, Ntozake

Smith, David

Snodgrass, W.D.

Snyder, Gary

Stern, Gerald

Strand, Mark

Van Duyn, Mona

Wakoski, Diane

Walcott, Derek

Wallace, Ron

Wilbur, Richard

Williams, C. K

Wright, James

SHORT FICTION

Barthelme, Donald. *Sixty Stories*

Beattie, Ann. *The Burning House*

Bellow, Saul. *Him with his Foot in his Mouth and Other Stories*

Bowles, Paul. *Things Gone and Things Still Here*

Boyle, T. Coraghessan. *Greasy Lake and Other Stories*

Brodkey, Harold. *Stories in an Almost Classical Mode*

Carver, Raymond. *Cathedral*

Cheever, John. *The Stories of John Cheever*

Friedman, Bruce Jay. *Let's Hear it for a Beautiful Guy*

Gilliat, Penelope. *Splendid Lives*

Gordimer, Nadine. *Something Out There* and *Selected Stories*

Hannah, Barry. *Airships*

Lessing, Doris. *Stories*

MacLeod, Alistair. *The Lost Salt Gift of Blood*

Malamud, Bernard. *The Stories of Bernard Malamud*

Mason, Bobbie Ann. *Shiloh and Other Stories*

Matthiessen, Peter. *Midnight Turning Gray*

Moore, Lorrie. *Self Help*

Oates, Joyce Carol. *All the Good People I've Left Behind*

Paley, Grace. *Later the Same Day*

Rhys, Jean. *Sleep it off, Lady*

Rush, Norman. *Whites*

Sillitoe, Alan. *The Second Chance and Other Stories*

Singer, Isaac Balshevis. *The Death of Methuselah*

Sontag, Susan. *I, Etcetera*

Spark, Muriel. *The Stories of Muriel Spark*

Updike, John. *Trust Me: Stories*

NOVELS

Atwood, Margaret. *The Handmaid's Tale, Cat's Eye*

Banks, Russell. *Continental Drift*

Barth, John. *The Tidewater Tales*

Bellow, Saul. *Humboldt's Gift*

Bradley, David. *The Chaneysville Incident*

Brown, Rosellen. *Civil Wars*

Davies, Robertson. *The Lyre of Orpheus*

De Lillo, Don. *White Noise*

deVries, Peter. *Sauce for the Goose*

Doctorow, E. L. *Billy Bathgate*

Drabble, Margaret. *The Middle Ground*

Erdrich, Louise. *Love Medicine*

Godwin, Gail. *Southern Family*

Golding, William. *Darkness Visible*

Gordon, Mary. *The Company of Women*

Greene, Graham. *The Captain and the Enemy*

Hawkes, John. *Whistlejacket*

Heller, Joseph. *Picture This*

Irving, John. *The World According to Garp*

Kennedy, William. *Ironweed*

Kingston, Maxine Hong. *The Woman Warrior, China Men*, and *Tripmaster Monkey: His Fake Book*

Knowles, John. *A Stolen Past*

Lessing, Doris. *The Fifth Child*

Mailer, Norman. *Executioner's Song*

Malamud, Bernard. *Dubin's Lives*

Miller, Sue. *The Good Mother*

Mortimer, John. *Paradise Postponed*

Murdoch, Iris. *The Good Apprentice* and *The Book and the Brotherhood*

Naylor, Gloria. *The Women of Brewster Place*

Oates, Joyce Carol. *You Must Remember This*

O'Brien, Tim. *Gone After Cacciato*

Percy, Walker. *The Second Coming*

Piercy, Marge. *Woman on the Edge of Time*

Pym, Barbara. *An Academic Question*

Robinson, Marilynne. *Housekeeping*

Silko, Leslie Marmon. *Ceremony.*

Spark, Muriel. *A Far Cry from Kensington*

Stegner, Wallace. *Crossing to Safety*

Stone, Robert. *A Flag for Sunrise*

Styron, William. *Sophie's Choice*

Taylor, Peter. *A Summons to Memphis*

Theroux, Paul. *The Mosquito Coast*

Tyler, Anne. *The Accidental Tourist*, *Dinner at the Homesick Restaurant*, and *Breathing Lessons*

Walker, Alice. *The Color Purple*

Wideman, John. *Hiding Place*

Wiesel, Eli. *Twilight*

Woiwode, Larry. *Born Brothers*

Wolff, Tobias. *In the Garden of the North American Martyrs*

WRITTEN ASSIGNMENT 13 (OPTIONAL)

POETRY

Write four to six pages on *one* of the following questions.

A. Compare and contrast the contemporary poems you selected with those by one poet you read earlier in the course (Bishop, Eliot, Frost, or Yeats). Discuss the similarities and differences between these two poets: note the moods, themes, imagery (both literal and figurative), literary devices (meter, rhyme, irony, etc.), and form (sonnet, free verse, etc.). Do you feel that the work of the earlier poet laid any sort of foundation for the later one? If you wish, close by explaining why you did or did not get something out of reading this new poet.

B. No one can be certain which contemporary poets will stand the test of time. If the choice were yours, would you place the contemporary poet you read in the same category with Eliot, Frost, and Yeats? Why or why not? Use examples from this contemporary poet and one or more poets from the first half of the course to explain your own criteria for "standing the test of time."

SHORT FICTION

Read three or more stories by one author from the reading list and answer A or B. Include in your essay the titles of the stories you read.

A. Characterization is somewhat similar in all fiction--both stories and novels. Compare characterization in the three contemporary stories you read with one of these fiction writers from the course: Faulkner, Hemingway, Morrison, Roth, Taylor, Welty, or Woolf. Consider such areas as how the characters are presented to the reader, whether the characters learn or change, whether they seem realistic, and whether they reveal the author's view of the world.

B. Assume you are a member of a faculty committee adding new works to this introductory course on twentieth-century English and American literature. Explain why you recommend including or excluding this author from the course. In your explanation, include comparisons and contrasts between this author and other works of fiction you read in the course.

NOVELS

Read one of the novels from the reading list and answer A or B.

A. Write a short paragraph summarizing the plot and characters of this novel. Then discuss this novel's similarities to one work of fiction from this course: Faulkner's "The Bear," Gordimer's *July's People*, Morrison's *Song of Solomon*, Roth's *The Ghost Writer*, or Woolf's *To the Lighthouse*. How are the two works alike in terms of characterization, style, and theme?

B. Which fiction writer from this course (Faulkner, Gordimer, Hemingway, Morrison, Roth, Taylor, Walker, Welty, or Woolf) seems most similar to the contemporary novelist you selected from the list? Compose a letter from one of these writers to the other, or create a dialogue between them. What might the two have to say to each other? Would the two share similar concerns about social issues, like the status of an oppressed group? Your answer should include specific examples from the contemporary novel you selected.

Glossary

Contents: abstract, abstract art, alliteration, allusion, ambiguity, anti-hero, apartheid, archetype, assonance, atonality, avant-garde, ballad, blank verse, caesura, canon, causality, character, connotation, couplet, cubism, cumulative sentence, diction, discontinuity, dramatic monologue, elegy, end-stopped lines, enjambment, epiphany, expressionism, figurative language, flashback, free verse, hyperbole, imagery, impressionism, interior monologue, irony, juxtaposition, lyric, metafiction, metaphor, meter, modernism, onomatopoeia, ottava rima, oxymoron, paradox, persona, personification, plot, point of view, protagonist, quatrain, rhetoric, rhetorical question, rhyme, romanticism, scansion, sestina, setting, simile, sonnet, speaker, stream of consciousness, surrealism, symbol, theme, tone, understatement, villanelle

Note: For further discussion of many of these terms, see *Modern Poems*, "Reading Poems" section.

abstract: lacking in concreteness or specific detail. In language, an abstract phrase such as "unattractive appearance" can be made concrete through the addition of specific details: "John's face had three warts and a greenish hue." Poets often use concrete imagery to illustrate abstract states, as in Shakespeare's "Jealousy is a green-eyed monster . . ."

abstract art: refers to visual art lacking in referential quality; abstract paintings often include shapes and designs not resembling known objects (as in Figure 3, "Gray Instrumentation," included in the General Introduction).

alliteration: a device in which consonants, especially those at the beginning of words, are repeated. Tongue-twisters often use alliteration in an extreme form, as in "Peter Piper picked a peck of pickled peppers." In literature, alliteration is used more subtly to create a sense of harmony ("_d_ark and _d_eep": Frost) or to make a phrase more memorable.

147

Glossary

allusion: an implied or indirect reference, often to another literary work, to mythology, or to a person or event. The purpose of an allusion is to enrich the original work by creating associations with other works or events. When Eliot alludes to Hamlet, Yeats alludes to Leda, Roth alludes to Dedalus, or Bishop alludes to the Nativity, they ask us to bring into our understanding of their work our knowledge of Shakespeare, classical mythology, James Joyce, and the Bible.

ambiguity: a situation in which more than one interpretation is possible. Critic William Empson defines ambiguity as a "verbal nuance, however slight, which gives room or alternative reactions to the same piece of language." Some writers create deliberate ambiguity (as in Bishop's lines, "Should we have stayed at home, wherever that may be?") in order to convey life's uncertainty and duality.

anti-hero: a character who is the opposite of the traditional hero (one capable of performing heroic deeds or possessing noble, almost superhuman attributes); anti-heroes generally fail, lack self-esteem, seem powerless to control their destinies and remain unable to reach insight. Eliot's character Prufrock is an example.

apartheid: (Afrikaans: "apartness") South Africa's policy of rigid racial segregation, in which members of different races are segregated for education, employment, housing, politics, and other activities. Apartheid has been the official South African policy since 1948, when the Afrikaner-dominated Nationalist Party gained control of the government.

archetype: a universal pattern of experience or type of character--one that is similar in different nations and cultures. The deadly enchantress is an example of an archetype, for it is an image found in most mythic traditions and literatures, from Circe to Eve to Cleopatra to Keats's *La Belle Dame sans Merci* to Roth's "Femme Fatale."

assonance: a technique in which similar vowel sounds are repeated, usually in order to achieve a harmonious effect. Examples would include "silent night" and "beechen green."

atonality: a characteristic of music no longer relying on the tonality, or sense of key and harmony, dominating Western composition for centuries; atonal music is often dissonant and without a sense of direction or resolution.

avant-garde: (French: "advance guard") a general term referring to modern artistic movements so pioneering or innovative that they seem ahead of (in advance of) their times.

ballad: a song that tells a story, originally a musical accompaniment to a dance. Ballads are often characterized by the use of dialogue and action, tragic themes, and an ending that returns to the ideas of the beginning (refrain). Ballads are a part of many folk cultures, transmitted orally from generation to generation. A literary ballad is a poet's conscious attempt to imitate this form for his or her own thematic purposes. Literary ballads often make use of legend and folklore. The ballad stanza generally consists of a four-line stanza with alternating four- and three-stress lines and a rhyme scheme of abcb or abab.

blank verse: poetry that employs unrhymed iambic pentameter (see meter).

caesura: (Latin: "a cutting") a pause within a line of poetry that results from the phrasing of the language. In Bishop's "One Art," for instance, a reader must pause in the middle of the line to indicate completion of thought:

> Lose something every day. // Accept the fluster
> Of lost door keys, the hour badly spent.

In these lines, a caesura, or pause, occurs after "day." A virgule, or double slash (//), is used to indicate a caesura.

canon: (Greek: "rod, rule") an authoritative list of accepted texts. The literary canon consists of works whose merit has been established over the years by scholars. Recently efforts are being made to reevaluate the accepted canon of literature routinely taught in schools and universities. Recognizing the bias of those who originally selected the canon, some educators today are expanding the canon to include third world and minority works.

causality: relationships determined by cause and effect. In a literary work governed by causality, actions in the first chapter may *cause* the actions in the second chapter; in contrast, works that avoid causality simply juxtapose or place together ideas, characters, thoughts, and events without implying any cause and effect relationship.

character: a person in a literary work. E.M. Forster distinguishes between flat characters, who do not change in the course of the work, and round characters, who change or develop. In *The Ghost Writer*, Mrs. Zuckerman is a flat character who remains a stereotypical Jewish mother throughout the novel. In contrast, Maureen Smales in *July's People* is a round character who changes and develops, revealing many dimensions.

connotation: ideas that are suggested or implied by a word or phrase that go beyond its dictionary definition, or denotation. A "bachelor" may have the denotation of "an unmarried man," but it also may carry with it the connotation of a swinging lifestyle and an unkempt dwelling; it has a very different connotation than "old maid," a term for an unmarried woman. In literature, writers often choose words with careful attention to the connotations, or associations, they evoke.

couplet: two lines of poetry. In a *closed couplet*, the lines conclude in sense at the end of the second line: two lines that do not reach a conclusion or stopping point are called an *open couplet*. A *heroic couplet* refers to a closed couplet written in rhymed iambic pentameter. The close of Frost's "Design" is an example: "What but design of darkness to appall?--/If design govern in a thing so small."

cubism: a school of painting and sculpture developed in Paris in the early twentieth century which avoided traditional approaches to form and space. Cubist painters such as Pablo Picasso and Georges Braque reduced natural forms to geometric shapes and elementary signs.

cumulative sentence: (Latin: "heaping") an often lengthy sentence in which details are accumulated, or piled on. In "The Bear," for instance, Faulkner writes: "It was of the men, not white nor black nor red but men, hunters, with the will and hardihood to endure and the humility and skill to survive, and the dogs and the bear and the bear and deer juxtaposed and reliefed against it, ordered and compelled by and within the wilderness in the ancient and unremitting contest according to the ancient and immitigable rules which voided all regrets and brooked no quarter;--the best game of all the best of all breathing and forever the best of all listening, the voices quiet and weighty and deliberate for retrospection and recollection and exactitude among the concrete trophies--the racked guns and the heads and skins--in the libraries of town houses or (and best of all) in the camps themselves where the intact and still-warm meat yet hung, the men who had slain it sitting before the burning logs on hearths when there were houses and hearths or about the smoky blazing of piled wood in front of stretched tarpaulins when there were not." This 172-word sentence is built upon the short declarative sentence "It was of the men"; the additional details elaborate and expand on the original statement, creating atmosphere.

diction: (Latin: "speaking style") speech or pronunciation; in literature, a writer's choice of words or vocabulary. We can distinguish between artificial poetic diction (such as a reference to the North as a "hyperborean clime") and colloquial diction, or language similar to common speech.

discontinuity: a term suggesting a lack of connection, or continuity, between parts or elements; gaps or breaks in thoughts; literary elements that shift abruptly rather than flow smoothly from one to the next.

dramatic monologue: a poem constructed as the speech of one person, often speaking to an audience. The dramatic monologue captures an intense moment or point of conflict. The speaker's remarks often reveal much about his/her character.

elegy: (Greek: "lament") a work of mourning or lament for a dead person or tragic event. Traditionally, elegies were poems of lament and often included references to nature; at the end, the poet moved away from grief toward joy and celebration, providing a sense of consolation and renewal. In *To the Lighthouse* Virginia Woolf appropriates the elegy form for fiction, writing an extended work of mourning for her parents' generation and its way of life.

end-stopped lines: unlike enjambed lines (see next entry), end-stopped lines conclude in sense at the end of a line or couplet of poetry. Alexander Pope uses end-stopped lines in his poem *An Essay on Man*, as in this couplet:

> Know then Thyself, presume not God to scan;
> The proper study of Mankind is Man.

The ending of the lines (scan/Man) corresponds to the ending of thoughts or ideas.

enjambment: (French: "to straddle") the running over of a sentence from one verse or couplet into another so that closely related words fall in different lines.

> Watch out! Oh! It has caught Miss Breen's
> skirt! There! Miss Breen is about seventy, . . .

These lines from Bishop's "Arrival at Santos" illustrate enjambment. The thought "It has caught Miss Breen's skirt" is divided into two lines, requiring the reader to continue through the lines without pause.

epiphany: (Greek: "manifestation") Originally a religious term, epiphany refers to a moment in which an individual achieves a spiritual vision, or manifestation of a higher realm. James Joyce first used the term in literature to refer to a character's glimpse of something beyond ordinary experience. Many modern short stories and poems attempt to capture these highly intense, visionary moments in which sudden insight comes to individuals. Bishop describes this sort of revelation in "The Fish."

expressionism: a movement (beginning with German painters) to project a personal vision rather than represent reality; expressionist works are more subjective than objective.

figurative language: the use of words to convey associations and other levels of meaning, unlike literal language, which uses words to convey their primary meaning directly. **Metaphors** and **similes** (see separate entries) are types of figurative language. "My wife died" is a literal statement; in figurative language, one might express this as "The light of my life went out." Yeats uses figurative language in "The Lake Isle of Innisfree" in the lines "There midnight's all a glimmer, and noon a purple glow."

flashback: an episode which is inserted in a literary work to show events that happened at an earlier time. In *July's People* Maureen has a flashback to an earlier time in her life when a photographer stopped her with her black servant, Lydia.

free verse: poetry with no regular meter, line length, or rhyme. Often free verse grows out of the rhythms of natural speech.

hyperbole: (Greek: "overcasting") an exaggerated statement, often used to emphasize a point or to create humor. We use hyperbole in everyday speech when we say, "I'm starving," or "He's as old as the hills." Elizabeth Bishop uses hyperbole in "In the Waiting Room" when she writes that "nothing stranger/had ever happened," and "nothing/stranger could ever happen."

imagery: a general term indicating the objects referred to either literally or figuratively in a work of literature. The term often is used to denote objects that appeal to the senses or create mind-pictures. Prose writers and poets use a variety of images: as in these lines from Bishop's "The Fish":

> ... Here and there
> is brown skin hung in strips
> like ancient wall paper
> and its pattern of darker brown
> was like wallpaper:

> shapes like full-blown roses
> stained and lost through age.

In these lines, Bishop uses both literal images (the fish's brown skin in strips, its pattern of darker brown) and figurative images (the skin like wallpaper; the shapes like roses). Patterns of imagery occur in a literary text when similar images are repeated: imagery of cold (Frost), fog (Eliot), singing (Morrison), and so on. When an image signifies something other than its literal reality, it may be called a symbol: e.g., the image of a golden bird in Yeats's "Sailing to Byzantium" may be a symbol of an immortal work of art.

impressionism: originally a movement in painting to capture fleeting impressions and points of view rather than a precise, fixed representation. In literature, impressionism refers to a writer's focus on mood and inner thoughts rather than external events.

interior monologue: a speech by a single character to himself or herself, almost as if thinking aloud.

irony: (Greek "dissimulation") In classical Greece, an *eiron* was one who dissembled or pretended in order to achieve a certain result. In literature, irony occurs when the intended meaning is different from what is actually stated. *Verbal irony* occurs when a character says one thing but means another. *Dramatic irony* occurs when a character says or does something that the audience interprets in a different way. Yeats's title "The Second Coming" is ironic because Bethlehem witnesses the approach of a monster rather than the reappearance of Christ. Dramatic irony occurs in "Petrified Man" when Mrs. Fletcher says "I ask Mr. Fletcher's advice . . . on something important, like is it time for a permanent--not that I've told him about the baby": we as readers sense that Mrs. Fletcher, contrary to her claim, hides important matters from her husband and shares only trivial matters.

juxtaposition: (Latin: "placing close together") the act of situating different elements or ideas side by side, without any necessary link or relationship between them.

lyric: (Greek: "a song accompanied by a lyre") a poem characterized by harmonious beauty and intense personal emotion. A lyric poem is often short and expresses the thoughts and meditations of one speaker.

metafiction: a fictional work about the making of fiction; one in which we are aware of the author standing behind the work and analyzing the process of creation.

metaphor: (Greek: "to transfer, or carry from one place to another") a figure of speech in which a word or phrase literally denoting one kind of object or idea is used in place of another to suggest a likeness or analogy between them. Unlike a **simile**, a **metaphor** makes the comparison implicit. When Yeats writes in "Sailing to Byzantium," "An aged man is but a paltry thing,/A tattered coat upon a stick," he is using a metaphor to compare an old man to a scarecrow. If this line were rewritten as a simile, the comparison would be explicit: "An aged man . . . is *like* a tattered coat upon a stick."

meter: (Greek: "measure") the pattern of stressed and unstressed syllables in verse. A metric line is named according to the number of feet it is composed of:

monometer: one foot
dimeter: two feet
trimeter: three feet
tetrameter: four feet
pentameter: five feet
hexameter: six feet (and so on)

A *poetic foot* is the recurring metric unit of a line, a combination of strong and weak stresses (strong stresses are capitalized in these examples):

iambic: weakSTRONG (uNITE, rePEAT)
trochaic: STRONGweak (UNit, REAPer)
anapestic: weakweakSTRONG (interRUPT, disarRANGE)
dactylic: STRONGweakweak (WASHington, HICKory)
spondaic: STRONGSTRONG (HEARTBREAK, HEADLINE)

A poem's meter indicates both the number of beats per line and the type of poetic foot used as the basic metric unit. One of the most common meters in English is *iambic pentameter*, or five-beat lines using iambic feet:

> The BLISS of MAN (could PRIDE that BLESsing
> FIND)
> Is NOT to ACT or THINK beYOND ManKIND;
> No POW'RS of BOdy OR of SOUL to SHARE;
> But WHAT his NAture AND his STATE can BEAR.

These lines from Alexander Pope's *An Essay on Man* are written in rhymed iambic pentameter. Frost often employed unrhymed iambic pentameter, also known as blank verse, in order to achieve an effect more closely resembling actual speech. Modern poets frequently deviate from this meter both in order to avoid creating a singsong effect and in order to emphasize certain words.

Other meters can be formed by combining a line length with a type of metric foot. A poet may use *trochaic tetrameter*:

> TYger! TYger! BURning BRIGHT
> IN the FORests OF the NIGHT. (Blake's "The Tyger")

or *anapestic tetrameter*:

> 'Twas the NIGHT before CHRISTmas and ALL
> through the HOUSE,
> Not a CREAture was STIRring, not Even a MOUSE.

or *iambic tetrameter*:

> The WOODS are LOVEly, DARK and DEEP,
> But I have PROMisES to KEEP,
> And MILES to GO beFORE i SLEEP . . .

(Frost's "Stopping by Woods on a Snowy Evening")

Meter is basic to the effect of poetry. To illustrate this, try to read Blake's "The Tyger" with the *wrong* meter:

> TyGER! TyGER! burNING bright
> In THE forESTS of THE night.

Or read Frost's "Stopping by Woods on a Snowy Evening" with the wrong meter:

> THE woods ARE loveLY dark AND deep
> BUT i HAVE promISes TO keep.

Obviously such a reading of these lines is worse than clumsy; disrupting the meter in this way destroys the musical sound of the poetry.

modernism: a very broad term referring to an international movement in all the arts in the late nineteenth and early twentieth centuries. Literary modernism has involved a reaction against established conventions and traditions, new ways of viewing humanity, nature, religion, and art, and radical experimentation with form and style.

onomatopoeia: (Greek: "name-making") the naming of a thing or action by a vocal imitation of the sound associated with it. In words such as "murmur," "hiss," or "crackle," the sound suggests the sense. "The buzz saw snarled and rattled" from Frost's "'Out, Out--'" exemplifies onomatopoeia.

ottava rima: (Italian: "eighth rhyme") a poetic form of apparent Italian origin consisting of eight-line iambic stanzas rhyming abababcc. Yeats chooses this form for "Sailing to Byzantium," "Among School Children," and "The Circus Animals' Desertion."

oxymoron: (Greek: "pointedly foolish") a combination of contradictory or incongruous words, often used by a writer to convey a sense of duality or ambiguity. Examples include "cruel kindness," "living death." "frozen warmth," "hateful love," and from Yeats's "Easter 1916," "terrible beauty."

paradox: (Greek: "contrary to expectations") a statement that seems contradictory or opposed to common sense and yet is true. An example from ordinary life would be a forty-year-old man who claims to have had only ten birthdays: paradoxically, both statements prove true when it is revealed that his birthday falls on February 29, a day included in the calendar only in leap years. In poetry, paradox is related to **ambiguity, oxymoron,** and **irony**. Bishop may paradoxically discover that she achieves greater visions at home than abroad; Eliot's Prufrock may discover that his life is more like death.

persona: (Greek: "mask") a character in a fictional presentation; plural is "personas" or "personae." At times we may talk about an author's multiple personae, or the many voices/masks the writer chooses to adopt in his/her poetry or fiction.

personification: a figure of speech or type of metaphor, in which a nonhuman object is represented or addressed as a human being. Frost personifies the buzz-saw in "'Out, Out--'" as a murderer. Bishop personifies the fish as a wise veteran ("The Fish") when she describes him as possessing "medals" and "a five-haired beard of wisdom."

plot: the design or plan of events in a fictional work, particularly the organization of events in order to create suspense. E.M. Forster in *Aspects of the Novel* distinguishes between a story ("The king died and then the queen died") and a plot ("The king died and then the queen died of grief"). In the second example, causality is implied: the king's death (event 1) caused the queen's death (event 2). In a mystery plot, this sentence might read, "The queen died and no one knew why, until it was discovered that she died out of grief for the king." A plot often consists of parts, such as a beginning, middle, and end, and contains a *climax*, or turning point. Suspense results when a reader is left uncertain and curious about the outcome of events. A plot is said to be rising if a character or situation moves from unhappiness to happiness; a falling plot moves from happiness to tragedy, as in the downfall of King Lear or the Biblical story of man's fall from

Paradise. If a story contains a secondary sequence of actions, this is called a *subplot*, as opposed to the main plot.

point of view: the outlook on the events of a story, or the relationship between the speaker and the characters. *The Ghost Writer* uses a first-person point of view (The "I" is Nathan Zuckerman), whereas *July's People* employs a third-person (or omniscient) point of view ("Maureen and Bam Smales . . .")

protagonist: (Greek: "first combatant") the principal or central character in a literary work, such as Nick Adams in *In Our Time*, Milkman Dead in *Song of Solomon*, or Maureen Smales in *July's People*.

quatrain: a verse stanza with four lines.

rhetoric: (Greek: "oratory") the art of using language skillfully, often in order to persuade others. In prose, a rhetorician employs a variety of devices to make the language effective. These may include exclamations ("Heaven help us!"), hyperbole ("This is the greatest injustice in human history."), rhetorical questions, or questions that imply answers ("Is it just to continue this cruel and demeaning slavery?") and parallelism, in which phrases or sentences of similar construction are placed side by side ("Give me liberty, or give me death!").

rhetorical question: a question to which no answer is expected, or to which only one answer can be made. The question "Can any decent, right-thinking American really be a supporter of the ridiculous Senator John Doe?" is rhetorical, as it implies that *no one* can (or should) support Senator Doe. Orators frequently use rhetorical questions as a device for controlling audience reaction.

rhyme: words in which the final sounds correspond or harmonize in sound, as in "sound/hound" or "word/bird." Types of rhyme include *eye rhyme*, in which words look as if they would rhyme but do not (daughter/laughter), and *near rhyme*, in which words approach the effect of rhyme (bird/dirt). If the rhyme occurs at the end of lines of poetry, it is called *end rhyme*, distinguishing it from *internal rhyme* that occurs within the lines of a poem. Types of end rhyme include *masculine rhyme*, in which the rhyme occurs on a single syllable (thorn/scorn), and *feminine rhyme*, in which words of two or more syllables rhyme (winding/binding). These terms reflect the sexism of the time they originated since the one-syllable masculine rhyme is so named because it occurs on a strong beat (STRONG/LONG), while the feminine rhyme often ends with an unstressed or weak syllable (SILly/HILly).

Glossary

romanticism: a broad term referring to a revolutionary cultural movement in the late eighteenth and early nineteenth centuries. Romantic writers, painters, composers, and philosophers emphasized emotion, imagination, spontaneity, freedom, originality, nature, and the importance of the individual; they reacted against order, reason, restraint, tyranny, imitation, and generalities. Some romantic writers advocated a return to a simpler, more natural style and way of life; others deliberately sought to escape reality through their imaginations.

scansion: the marking off of lines of poetry into feet, indicating the stressed and unstressed syllables. For example, read these lines aloud:

> I think that I shall never see
> A poem lovely as a tree. (Joyce Kilmer)

When you scan these lines, you will observe an even rhythmic pattern of accented and unaccented syllables:

> I THINK that I shall NEver SEE
> A POem LOVEly AS a TREE.

As you scan poetry, you will find that poets frequently deviate from the basic meter they have adopted and that there are times when the exact rhythm is ambiguous. A good technique for beginning to scan a poem is to mark the stresses of polysyllabic words, or those words with more than one syllable. In Kilmer's verse these words would be NEver, POem, and LOVEly. There is no ambiguity in marking these words, and the remaining one-syllable words in the two lines quickly fall into place around them, revealing a clear metric pattern.

sestina: (Italian: "sixth") a complicated verse form first developed by the troubadours, or French poets who celebrated courtly love; the form consists of six six-line stanzas and a final three-line stanza, or *envoi*. The form also involves an intricate word scheme: the same six end words must appear in each stanza but in a different order.

setting: the time, place, and context in which the action of a story or poem occurs. A writer's choice of season, time of day, period in history, geographic region, building, etc., contributes to the mood, atmosphere, and themes of the work. The setting of "The Bear"-- northern Mississippi in the early 1880s--allows Faulkner to explore the American South at a turning point between past traditions and the coming of the modern age. The setting of Bishop's "First Death in Nova Scotia" is a parlor in a house in "and the roads deep in snow") convey the child's discovery of the silent coldness of death.

simile: (Latin: "likeness") a figure of speech in which one thing is explicitly likened or compared to another, usually with the words "like" or "as." Example: "streets that follow *like* a tedious argument" (Eliot).

sonnet: a fourteen-line poem, usually in iambic pentameter (see **meter**) that allows a precise pattern of rhyme. Two common types of sonnets are:

Petrarchan sonnet, in which the first eight lines (octet) rhyme abbabba and the last six lines (sestet) rhyme cdecde or cdcdcd. The octet and sestet often divide two major thoughts or approaches to a subject.

Shakespearean sonnet, in which the fourteen-line sonnet consists of three quatrains and a couplet, often rhyming ababcdcdefefgg. The couplet sometimes seems detachable, providing a summation or moral conclusion.

Later writers often imitated these forms, combined them, or invented forms of their own. Frost's "Design," for instance, uses both the octet/sestet structures of the Petrarchan sonnet and the final heroic couplet of the Shakespearean sonnet.

speaker: the teller of a story or the speaking voice in a poem, also referred to as a *narrator* or **persona**. At times the speaker appears to be the direct voice of the writer, as in Bishop's "In the Waiting Room" ("I, Elizabeth") or Malcolm X's *Autobiography*. Elsewhere the speaker is a character who is not the writer, as in Roth's *The Ghost Writer* or Eliot's "The Love Song of J. Alfred Prufrock."

stream of consciousness: a technique which tries to capture the varied and fluid thoughts and ideas passing through the mind. Also called **interior monologue**, stream of consciousness makes use of free association, fragmented phrases, run-together ideas, and unconventional punctuation to capture the complex workings of the mind.

surrealism: (French: "super realism") an early twentieth-century movement in art and literature to free the mind from logic and reason and delve the workings of the unconscious. Surrealist artists attempt to create forms and images through impulse, illogical feelings, or accident; hypnosis, dreams, hallucinations sometimes provided the gateway to surrealist visions.

symbol: (Greek: "sign" or "emblem") an object which represents or stands for something else. On the American flag, for instance, the fifty stars symbolize the fifty states. In Frost's "Mending Wall," the stone wall may be interpreted as a symbol, or representation, of artificial, unnatural divisions between people.

theme: the central idea of a literary work. We might say that the theme of Bishop's "Questions of Travel" is that one can achieve visions both through traveling and through one's own imagination.

tone: the mood or attitude of a writer or speaker, reflected in the choice of language. The tone of a poem may be bitter, humorous, ironic, reflective, and so forth. Contrast Yeats's tone in "The Wild Swans at Coole": and "Crazy Jane Talks with the Bishop": the first is reflective, dreamy; the second is informal and argumentative.

understatement: the deliberate expression of an idea without the emphasis or completeness it deserves, as opposed to **hyperbole**, in which a situation is exaggerated. Bishop uses understatement in "One Art" when she claims losing a loved one is no disaster.

villanelle: (Italian: "rustic song") a poetic form consisting of five three-lined stanzas (called *tercets*) and a final **quatrain**, or four-lined stanza. The first and third lines of the first tercet are alternatively repeated in later stanzas as a refrain and also form a final couplet. Elizabeth Bishop uses the villanelle form in "One Art."

ANTHOLOGY

ANTHOLOGY
CONTENTS

PART ONE: LITERATURE 1900-1944

Unit 3: William Butler Yeats

      "Adam's Curse" / 165

Unit 5: Robert Frost

      "'Out, Out--'" / 166

PART TWO: LITERATURE AFTER WORLD WAR II

Unit 7: Contemporary Southern Writers

      Eudora Welty, "Petrified Man" / 167
      Peter Taylor, "A Wife of Nashville" / 181
      Alice Walker, "Strong Horse Tea" / 203
        "In Search of Our Mothers' Gardens" / 211

Unit 10: Elizabeth Bishop

      "Over 2000 Illustrations and a Complete Concordance" / 220
      "At the Fishhouses" / 222
      "Arrival at Santos" / 224
      "Questions of Travel" / 225
      "Sestina" / 227
      "First Death in Nova Scotia" / 228
      "In the Waiting Room" / 230
      "One Art" / 232

WILLIAM BUTLER YEATS

Adam's Curse

We sat together at one summer's end,
That beautiful mild woman, your close friend,
And you and I, and talked of poetry.
I said: 'A line will take us hours maybe;
Yet if it does not seem a moment's thought,
Our stitching and unstitching has been naught.

Better go down upon your marrow-bones
And scrub a kitchen pavement, or break stones
Like an old pauper, in all kinds of weather;
For to articulate sweet sounds together
Is to work harder than all these, and yet
Be thought an idler by the noisy set
Of bankers, schoolmasters, and clergymen
The martyrs call the world.'

                              And thereupon
That beautiful mild woman for whose sake
There's many a one shall find out all heartache
On finding that her voice is sweet and low
Replied: 'To be born woman is to know--
Although they do not talk of it at school--
That we must labour to be beautiful.'

I said: 'It's certain there is no fine thing
Since Adam's fall but needs much labouring.
There have been lovers who thought love should be
So much compounded of high courtesy
That they would sigh and quote with learned looks
Precedents out of beautiful old books;
Yet now it seems an idle trade enough.'

We sat grown quiet at the name of love;
We saw the last embers of daylight die,
And in the trembling blue-green of the sky
A moon, worn as if it had been a shell
Washed by time's waters as they rose and fell
About the stars and broke in days and years.

I had a thought for no one's but your ears:
That you were beautiful, and that I strove
To love you in the old high way of love;
That it had all seemed happy, and yet we'd grown
As weary-hearted as that hollow moon.

ROBERT FROST

"'Out, Out--'"

The buzz saw snarled and rattled in the yard
And made dust and dropped stove-length sticks of
wood,
Sweet-scented stuff when the breeze drew across it.
And from there those that lifted eyes could count
Five mountain ranges one behind the other
Under the sunset far into Vermont.
And the saw snarled and rattled, snarled and
rattled,
As it ran light, or had to bear a load.
And nothing happened: day was all but done.
Call it a day, I wish they might have said
To please the boy by giving him the half hour
That a boy counts so much when saved from work.
His sister stood beside them in her apron
To tell them "Supper." At the word, the saw,
As if to prove saws knew what supper meant,
Leaped out at the boy's hand, or seemed to leap--
He must have given the hand. However it was,
Neither refused the meeting. But the hand!
The boy's first outcry was a rueful laugh,
As he swung toward them holding up the hand,
Half in appeal, but half as if to keep
The life from spilling. Then the boy saw all--
Since he was old enough to know, big boy
Doing man's work, though a child at heart--
He saw all spoiled. "Don't let him cut my hand off--
The doctor, when he comes. Don't let him, sister!"
So. But the hand was gone already.
The doctor put him in the dark of ether.
He lay and puffed his lips out with his breath.
And then--the watcher at his pulse took fright.
No one believed. They listened at his heart.
Little--less--nothing!--and that ended it.
No more to build on there. And they, since they
Were not the one dead, turned to their affairs.

PETRIFIED MAN

Eudora Welty

"Reach in my purse and git me a cigarette without no powder in it if you kin, Mrs. Fletcher, honey," said Leota to her ten o'clock shampoo-and-set customer, "I don't like no perfumed cigarettes."

Mrs. Fletcher gladly reached over to the lavender shelf under the lavender-framed mirror, shook a hair net loose from the clasp of the patent-leather bag, and slapped her hand down quickly on a powder puff which burst out when the purse was opened.

"Why, look at the peanuts, Leota!" said Mrs. Fletcher in her marvelling voice.

"Honey, them goobers has been in my purse a week if they's been in it a day. Mrs. Pike bought them peanuts."

"Who's Mrs. Pike?" asked Mrs. Fletcher, settling back. Hidden in this den of curling fluid and henna packs, separated by a lavender swing-door from the other customers, who were being gratified in other booths, she could give her curiosity its freedom. She looked expectantly at the black part in Leota's yellow curls as she bent to light the cigarette.

"Mrs. Pike is this lady from New Orleans," said Leota, puffing, and pressing into Mrs. Fletcher's scalp with strong red-nailed fingers. "A friend, not a customer. You see, like maybe I told you last time, me and Fred and Sal and Joe all had us a fuss, so Sal and Joe up and moved out, so we didn't do a thing but rent out their room. So we rented it to Mrs. Pike. And Mr. Pike." She flicked an ash into the basket of dirty towels. "Mrs. Pike is a very decided blonde. *She* bought me the peanuts."

"She must be cute," said Mrs. Fletcher.

"Honey, 'cute' ain't the word for what she is. I'm tellin' you, Mrs. Pike is attractive. She has her a good time. She's got a sharp eye out, Mrs. Pike has."

She dashed the comb through the air, and paused dramatically as a cloud of Mrs. Fletcher's hennaed hair floated out of the lavender teeth like a small storm-cloud.

"Hair fallin'."

"Aw, Leota."

"Uh-huh, commencin' to fall out," said Leota, combing again, and letting fall another cloud.

"Is it any dandruff in it?" Mrs. Fletcher was frowning, her hair-line eyebrows diving down toward her nose, and her wrinkled, beady-lashed eyelids batting with concentration.

"Nope." She combed again. "Just fallin' out."

"Bet it was that last perm'nent you gave me that did it," Mrs. Fletcher said cruelly. "Remember you cooked me fourteen minutes."

"You had fourteen minutes comin' to you," said Leota with finality.

"Bound to be somethin'," persisted Mrs. Fletcher. "Dandruff, dandruff. I couldn't of caught a thing like that from Mr. Fletcher, could I?"

"Well," Leota answered at last, "you know what I heard in here yestiddy, one of Thelma's ladies was settin' over yonder in Thelma's booth gittin' a machineless, and I don't mean to insist or insinuate or anything, Mrs. Fletcher, but Thelma's lady just happ'med to throw out--I forgotten what she was talkin' about at the time--that you was p-r-e-g., and lots of times that'll make your hair do awful funny, fall out and God knows what all. It just ain't our fault, is the way I look at it."

There was a pause. The women stared at each other in the mirror.

"Who was it?" demanded Mrs. Fletcher.

"Honey, I really couldn't say," said Leota. "Not that you look it."

"Where's Thelma? I'll get it out of her," said Mrs. Fletcher.

"Now, honey, I wouldn't go and git mad over a little thing like that," Leota said, combing hastily, as though to hold Mrs. Fletcher down by the hair. "I'm sure it was somebody didn't mean no harm in the world. How far gone are you?"

"Just wait," said Mrs. Fletcher, and shrieked for Thelma, who came in and took a drag from Leota's cigarette.

"Thelma, honey, throw your mind back to yestiddy if you kin," said Leota, drenching Mrs. Fletcher's hair with a thick fluid and catching the overflow in a cold wet towel at her neck.

"Well, I got my lady half wound for a spiral," said Thelma doubtfully.

"This won't take but a minute," said Leota. "Who is it you got in there, old Horse Face? Just cast your mind back and try to remember who your lady was yestiddy who happ'm to mention that my customer was pregnant, that's all. She's dead to know."

Thelma drooped her blood-red lips and looked over Mrs. Fletcher's head into the mirror. "Why, honey, I ain't got the faintest," she breathed. "I really don't recollect the faintest. But I'm sure she meant no harm. I declare, I forgot my hair finally got combed and thought it was a stranger behind me."

"Was it that Mrs. Hutchinson?" Mrs. Fletcher was tensely polite.

"Mrs. Hutchinson? Oh, Mrs. Hutchinson." Thelma batted her eyes. "Naw, precious, she come on Thursday and didn't ev'm mention your name. I doubt if she ev'm knows you're on the way."

"Thelma!" cried Leota staunchly.

"All I know is, whoever it is 'll be sorry some day. Why, I just barely knew it myself!" cried Mrs. Fletcher. "Just let her wait!"

"Why? What're you gonna do to her?"

It was a child's voice, and the women looked down. A little boy was making tents with aluminum wave pinchers on the floor under the sink.

"Billy Boy, hon, mustn't bother nice ladies," Leota smiled. She slapped him brightly and behind her back waved Thelma out of the booth. "Ain't Billy Boy a sight? Only three years old and already just nuts about the beauty-parlor business."

"I never saw him here before," said Mrs. Fletcher, still unmollified.

"He ain't been here before, that's how come," said Leota. "He belongs to Mrs. Pike. She got her a job but it was Fay's Millinery. He oughtn't to try on those ladies' hats, they come down over his eyes like I don't know what. They just git to look ridiculous, that's what, an' of course he's gonna put 'em on: hats. They tole Mrs. Pike they didn't appreciate him hangin' around there. Here, he couldn't hurt a thing."

"Well! I don't like children that much," said Mrs. Fletcher.

"Well!" said Leota moodily.

"Well! I'm almost tempted not to have this one," said Mrs. Fletcher. "That Mrs. Hutchinson! Just looks straight through you when she sees you on the street and then spits at you behind your back."

"Mr. Fletcher would beat you on the head if you didn't have it now," said Leota reasonably. "After going this far."

Mrs. Fletcher sat up straight. "Mr. Fletcher can't do a thing with me."

"He can't!" Leota winked at herself in the mirror.

"No, siree, he can't. If he so much as raises his voice against me, he knows good and well I'll have one of my sick headaches, and then I'm just not fit to live with. And if I really look that pregnant already--"

"Well, now, honey, I just want you to know--I habm't told any of my ladies and I ain't goin' to tell 'em--even that you're losin' your hair. You just get you one of those Stork-a-Lure dresses and stop worryin'. What people don't know don't hurt nobody, as Mrs. Pike says."

"Did you tell Mrs. Pike?" asked Mrs. Fletcher sulkily.

"Well, Mrs. Fletcher, look, you ain't ever goin' to lay eyes on Mrs. Pike or her lay eyes on you, so what diffunce does it make in the long run?"

"I knew it!" Mrs. Fletcher deliberately nodded her head so as to destroy a ringlet Leota was working on behind her ear. "Mrs. Pike!"

Leota sighed. "I reckon I might as well tell you. It wasn't any more Thelma's lady tole me you was pregnant than a bat."

"Not Mrs. Hutchinson?"

"Naw, Lord! It was Mrs. Pike."

"Mrs. Pike!" Mrs. Fletcher could only sputter and let curling fluid roll into her ear. "How could Mrs. Pike possibly know I was pregnant or otherwise, when she doesn't even know me? The nerve of some people!"

"Well, here's how it was. Remember Sunday?"

"Yes," said Mrs. Fletcher.

"Sunday, Mrs. Pike an' me was all by ourself. Mr. Pike and Fred had gone over to Eagle Lake, sayin' they was goin' to catch 'em some fish, but they didn't a course. So we was settin' in Mrs. Pike's car, it's a 1939 Dodge--"

"1939, eh," said Mrs. Fletcher.

"--An' we was gettin' us a Jax beer apiece--that's the beer that Mrs. Pike says is made right in N.0., so she won't drink no other kind. So I seen you drive up to the drugstore an' run in for just a secont, leavin' I reckon Mr. Fletcher in the car, an' come runnin' out with looked like a perscription. So I says to Mrs. Pike, just to be makin' talk, 'Right yonder's Mrs. Fletcher, and I reckon that's Mr. Fletcher--she's one of my regular customers,' I says."

"I had on a figured print," said Mrs. Fletcher tentatively.

"You sure did," agreed Leota. "So Mrs. Pike, she give you a good look--she's very observant, a good judge of character, cute as a minute, you know--and she says, 'I bet you another Jax that lady's three months on the way.'"

"What gall!" said Mrs. Fletcher. "Mrs. Pike!"

"Mrs. Pike ain't goin' to bite you," said Leota. "Mrs. Pike is a lovely girl, you'd be crazy about her, Mrs. Fletcher. But she can't sit still a minute. We went to the travellin' freak show yestiddy after work. I got through early--nine o'clock. In the vacant store next door. What, you ain't been?"

"No, I despise freaks," declared Mrs. Fletcher.

"Aw. Well, honey, talkin' about bein' pregnant an' all, you ought to see those twins in a bottle, you really owe it to yourself."

"What twins?" asked Mrs. Fletcher out of the side of her mouth.

"Well, honey, they got these two twins in a bottle, see? Born joined plumb together--dead a course." Leota dropped her voice into a soft lyrical hum. "They was about this long--pardon--must of been full time, all right, wouldn't you say?--an' they had these two heads an' two

171

faces an' four arms an' four legs, all kind of joined *here*. See, this face looked this-a-way, and the other face looked that-a-way, over their shoulder, see. Kinda pathetic."

"Glah!" said Mrs. Fletcher disapprovingly.

"Well, ugly? Honey, I mean to tell you--their parents was first cousins and all like that. Billy Boy, git me a fresh towel from off Teeny's stack--this 'n's wringin' wet--an' quit ticklin' my ankles with that curler, I declare! He don't miss nothin'."

"Me and Mr. Fletcher aren't one speck of kin, or he could never of had me," said Mrs. Fletcher placidly.

"Of course not!" protested Leota. "Neither is me an' Fred, not that we know of. Well, honey, what Mrs. Pike liked was the pygmies. They've got these pygmies down there, too, an' Mrs. Pike was just wild about 'em. You know, the teeniniest men in the universe? Well, honey, they can just rest back on their little bohunkus an' roll around an' you can't hardly tell if they're sittin' or standin'. That'll give you some idea. They're about forty-two years old. Just suppose it was your husband!"

"Well, Mr. Fletcher is five foot nine and one half," said Mrs. Fletcher quickly.

"Fred's five foot ten," said Leota, "but I tell him he's still a shrimp, account of I'm so tall." She made a deep wave over Mrs. Fletcher's other temple with the comb. "Well, these pygmies are a kind of a dark brown, Mrs. Fletcher. Not bad lookin' for what they are, you know."

"I wouldn't care for them," said Mrs. Fletcher. "What does that Mrs. Pike see in them?"

"Aw, I don't know," said Leota. "She's just cute, that's all. But they got this man, this petrified man, that ever'thing ever since he was nine years old, when it goes through his digestion, see, somehow Mrs. Pike says it goes to his joints and has been turning to stone."

"How awful!" said Mrs. Fletcher.

"He's forty-two too. That looks like a bad age."

"Who said so, that Mrs. Pike? I bet she's forty-two," said Mrs. Fletcher.

"Naw," said Leota, "Mrs. Pike's thirty-three, born in January, an Aquarian. He could move his head--like this. A course his head and mind ain't a joint, so to speak, and I guess his stomach ain't, either-- not yet, anyways. But see--his food, he eats it, and it goes down, see, and then he digests it"--Leota rose on her toes for an instant--"and it goes out to his joints and before you can say 'Jack Robinson,' it's stone-- pure stone. He's turning to stone. How'd you like to be married to a guy like that? All he can do, he can move his head just a quarter of an inch. A course he *looks* just *terrible*."

"I should think he would," said Mrs, Fletcher frostily. "Mr. Fletcher takes bending exercises every night of the world. I make him."

"All Fred does is lay around the house like a rug. I wouldn't be surprised if he woke up some day and couldn't move. The petrified man just sat there moving his quarter of an inch though," said Leota reminiscently.

"Did Mrs. Pike like the petrified man?" asked Mrs. Fletcher.

"Not as much as she did the others," said Leota deprecatingly, "And then she likes a man to be a good dresser, and all that."

"Is Mr. Pike a good dresser?" asked Mrs. Fletcher sceptically.

"Oh, well, yeah," said Leota, "but he's twelve or fourteen years older'n her. She ast Lady Evangeline about him."

"Who's Lady Evangeline?" asked Mrs. Fletcher.

"Well, it's this mind reader they got in the freak show," said Leota. "Was real good. Lady Evangeline is her name, and if I had another dollar I wouldn't do a thing but have my other palm read. She had what Mrs. Pike said was the 'sixth mind' but she had the worst manicure I ever saw on a living person."

"What did she tell Mrs. Pike?" asked Mrs. Fletcher.

"She told her Mr. Pike was as true to her as he could be and besides, would come into some money."

"Humph!" said Mrs. Fletcher. "What does he do?"

"I can't tell," said Leota, "because he don't work. Lady Evangeline didn't tell me enough about my nature or anything. And I would like to go back and find out some more about this boy. Used to go with this boy until he got married to this girl, Oh, shoot, that was about three and a half years ago, when you was still goin' to the Robert E. Lee Beauty Shop in Jackson. He married her for her money. Another fortune-teller tole me that at the time. So I'm not in love with him any more, anyway, besides being married to Fred, but Mrs. Pike thought, just for the hell of it, see, to ask Lady Evangeline was he happy."

"Does Mrs. Pike know everything about you already?" asked Mrs. Fletcher unbelievingly. "Mercy!"

"Oh, yeah, I tole her ever'thing about ever'thing, from now on back to I don't know when--to when I first started goin' out, said Leota. "So I ast Lady Evangeline for one of my questions, was he happily married, and she says, just like she was glad I ask her, 'Honey,' she says, 'naw, he idn't. You write down this day, March 8, 1941,' she says, 'and mock it down: three years from today him and her won't be occupyin' the same bed.' There it is, up on the wall with them other dates--see, Mrs. Fletcher? And she says, 'Child, you ought to be glad you didn't git him, because he's so mercenary.' So I'm glad I married Fred. He sure ain't mercenary, money don't mean a thing to him. But I sure would like to go back and have my other palm read."

"Did Mrs. Pike believe in what the fortune-teller said?" asked Mrs. Fletcher in a superior tone of voice.

"Lord, yes, she's from New Orleans. Ever'body in New Orleans believes ever'thing spooky. One of 'em in New Orleans before it was raided says to Mrs. Pike one summer she was goin' to go from State to State and meet some grey-headed men, and, sure enough, she says she went on a beautician convention up to Chicago. . . ."

"Oh!" said Mrs. Fletcher. "Oh, is Mrs. Pike a beautician too?"

"Sure she is," protested Leota. "She's a beautician. I'm goin' to git her in here if I can. Before she married. But it don't leave you. She says sure enough, there was three men who was a very large part of making her trip what it was, and they all three had grey in their hair and they went in six States. Got Christmas cards from 'em. Billy Boy, go see if Thelma's got any dry cotton. Look how Mrs. Fletcher's a-drippin'."

"Where did Mrs. Pike meet Mr. Pike?" asked Mrs. Fletcher primly.

"On another train," said Leota.

"I met Mr. Fletcher, or rather he met me, in a rental library," said Mrs. Fletcher with dignity, as she watched the net come down over her head.

"Honey, me an' Fred, we met in a rumble seat eight months ago and we was practically on what you might call the way to the altar inside of half an hour," said Leota in a guttural voice, and bit a bobby pin open. "Course it don't last, Mrs. Pike says nothin' like that ever lasts."

"Mr. Fletcher and myself are as much in love as the day we married," said Mrs. Fletcher belligerently as Leota stuffed cotton into her ears.

"Mrs. Pike says it don't last," repeated Leota in a louder voice. "Now go git under the dryer. You can turn yourself on, can't you? I'll be back to comb you out. Durin' lunch I promised to give Mrs. Pike a facial. You know--free. Her bein' in the business, so to speak."

"I bet she needs one," said Mrs. Fletcher, letting the swing-door fly back against Leota. "Oh, pardon me."

A week later, on time for her appointment, Mrs. Fletcher sank heavily into Leota's chair after first removing a drug-store rental book, called *Life Is Like That*, from the seat. She stared in a discouraged way into the mirror.

"You can tell it when I'm sitting down, all right," she said.

Leota seemed preoccupied and stood shaking out a lavender cloth. She began to pin it around Mrs. Fletcher's neck in silence.

"I said you sure can tell it when I'm sitting straight on and coming at you this way," Mrs. Fletcher said.

"Why, honey, naw you can't," said Leota gloomily. "Why, I'd never know. If somebody was to come up to me on the street and say, 'Mrs. Fletcher is pregnant!' I'd say, 'Heck, she don't look it to me.'"

"If a certain party hadn't found it out and spread it around, it wouldn't be too late even now," said Mrs. Fletcher frostily, but Leota was almost choking her with the cloth, pinning it so tight, and she couldn't speak clearly. She paddled her hands in the air until Leota wearily loosened her.

"Listen, honey, you're just a virgin compared to Mrs. Montjoy," Leota was going on, still absent-minded. She bent Mrs. Fletcher back in the chair and, sighing, tossed liquid from a teacup on to her head and dug both hands into her scalp. "You know Mrs. Montjoy--her husband's that premature-grey-headed fella?"

"She's in the Trojan Garden Club, is all I know," said Mrs. Fletcher.

"Well, honey," said Leota, but in a weary voice, "she come in here not the week before and not the day before she had her baby--she come in here the very selfsame day, I mean to tell you. Child, we was all plumb scared to death. There she was! Come for her shampoo an' set. Why, Mrs. Fletcher, in an hour an' twenty minutes she was layin' up there in the Babtist Hospital with a seb'm-pound son. It was that close a shave. I declare, if I hadn't been so tired I would of drank up a bottle of gin that night."

"What gall," said Mrs. Fletcher. "I never knew her at all well."

"See, her husband was waitin' outside in the car, and her bags was all packed an' in the back seat, an' she was all ready, 'cept she wanted her shampoo an' set. An' havin' one pain right after another. Her husband kep' comin' in here, scared-like, but couldn't do nothin' with her a course. She yelled bloody murder, too, but she always yelled her head off when I give her a perm'nent."

"She must of been crazy," said Mrs. Fletcher. "How did she look?"

"Shoot!" said Leota.

"Well, I can guess," said Mrs. Fletcher. "Awful."

"Just wanted to look pretty while she was havin' her baby, is all," said Leota airily. "Course, we was glad to give the lady what she was after--that's our motto--but I bet a hour later she wasn't payin' no mind to them little end curls. I bet she wasn't thinkin' about she ought to have on a net. It wouldn't of done her no good if she had."

"No, I don't suppose it would," said Mrs. Fletcher.

"Yeah man! She was a-yellin'. Just like when I give her perm'nent."

"Her husband ought to make her behave. Don't it seem that way to you?" asked Mrs. Fletcher. "He ought to put his foot down."

"Ha," said Leota. "A lot he could do. Maybe some women is soft."

"Oh, you mistake me, I don't mean for her to get soft--far from it! Women have to stand up for themselves, or there's just no telling. But now you take me--I ask Mr. Fletcher's advice now and then, and he appreciates it, especially on something important, like is it time for a permanent--not that I've told him about the baby. He says, 'Why, dear, go ahead!' Just ask their *advice*."

"Huh! If I ever ast Fred's advice we'd be floatin' down the Yazoo River on a houseboat or somethin' by this time," said Leota. "I'm sick of Fred. I told him to go over to Vicksburg."

"Is he going?" demanded Mrs. Fletcher.

"Sure. See, the fortune-teller--I went back and had my other palm read, since we've got to rent the room agin--said my lover was goin' to work in Vicksburg, so I don't know who she could mean, unless she meant Fred. And Fred ain't workin' here--that much is so."

"Is he going to work in Vicksburg?' asked Mrs. Fletcher. "And--"

"Sure. Lady Evangeline said so. Said the future is going to be brighter than the present. He don't want to go, but I ain't gonna put up with nothin' like that. Lays around the house an' bulls--did bull-- with that good-for-nothin' Mr. Pike. He says if he goes who'll cook, but I says I never get to eat anyway--not meals. Billy Boy, take Mrs. Grover that *Screen Secrets* and leg it."

Mrs. Fletcher heard stamping feet go out the door.

"Is that that Mrs. Pike's little boy here again?" she asked, sitting up gingerly.

"Yeah, that's still him." Leota stuck out her tongue.

Mrs. Fletcher could hardly believe her eyes.

"Well! How's Mrs. Pike, your attractive new friend with the sharp eyes who spreads it around town that perfect strangers are pregnant?" she asked in a sweetened tone.

"Oh, Mizziz Pike." Leota combed Mrs. Fletcher's hair with heavy strokes.

"You act like you're tired," said Mrs. Fletcher.

"Tired? Feel like it's four o'clock in the afternoon already," said Leota. "I ain't told you the awful luck we had, me and Fred? It's the worst thing you ever heard of. Maybe *you* think Mrs. Pike's got sharp eyes. Shoot, there's a limit! Well, you know, we rented out our room to this Mr. and Mrs. Pike from New Orleans when Sal an' Joe Fentress got mad at us 'cause they drank up some home-brew we had in the closet--Sal an' Joe did. So, a week ago Sat'day Mr. and Mrs. Pike moved in. Well, I kinda fixed up the room, you know--put a sofa pillow on the couch and picked some ragged robbins and put in a vase, but they never did say they appreciated it. Anyway, then I put some old magazines on the table."

"I think that was lovely," said Mrs. Fletcher.

"Wait. So, come night 'fore last, Fred and this Mr. Pike, who Fred just took up with, was back from they said they was fishin', bein' as neither one of 'em has got a job to his name, and we was all settin' around in their room. So Mrs. Pike was settin' there, readin' a old *Startling G-Man Tales* that was mine, mind you, I'd bought it myself, and all of a sudden she jumps!--into the air--you'd 'a' thought she'd set on a spider--an' says, 'Canfield'--ain't that silly, that's Mr. Pike-- 'Canfield, my God A'mighty,' she says, 'honey,'she says, 'we're rich, and you won't have to work.' Not that he turned one hand anyway. Well, me and Fred rushes over to her, and Mr. Pike, too, and there she sets, pointin' her finger at a photo in my copy of *Startling G-Man*. 'See that man?' yells Mrs. Pike. 'Remember him, Canfield?' 'Never forget a face,' says Mr. Pike. 'It's Mr. Petrie, that we stayed with him in the apartment next to ours in Toulouse Street in N.O. for six weeks. Mr. Petrie.' 'Well,' says Mrs. Pike, like she can't hold out one secont longer, 'Mr. Petrie is wanted for five hundred dollars cash, for rapin' four women in California, and I know where he is.'"

"Mercy!" said Mrs. Fletcher. "Where was he?"

At some time Leota had washed her hair and now she yanked her up by the back locks and sat her up.

"Know where he was?"

"I certainly don't," Mrs. Fletcher said. Her scalp hurt all over.

Leota flung a towel around the top of her customer's head. "Nowhere else but in that freak show! I saw him just as plain as Mrs. Pike. *He* was the petrified man!"

"Who would ever have thought that!" cried Mrs. Fletcher sympathetically.

"So Mr. Pike says, 'Well whatta you know about that,' an' he looks real hard at the photo and whistles. And she starts dancin' and singin' about their good luck. She meant our bad luck! I made a point of tellin' that fortune-teller the next time I saw her. I said, 'Listen, that magazine was layin' around the house for a month, and there was the freak show runnin' night an' day, not two steps away from my own beauty parlor, with Mr. Petrie just settin' there waitin'. An' it had to be Mr. and Mrs. Pike, almost perfect strangers."

"What gall," said Mrs. Fletcher. She was only sitting there, wrapped in a turban, but she did not mind.

"Fortune-tellers don't care. And Mrs, Pike, she goes around actin' like she thinks she was Mrs. God," said Leota. "So they're goin' to leave tomorrow, Mr. and Mrs. Pike. And in the meantime I got to keep that mean, bad little ole kid here, gettin' under my feet ever' minute of the day an' talkin' back too."

"Have they gotten the five hundred dollars' reward already?" asked Mrs. Fletcher.

"Well," said Leota, "at first Mr. Pike didn't want to do anything about it. Can you feature that? Said he kinda liked that ole bird and said he was real nice to 'em, lent 'em money or somethin'. But Mrs. Pike simply tole him he could just go to hell, and I can see her point. She says, 'You ain't worked a lick in six months, and here I make five hundred dollars in two seconts, and what thanks do I get for it? You go to hell, Canfield,' she says. So," Leota went on in a despondent voice, "they called up the cops and they caught the ole bird, all right, right there in the freak show where I saw him with my own eyes, thinkin' he was petrified. He's the one. Did it under his real name--Mr. Petrie. Four women in California, all in the month of August. So Mrs. Pike gits five hundred dollars. And my magazine, and right next door to my beauty parlor. I cried all night, but Fred said it wasn't a bit of use and to go to sleep, because the whole thing was just a sort of coincidence-- you know: can't do nothin' about it. He says it put him clean out of the notion of goin' to Vicksburg for a few days till we rent out the room agin--no tellin' who we'll git this time."

"But can you imagine anybody knowing this old man, that's raped four women?" persisted Mrs. Fletcher, and she shuddered audibly. "Did Mrs. Pike *speak* to him when she met him in the freak show?"

Leota had begun to comb Mrs. Fletcher's hair. "I says to her, I says, 'I didn't notice you fallin' on his neck when he was the petrified man--don't tell me you didn't recognize your fine friend?' And she says, 'I didn't recognize him with that white powder all over his face. He just looked familiar.' Mrs. Pike says, 'and lots of people look familiar.' But she says that ole petrified man did put her in mind of somebody. She wondered who it was! Kep' her awake, which man she'd ever knew it reminded her of. So when she seen the photo, it all come to her.

Like a flash. Mr. Petrie. The way he'd turn his head and look at her when she took him in his breakfast."

"Took him in his breakfast!" shrieked Mrs. Fletcher. "Listen-- don't tell me. I'd 'a' felt something."

"Four women. I guess those women didn't have the faintest notion at the time they'd be worth a hunderd an' twenty-five bucks a piece some day to Mrs. Pike. We ast her how old the fella was then, an' she says he musta had one foot in the grave, at least. Can you beat it?"

"Not really petrified at all, of course," said Mrs. Fletcher meditatively. She drew herself up. "I'd 'a' felt something," she said proudly.

"Shoot! I did feel somethin'," said Leota. "I tole Fred when I got home I felt so funny. I said, 'Fred, that ole petrified man sure did leave me with a funny feelin'.' He says, 'Funny-haha or funny peculiar?' and I says, 'Funny-peculiar.'" She pointed her comb into the air emphatically.

"I'll bet you did," said Mrs. Fletcher.

They both heard a crackling noise.

Leota screamed, "Billy Boy! What you doin' in my purse?"

"Aw, I'm just eatin' these ole stale peanuts up," said Billy Boy.

"You come here to me!" screamed Leota, recklessly flinging down the comb, which scattered a whole ashtray full of bobby pins and knocked down a row of Coca-Cola bottles. "This is the last straw!"

"I caught him! I caught him!" giggled Mrs. Fletcher. "I'll hold him on my lap. You bad, bad boy, you! I guess I better learn how to spank little old bad boys," she said.

Leota's eleven o'clock customer pushed open the swing-door upon Leota paddling him heartily with the brush, while he gave angry but belittling screams which penetrated beyond the booth and filled the whole curious beauty parlor. From everywhere ladies began to gather round to watch the paddling. Billy Boy kicked both Leota and Mrs. Fletcher as hard as he could, Mrs. Fletcher with her new fixed smile.

Billy Boy stomped through the group of wild-haired ladies and went out the door, but flung back the words, "If you're so smart, why ain't you rich?"

A WIFE OF NASHVILLE

Peter Taylor

The Lovells' old cook Sarah had quit to get married in the spring, and they didn't have anybody else for a long time--not for several months. It was during the Depression, and when a servant quit, people in Nashville (and even people out at Thornton, where the Lovells came from) tried to see how long they could go before they got another. All through the summer, there would be knocks on the Lovells' front door or on the wooden porch floor, by the steps. And when one of the children or their mother went to the door, some Negro man or woman would be standing there, smiling and holding out a piece of paper. A recommendation it was supposed to be, but the illegible note scribbled with a blunt lead pencil was something no white person could have written if he had tried. If Helen Ruth, the children's mother, went to the door, she always talked a while to whoever it was, but she hardly ever even looked at the note held out to her. She would give a piece of advice or say to meet her around at the back door for a handout. If one of the boys--there were three Lovell boys, and no girls--went to the door, he always brought the note in to Helen Ruth, unless John R., their father, was at home, sick with his back ailment. Helen Ruth would shake her head and say to tell whoever it was to go away! "Tell him to go back home," she said once to the oldest boy, who was standing in the sun parlor doorway with a smudged scrap of paper in his hand. "Tell him if he had any sense, he never would have left the country."

"He's probably not from the country, Mother."

"They're all from the country," Helen Ruth said. "When they knock on the porch floor like that, they're bound to be from the country, and they're better off at home, where somebody cares something about them. I don't care anything about them anymore than you do."

But one morning Helen Ruth hired a cheerful-looking and rather plump, light-complexioned young Negro girl named Jess McGehee, who had come knocking on the front-porch floor just as the others had. Helen Ruth talked to her at the front door for a while; then she told her to come around to the kitchen, and they talked there for nearly an hour. Jess stayed to fix lunch and supper, and after she had been

181

there a few days, the family didn't know how they had ever got along without her.

In fact, Jess got on so well with the Lovells that Helen Ruth even decided to let her come and live on the place, a privilege she had never before allowed a servant of hers. Together, she and Jess moved all of John R.'s junk--a grass duck-hunting outfit, two mounted stags' heads, an outboard motor, and so on--from the little room above the garage into the attic of the house. John R. lent Jess the money for the down payment on a "suit" of furniture, and Jess moved in. "You would never know she was out there," Helen Ruth told her friends. "There is never any rumpus. And her room! It's as clean as yours or mine."

Jess worked for them for eight years. John R. got so one of his favorite remarks was, "The honeymoon is over, but this is the real thing this time." Then he would go on about what he called Helen Ruth's "earlier affairs." The last one before Jess was Sarah, who quit to get married and go to Chicago at the age of sixty-eight. She had been with them for six years and was famous for her pies and her banana dishes.

Before Sarah, there was Carrie. Carrie had been with them when the two younger boys were born, and it was she who had once tried to persuade Helen Ruth not to go to the hospital but to let her act as midwife. She had quit them after five years, to become an undertaker. And before Carrie there was Jane Blakemore, the very first of them all, whom John R. and Helen Ruth had brought with them from Thornton to Nashville when they married. She lasted less than three years; she quit soon after John R., Jr., was born, because, she said, the baby made her nervous.

"It's an honorable record," John R. would say. "Each of them was better than the one before, and each one stayed with us longer. It proves that experience is the best teacher."

Jess's eight years were the years when the boys were growing up; the boys were children when she came, and when she left, the youngest, little Robbie, had learned to drive the car. In a sense, it was Jess who taught all three boys to drive. She didn't give them their first lessons, of course, because, like Helen Ruth, she had never sat at the wheel of an automobile in her life. She had not ridden in a car more than half a dozen times when she came to the Lovells, but just by chance, one day, she was in the car when John R. let John R., Jr., take the wheel. The car would jerk and lunge forward every time the boy shifted gears, and his father said, "Keep your mind on what you're doing."

"I am," John R., Jr., said, "but it just does that. What makes it do it?"

"Think!" John R. said. "Think! . . . *Think*!"

"I *am* thinking, but what makes it do it?"

Suddenly, Jess leaned forward from the back seat and said, "You letting the clutch out too fast, honey."

Both father and son were so surprised they could not help laughing. They laughed harder, of course, because what Jess said was true. And Jess laughed with them. When they had driven another block, they reached a boulevard stop, and in the process of putting on the brake John R., Jr., killed the engine and then flooded the motor. His father shouted, "Well, let it rest! We're just stuck here for about twenty minutes!"

Jess, who was seated with one arm around a big bag of groceries, began to laugh again. "Turn off the key," she said. "Press down on the starter a spell. Then torectly you turn on the key and she'll start."

John R. looked over his shoulder at her, not smiling, but not frowning, either. Presently, he gave the order, "Try it."

"Try what *Jess said?*" John R., Jr., asked.

"Try what Jess said."

The boy tried it, and in a moment he was racing the motor and grinning at his father. When they had got safely across the boulevard, John R. turned around to Jess again. He asked in a quiet, almost humble manner--the same manner he used when describing the pains in his back to Helen Ruth--where she had learned these things about an automobile. "Law," she said, "I learnt them listening to my brother-in-law that drives a truck talk. I don't reckon I really know'm, but I can say them."

John R. was so impressed by the incident that he did not make it one of his stories. He told Helen Ruth about it, of course, and he mentioned it sometimes to his close friends when they were discussing "the good things" about Negroes. With his sons, he used it as an example of how much you can learn by listening to other people talk, and after that day he would permit John R., Jr., to go for drives in the car without him provided Jess went along in his place. Later on, when the other boys got old enough to drive, there were periods when he turned their instruction over to Jess. Helen Ruth even talked of learning to drive, herself, with the aid of Jess.

But it never came to more than talk with Helen Ruth, though John R. encouraged her, saying he thought driving was perhaps a serious strain on his back. She talked about it for several months, but in the end she said that the time had passed when she could learn new skills. When John R. tried to encourage her in the idea, she would sometimes look out one of the sun-parlor windows toward the street and think of how much she had once wanted to learn to drive. But that had been long ago, right after they were married, in the days when John R. had owned a little Ford coupé. John R. was on the road for the Standard Candy Company then, and during most of the week she was alone in their apartment at the old Vaux Hall. While he was away John R. kept the coupé stored in a garage only two blocks east, on Broad Street; in those days traveling men still used the railroads, because Governor Peay hadn't yet paved Tennessee's highways. At that time, John R. had not believed in women driving automobiles, and Helen Ruth had felt that he must be right about it; she had even made fun of women who went *whizzing* about town, blowing horns at every intersection. Yet in her heart she had longed to drive that coupé! Jane Blakemore was working for them then, and one day Jane had put Helen Ruth's longings into words. "Wouldn't it be dandy," she said, "if me and you clomb in that car one of these weekdays and toured out to Thornton to see all the folks--white and black?"

Without a moment's hesitation, however, Helen Ruth gave the answer that she knew John R. would have given. "Now, think what you're saying, Jane!" she said. "Wouldn't we be a fool-looking pair pulling into the Square at Thornton? *Think* about it. What if we should have a flat tire when we got out about as far as Nine Mile Hill? Who would change it? *You* certainly couldn't! Jane Blakemore, I don't think you use your head about anything!"

That was the way Helen Ruth had talked to Jane on more occasions than one. She was a plain-spoken woman, and she never spoke plainer to anyone than she did to Jane Blakemore during the days when they were shut up together in that apartment at the Vaux Hall. Since Jane was from Thornton and knew how plain-spoken all Helen Ruth's family were, she paid little attention to the way Helen Ruth talked to her. She would smile, or else sneer, and go on with her work of cooking and cleaning. Sometimes she would rebel and speak just as plainly as Helen Ruth did. When Helen Ruth decided to introduce butter plates to their table, Jane said, "I ain't never heard tell of no butter dishes."

Helen Ruth raised her eyebrow. "That's because you are an ignoramus from Thornton, Tennessee," she said.

"I'm ignoramus enough to know ain't no need in nastying up all them dishes for me to wash."

Helen Ruth had, however, made Jane Blakemore learn to use butter plates and had made her keep the kitchen scrubbed and the other rooms of the apartment dusted and polished and in such perfect order that even John R. had noticed it when he came on week ends. Sometimes he had said, "You drive yourself too hard, Helen Ruth."

Jess McGehee was as eager and quick to learn new things as Jane Blakemore had been unwilling and slow. She would even put finger bowls on the breakfast table when there was grapefruit. And how she did spoil the three boys about their food! There were mornings when she cooked the breakfast eggs differently for each one of them while John R. sat and shook his head in disgust at the way she was pampering his sons. John R.'s "condition" in his back kept him at home a lot of the time during the eight years Jess was with them. He had long since left off traveling for the candy company; soon after the first baby came, he had opened an insurance agency of his own.

When Jane Blakemore left them and Helen Ruth hired Carrie (after fifteen or twenty interviews with other applicants), she had had to warn Carrie that John R.'s hours might be very irregular, because he was in business for himself and wasn't able merely to punch a time clock and quit when the day ended. "He's an onsurance man, ain't he?" Carrie had asked and had showed by the light in her eyes how favorably impressed she was. "I know about him," she had said. "He's a life onsurance man, and that's the best kind to have."

At that moment, Helen Ruth thought perhaps she had make a mistake in Carrie. "I don't like my servant to discuss my husband's business," she said.

"No'm!" Carrie said with enthusiasm. "No, *ma'am!*" Helen Ruth was satisfied, but afterward she had often to tell herself that her first suspicion had been right. Carrie was nosy and prying and morbid--and she gossiped with other people's servants. Her curiosity and her gossiping were especially trying for Helen Ruth during her and John R.'s brief separation. They actually had separated for nearly two months right after Kenneth, the middle boy, was born. Helen Ruth had gone to her father's house at Thornton, taking the two babies and Carrie with her. The boys never knew about the trouble between their parents, of course, until Kenneth pried it out of his mother after they were all grown, and, at the time, people in Nashville and Thornton were not perfectly sure that it was a real separation. Helen Ruth had tried to tell herself that possibly Carrie didn't know it was a real separation. But she was never able to deny completely the significance of Carrie's behavior while they were at Thornton. Carrie's whole disposition had seemed to change the afternoon they left Nashville. Up until then, she had been a moody, shifty, rather loud-mouthed brown woman, full of darky compliments for white folks and of gratuitous promises of extra services she seldom rendered. But at Thornton she had put the old family servants to shame with her industriousness and her respectful, unassuming manner. "You don't find them like Carrie in Thornton any more," Helen Ruth's mother said. "The good ones all go to Nashville or Memphis." But Helen Ruth, sitting by an upstairs window one afternoon, saw her mother's cook and Carrie sauntering toward the back gate to meet a caller. She saw Carrie being introduced and then she recognized the caller as Jane Blakemore. Presently the cook returned to the kitchen and Helen Ruth saw Carrie and Jane enter the servants' house in the corner of the yard. During the hour that they visited there, Helen Ruth sat quietly by the window in the room with her two babies. It seemed to her the most terrible hour of her separation from John R. When Carrie and Jane reappeared on the stoop of the servants' house and Carrie was walking with Jane to the gate, there was no longer any doubt in Helen Ruth's mind but that she would return to her husband, and return without any complaints or stipulations. During that hour she had tried to imagine exactly what things the black Jane and the brown Carrie were talking about, or, rather, *how* and in what terms they were talking about the things they must be talking about. In her mind, she reviewed the sort of difficulties she had had with Jane and the sort she had with Carrie and tried to imagine what defense they would make for themselves--Jane for her laziness and contrariness, Carrie for her usual shiftiness and negligence. Would they blame her for these failings of theirs? Or would they blandly pass over their own failings and find fault with her for things that she was not even aware of, or that she could not help and could not begin to set right? Had she really misused these women, either the black one or the brown one? It seemed to her then that she had so little in life that she was entitled to the satisfaction of keeping an orderly house and to the luxury of efficient help. There was too much else she had not had--an "else" nameless to her, yet sorely missed--for her to be denied these small satisfactions. As she sat alone with her two babies in the old nursery and thought of the two servants gossiping about her, she became an object of pity to herself. And presently John R., wherever he might be at that moment--in his office or at the club or, more likely, on a hunting or fishing trip somewhere-- became an object of pity, too . And her two babies, one in his crib and the other playing on the carpet with a string of spools, were objects of pity. Even Carrie, standing alone by the gate after Jane had gone, seemed a lone and pitiful figure.

A few days later, Helen Ruth and Carrie and the two baby boys returned to Nashville.

In Nashville, Carrie was herself again everything was done in her old slipshod fashion. Except during that interval at Thornton, Carrie was never known to perform any task to Helen Ruth's complete satisfaction. Hardly a meal came to the table without the soup or the dessert or some important sauce having been forgotten; almost every week something important was left out of the laundry; during a general cleaning the upper sashes of two or three windows were invariably left unwashed. Yet never in her entire five years did Carrie answer back or admit an unwillingness to do the most menial or the most nonessential piece of work. In fact, one of her most exasperating pronouncements was, "You are exactly right," which was often followed by a lengthy description of how she would do the thing from then on, or an explanation of how it happened that she had forgotten to do it. Not only that, she would often undertake to explain to Helen Ruth Helen Ruth's reason for wanting it done. "You are exactly right and I know how you mean. You want them drapes shut at night so it can seem like we're living in a house out in the Belle Meade instead of this here Vox Hall flat, and some fool might be able to look in from the yard."

"Never mind the reasons, Carrie" was Helen Ruth's usual reply. But her answers were not always so gentle--not when Carrie suggested that she have the second baby at home with Carrie acting as midwife, not when Carrie spoke to her about having the third baby circumcised. And the day that Helen Ruth began packing her things to go to Thornton, she was certain that Carrie would speak out of turn with some personal advice. That would have been more than she could bear, and she was prepared to dismiss Carrie from her service and make the trip alone. But neither then nor afterward did Carrie give any real evidence of understanding the reasons for the trip to Thornton.

In fact, it was not until long afterward, when Carrie had quit them to become an undertaker, that Helen Ruth felt that Carrie's gossip with other Nashville servants had, by accident, played a part in her separation from John R. She and John R. had talked of separation and divorce more than once during the first two years they were married, in the era of Jane Blakemore. It was not that any quarreling led to this talk but that each accused the other of being dissatisfied with their marriage, When John R. came in from traveling, on a week

187

end or in the middle of the week--he was sometimes gone only two or three days at a time--he would find Helen Ruth sitting alone in the living room, without a book or even a deck of cards to amuse herself with, dressed perhaps in something new her mother had sent her, waiting for him. She would rise from her chair to greet him, and he would smile in frank admiration of the tall, graceful figure and of the countenance whose features seemed always composed, and softened by her hair, which was beginning to be gray even at the time of their marriage. But he had not come home many times before Helen Ruth was greeting him with tears instead of smiles. At first, he had been touched, but soon he began to complain that she was unhappy. He asked her why she did not see something of other people while he was away--the wives of his business and hunting friends, or some of the other Thornton girls who were married and living in Nashville. She replied that she did see them occasionally but that she was not the sort of woman who enjoyed having a lot of women friends. Besides, she was perfectly happy with her present life; it was only that she believed that he must be unhappy and that he no longer enjoyed her company. She understood that he had to be away most of the week, but even when he was in town, she saw very little of him. When he was not at his office, he was fishing out on Duck River or was off to a hunt up at Gallatin. And at night he either took her to parties with those hunting people, with whom she had little or nothing in common, or piled up on the bed after supper and slept. All of this indicated that he was not happy being married to her, she said, and so they talked a good deal about separating.

After the first baby came, there was no such talk for a long time--not until after the second baby. After the first baby came, Helen Ruth felt that their marriage must be made to last, regardless of hers or John R.'s happiness. Besides, it was at that time that one of John R.'s hunting friends--a rich man named Rufus Brantley--had secured the insurance agency for him; and almost before John R. opened his office, he had sold policies to other rich hunting friends that he had. For a while, he was at home more than he had ever been before. But soon, when his business was established, he began to attend more and more meets and trials, all over Tennessee and Alabama and Kentucky. He even acquired a few dogs and a horse of his own. With his friends he began to go on trips to distant parts of the country. It seemed that when he was not deer hunting in the State of Maine, he was deep-sea fishing in the Gulf. Helen Ruth did sometimes go with him to the local horse shows, but one night, at the Spring Horse Show, she had told Mrs. Brantley that she had a new machine, and Mrs. Brantley had thought she meant an automobile instead of a sewing machine. That, somehow, had been the last straw. She would never go out with "people like the Brantleys" after that. She was pregnant again before

188

the first baby was a year old, and this soon became her excuse for going nowhere in the evening. The women she did visit with very occasionally in the daytime were those she had known as girls in Thornton, women whose husbands were bank tellers and office managers and were barely acquainted with John R. Lovell.

After the second baby came, Helen Ruth saw these women more frequently. She began to feel a restlessness that she could not explain in herself. There were days when she could not stay at home. With Carrie and the two babies, she would traipse about town, on foot or by streetcar, to points she had not visited since she was a little girl and was in Nashville with her parents to attend the State Fair or the Centennial. She went to the Capitol, to Centennial Park and the Parthenon, even out to the Glendale Zoo. Once, with Nancy Tolliver and Lucy Parkes, two of her old Thornton friends, she made an excursion to Cousin Mamie Lovell's farm, which was several miles beyond the town of Franklin. They went by the electric inter-urban to Franklin, and from there they took a taxi to the farm. Cousin Mamie's husband had been a second cousin of John R.'s father, and it was a connection the Thornton Lovells had once been very proud to claim. But for a generation this branch of the family had been in decline. Major Lovell had been a prominent lawyer in Franklin and had been in politics, but when he died, he left his family "almost penniless." His boys had not gone to college; since the farm was supposed to have been exhausted, they did not try to farm it but clerked in stores in Franklin. There was said to be a prosperous son-in-law in St. Louis, but the daughter was dead and Cousin Mamie was reported to have once called her son-in-law a parvenu to his face. Helen Ruth and her friends made the excursion because they wanted to see the house, which was one of the finest old places in the country and full of antiques.

But Cousin Mamie didn't even let them inside the house. It was a hot summer day, and she had all the blinds closed and the whole L-shaped house shut up tight, so that it would be bearable at night. She received them on the long ell porch. Later, they moved their chairs out under a tree in the yard, where Cousin Mamie's cook brought them a pitcher of iced tea. While they were chatting under the tree that afternoon, they covered all the usual topics that are dealt with when talking to an old lady one doesn't know very well--the old times, mutual friends and family connections, country living and city living, and always, of course, the lot of woman as it relates to each topic.

"Where are you and John R. living?" Cousin Mamie asked Helen Ruth.

"We're still at the Vaux Hall, Cousin Mamie."

"I'd suppose the trains would be pretty bad for noise there, that close to the depot."

"They're pretty bad in the summer."

"I'd suppose you had a place out from town, seeing how often John R.'s name's in the paper with the hound and hunt set."

"That's John R.'s life," Helen Ruth said, "not mine."

"He runs with a fine pack, I must say," said Cousin Mamie.

Nancy Tolliver and Lucy Park nodded and smiled. Lucy said, "The swells of Nashville, Miss Mamie."

But Cousin Mamie said, "There was a day when they weren't the swells. Forty years ago, people like Major Lovell didn't know people like the Brantleys. I think the Brantleys quarried limestone, to begin with. I guess it don't matter though, for when I was a girl in upper East Tennessee, people said the Lovells started as land speculators hereabouts and at Memphis. But I don't blame you for not wanting to fool with Brantleys, Helen Ruth."

"John R. and I each live our own life, Cousin Mamie."

"Helen Ruth is a woman with a mind of her own, Miss Mamie," Nancy Tolliver said. "It's too bad more marriages can't be like theirs, each living their own life. Everyone admires it as a real achievement."

And Lucy Parks said, "Because a woman's husband hunts is no reason for her to hunt, any more than because a man's wife sews is any reason for him to sew."

"Indeed not," Cousin Mamie said, actually paying little attention to what Lucy and Nancy were saying. Presently, she continued her own train of thought. "Names like Brantley and Partee and Hines didn't mean a thing in this state even thirty years ago."

What Lucy and Nancy said about her marriage that day left Helen Ruth in a sort of daze and at the same time made her see her situation more clearly. She had never discussed her marriage with anybody, and hearing it described so matter-of-factly by these two women made her understand for the first time what a special sort of marriage it was and how unhappy she was in it. At the time, John R. was away on a fishing trip to Tellico Plains. She did not see him again before she took the babies and Carrie to Thornton. She sent a note to his office saying that she would return when he decided to devote his time to his wife and children instead of to his hounds and horses.

While she was at Thornton her letters from John R. made no mention of her note. He wrote about his business, about his hounds and horses, about the weather, and he always urged her to hurry home as soon as she had seen everybody and had a good visit. Meanwhile, he had a room at the Hermitage Club.

When Helen Ruth returned to Nashville, their life went on as before. A year later, the third boy, Robbie, was born, and John R. bought a large bungalow on Sixteenth Avenue, not too far from the Tarbox School, where they planned to send the boys. Carrie was with them for three years after the separation, and though her work did not improve, Helen Ruth found herself making excuses for her. She began to attribute Carrie's garrulity to a "certain sort of bashfulness, or the Negro equivalent to bashfulness." And with the three small boys and the yard to keep, too, there was so much more for Carrie to do than there had been before! Despite the excuses she made for her, Helen Ruth could see that Carrie was plainly getting worse about everything and that she now seemed to take pleasure in lying about the smallest, most unimportant things. But Helen Ruth found it harder to confront Carrie with her lies or to reprimand her in any way.

During the last months before Carrie quit, she would talk sometimes about the night work she did for a Negro undertaker. To make Helen Ruth smile, she would report things she had heard about the mourners. Her job, Carrie always said, was to sweep the parlors after the funeral and to fold up the chairs. It was only when she finally gave notice to Helen Ruth that she told her what she professed was the truth. She explained that during all those months she had been learning to embalm. "Before you can get a certificate," she said, "you has to handle a bad accident, a sickness, a case of old age, a drowning, a burning, and a half-grown child or less. I been waiting on the child till last night, but now I'll be getting my certificate."

Helen Ruth would not even let Carrie go to the basement to get her hat and coat. "You send somebody for them, " she said. "But, *you*, you get off these premises, Carrie!" She was sincerely outraged by what Carrie had told her, and when she looked at Carrie's hands she was filled with new horror. Yet something kept her from saying all the things that one normally said to a worthless, lying servant who had been guilty of one final outrage. "*Leave*, Carrie!" she said, consciously restraining herself. "*Leave* this place!" Carrie went out the kitchen door and down the driveway to the street, bareheaded, coatless, and wearing her kitchen slippers.

191

After Carrie, there was old Sarah, who stayed with them for six years and then quit them to get married and go to Chicago. Sarah was too old to do heavy work even when she first came, and before she had been there a week, John R. had been asked to help move the sideboard and to bring the ladder up from the basement. He said it seemed that every minute he was in the house, he was lifting or moving something that was too much for Sarah. Helen Ruth replied that perhaps she should hire a Negro man to help in the house and look after the yard. But John R. said no, he was only joking, he thought Sarah far and away the best cook they had ever had, and besides business conditions didn't look too good and it was no time to be taking on more help. But he would always add he did not understand why Helen Ruth babied Sarah so. "From the first moment old Sarah set foot in this house, Helen Ruth has babied her," he would say to people in Helen Ruth's presence.

Sarah could neither read nor write. Even so, it took her only a short while to learn all Helen Ruth's special recipes and how to cook everything the way the Lovells liked it. For two weeks, Helen Ruth stayed in the kitchen with Sarah, reading to her from *How We Cook in Tennessee* and giving detailed instructions for every meal. It was during that time that her great sympathy for Sarah developed. Sarah was completely unashamed of her illiteracy, and it was this that first impressed Helen Ruth. She admired Sarah for having no false pride and for showing no resentment of her mistress's impatience. She observed Sarah's kindness with the children. And she learned from Sarah about Sarah's religious convictions and about her long, unhappy marriage to a Negro named Morse Wilkins, who had finally left her and gone up North.

While Sarah was working for them, John R. and Helen Ruth lived the life that Helen Ruth had heard her friends describe to John R.'s Cousin Mamie. It was not until after Sarah had come that Helen Ruth, recalling the afternoon at Cousin Mamie's, identified Lucy Parkes's words about a wife's sewing and a husband's hunting as the very answer she had once given to some of Carrie's impertinent prying. That afternoon, the remark had certainly sounded familiar, but she had been too concerned with her own decision to leave her husband to concentrate upon anything so trivial. And after their reconciliation, she tried not to dwell on things that had led her to leave John R. Their reconciliation, whatever it meant to John R., meant to her the acceptance of certain mysteries--the mystery of his love of hunting, of his choice of friends, of his desire to maintain a family and home of which he saw so little, of his attachment to her, and of her own devotion to him. Her babies were now growing into little boys. She felt that there was much to be thankful for, not the least of which was a servant as fond of her and of her children as Sarah was. Sarah's affection for the three little boys often reminded Helen Ruth how lonely Sarah's life must be.

One day, when she had watched Sarah carefully wrapping up little Robbie in his winter play clothes before he went out to play in the snow, she said, "You love children so much, Sarah, didn't you ever have any of your own?"

Sarah, who was a yellow-skinned woman with face and arms covered with brown freckles, turned her gray eyes and fixed them solemnly on Helen Ruth. "Why, I had the cutest little baby you ever did see," she said, "and Morse went and killed it."

"Morse *killed* your baby?"

"He rolled over on it in his drunk sleep and smothered it in the bed."

After that, Helen Ruth would never even listen to Sarah when she talked about Morse, and she began to feel a hatred toward any and all of the men who came to take Sarah home at night. Generally, these men were the one subject Sarah did not discuss with Helen Ruth, and their presence in Sarah's life was the only serious complaint Helen Ruth made against her. They would come sometimes as early as four in the afternoon and wait on the back porch for Sarah to get through. She knew that Sarah was usually feeding one of them out of her kitchen, and she knew that Sarah was living with first one and then another of them, but when she told John R. she was going to put her foot down on it, he forbade her to do so. And so through nearly six years she tolerated this weakness of Sarah's. But one morning in the late spring Sarah told her that Morse Wilkins had returned from up North and that she had taken him back as her husband. Helen Ruth could not find anything to say for a moment, but after studying the large diamond on her engagement ring for awhile she said, "My servant's private life is her own affair, but I give you fair warning now, Sarah, I want to see no more of your men friends--Morse or *any other*-- on this place again."

From that time, she saw no more men on the place until Morse himself came, in a drunken rage, in the middle of a summer's day. Helen Ruth had been expecting something of the sort to happen. Sarah had been late to work several times during the preceding three weeks. She had come one morning with a dark bruise on her cheek and said she had fallen getting off the streetcar. Twice, Helen Ruth had found Sarah on her knees, praying in the kitchen. The day Helen Ruth heard the racket at the back-porch door, she knew at once that it was Morse. She got up from her sewing machine and went directly to the kitchen. Sarah was on the back porch, and Morse was outside the screen door of the porch, which was hooked on the inside. He was a little man, shriveled up, baldheaded, not more than five feet tall, and of a complexion very much like Sarah's. Over his white shirt he wore a dark sleeveless sweater. "You come on home," he was saying as he shook the screen door.

Helen Ruth stepped to the kitchen door. "Is that her?" Morse asked Sarah, motioning his head toward Helen Ruth.

When Sarah turned her face around, her complexion seemed several shades lighter than Morse's. "I got to go," she said to Helen Ruth.

"No, Sarah, *he's* got to go. But *you* don't."

"He's gonna leave me again."

"That's the best thing that could happen to you, Sarah."

Sarah said nothing, and Morse began shaking the door again.

"Is he drunk, Sarah?" Helen Ruth asked.

"He's so drunk I don't know how he find his way here."

Helen Ruth went out onto the porch. "Now, you get off this place, and quick about it," she said to Morse.

He shook the screen door again. "You didn't make me come here, Mrs. Lovellel, and you can't make me leave, Mrs. Lovellel."

"I can't make you leave," Helen Ruth said at once, "but there's a bluecoat down on the corner who can."

Suddenly Sarah dropped to her knees and began praying. Her lips moved silently, and gradually she let her forehead come to rest on the top of the rickety vegetable bin. Morse looked at her through the screen, putting his face right against the wire. "Sarah," he said, "you come on home. You better come on now if you think I be there."

Sarah got up off her knees.

"I'm going to phone the police," Helen Ruth said, pretending to move toward the kitchen.

Morse left the door and staggered backward toward the driveway. "Come on, Sarah," he shouted.

"I got to go," Sarah said.

"I won't let you go, Sarah!"

"She can't make you stay!" Morse shouted. "You better come on if you coming!"

"It will be the worst thing you ever did in your life, Sarah," said Helen Ruth. "And if you go with him, you can't ever come back here. He'll kill you someday, too--the way he did your baby."

Sarah was on her knees again, and Morse was out of sight but still shouting as he went down the driveway. Suddenly, Sarah was on her feet. She ran into the kitchen and on through the house to the front porch.

Helen Ruth followed, calling her back. She found Sarah on the front porch waving to Morse, who was halfway down the block, running in a zigzag down the middle of the street, still shouting at the top of his voice. Sarah cried out to him, "Morse! Morse!"

"Sarah!" Helen Ruth said.

"Morse!" Sarah cried again, and then she began mumbling words that Helen Ruth could not quite understand at the time. Afterward, going over it in her mind, Helen Ruth realized that what Sarah had been mumbling was, "If I don't see you no more on this earth, Morse, I'll see you in Glory."

Sarah was with the Lovells for four more months, and then one night she called up on the telephone and asked John R., Jr., to tell his mother that she was going to get married to a man named Racecar and they were leaving for Chicago in the morning.

Jess McGehee came to them during the Depression. Even before Sarah left the Lovells, John R. had had to give up all of his "activities" and devote his entire time to selling insurance. Rufus Brantley had shot himself through the head while cleaning a gun at his hunting lodge, and most of John R.'s other hunting friends had suffered the same financial reverses that John R. had. The changes in the Lovells' life had come so swiftly that Helen Ruth did not realize for awhile what the changes meant in her relationship with John R. It seemed as though she woke up on day and discovered that she was not married to the same man. She found herself spending all her evenings playing Russian bank with a man who had no interest in anything but his home, his wife, and his three boys. Every night, he would give a brief summary of the things that had happened at his office or on his calls, and then he would ask her and the boys for an account of everything they had done that day. He took an interest in the house and the yard, and he and the boys made a lily pool in the back yard, and singlehanded he screened in the entire front porch. Sometimes he took the whole family to Thornton for a week end, and he and Helen Ruth never missed the family reunions there in September.

In a sense, these were the happiest years of their married life. John R.'s business got worse and worse, of course, but since part of their savings was in the bank at Thornton that did not fail, they never had any serious money worries. Regardless of their savings, however, John R.'s loss of income and his having to give up his friends and his hunting wrought very real, if only temporary changes in him. There were occasions when he would sit quietly and listen to his family's talk without correcting them or pointing out how foolish they were. He gave up saying "Think!" to the boys, and instead would say, "Now, let's see if we can't reason this thing out." He could never bring himself to ask for any sympathy from Helen Ruth for his various losses, but as it was during this time that he suffered so from the ailment in his back (he and Helen Ruth slept with boards under their mattress for ten years), the sympathy he got for his physical pain was more than sufficient. All in all, it was a happy period in their life, and in addition to their general family happiness they had Jess.

Jess not only cooked and cleaned, she planned the meals, did the marketing, and washed everything, from handkerchiefs and socks to heavy woolen blankets. When the boys began to go to dances, she even learned to launder their dress shirts. There was nothing she would not do for the boys or for John R. or for Helen Ruth. The way she idealized the family became the basis for most of the "Negro jokes" told by the Lovells during those years. In her room she had a picture of the family, in a group beside the lily pool, taken with her own box Brownie; she had tacked it and also a picture of each of them on the wall above her washstand. In her scrapbook she had pasted every old snapshot and photograph that Helen Ruth would part with, as well as old newspaper pictures of John R. on horseback or with a record-breaking fish he had caught. She had even begged from Helen Ruth an extra copy of the newspaper notice of their wedding.

Jess talked to the family a good deal at mealtime, but only when they had addressed her first and had shown that they wanted her to talk. Her remarks were mostly about things that related to the

196

Lovells. She told a sad story about a "very loving white couple" from Brownsville, her home town, who had been drowned in each other's arms when their car rolled off the end of a river ferry. The point of the story was that those two people were the same, fine, loving sort of couple that John R. and Helen Ruth were. All three of the boys made good grades in school, and every month Jess would copy their grades in her scrapbook, which she periodically passed around for the family to appreciate. When Kenneth began to write stories and articles for his high-school paper, she would always borrow the paper overnight; soon it came out that she was copying everything he wrote onto the big yellow pages of her scrapbook.

After three or four years, John R. began to say that he thought Jess would be with them always and that they would see the day when the boys' children would call her "Mammy." Helen Ruth said she would like to agree with him about that, but actually she worried, because Jess seemed to have no life of her own, which wasn't at all natural. John R. agreed that they should make her take a holiday now and then. Every summer, they would pack Jess off to Brownsville for a week's visit with her kinfolks, but she was always back in her room over the garage within two or three days; she said that her people fought and quarreled so much that she didn't care for them. Outside her life with the Lovells, she had only one friend. Her interest was the movies, and her friend was "the Mary who works for Mrs. Dunbar." Jess and Mary went to the movies together as often as three or four times a week, and on Sunday afternoons Mary came to see Jess or Jess went to see Mary, who lived over the Dunbar's garage. Jess always took along her scrapbook and her most recent movie magazines. She and Mary swapped movie magazines, and it was apparent from Jess's talk on Monday mornings that they also swapped eulogies of their white families.

Sometimes Helen Ruth would see Mrs. Dunbar downtown or at a P.T.A. meeting; they would discuss their cooks and smile over the reports that each had received of the other's family. "I understand that your boys are all growing into very handsome men," Mrs. Dunbar said once, and she told Helen Ruth that Jess was currently comparing one of the boys--Mrs. Dunbar didn't know which one--to Neil Hamilton, and that she was comparing Helen Ruth to Irene Rich, and John R. to Edmund Lowe. As the boys got older, they began to resent the amount of authority over them--though it was small--that Jess had been allowed by their parents and were embarrassed if anyone said Jess had taught them to drive the car. When John R., Jr., began at the university, he made his mother promise not to let Jess know what grades he received, and none of the boys would let Jess take snapshots of them any more. Their mother tried to comfort Jess by saying that the boys were only going through a phase and that it would pass in time. One day, she even said this in the presence of Robbie, who promptly reported it to the older boys, and it ended with John R., Jr's, complaining to his father that their mother ought not to make fun of them to Jess. His father laughed at him but later told Helen Ruth that he thought she was making a mistake, that the boys were getting big enough to think about their manly dignity, and that she would have to take that into consideration.

She didn't make the same mistake again, but although Jess never gave any real sign of her feelings being hurt, Helen Ruth was always conscious of how the boys were growing away from their good-natured servant. By the time Robbie was sixteen, they had long since ceased to have any personal conversation with Jess, and nothing would have induced Robbie to submit to taking drives with her but the knowledge that his father would not allow him to use the car on dates until he had had months of driving practice. Once, when Robbie and Jess returned from a drive, Jess reported, with a grin, that not a word had passed between them during the entire hour and a half. Helen Ruth only shook her head sadly. The next day she bought Jess a new bedside radio.

The radio was the subject of much banter among the boys and their father. John R. said Helen Ruth had chosen the period of hard times and the Depression to become more generous with her servant than she had ever been before in her life. They recalled other presents she had given Jess recently, and from that time on they teased her regularly about how she spoiled Jess. John R. said that if Jess had had his back trouble, Helen Ruth would have retired her at double pay and nursed her with twice the care that he received. The boys teased her by saying that at Christmas time she reversed the custom of shopping for the servant at the ten-cent stores and for the family at the department stores.

Yet as long as Jess was with them, they all agreed that she was the best help they had ever had. In fact, even afterward, during the war years, when John R.'s business prospered again and his back trouble left him entirely and the boys were lucky enough to be stationed near home and, later, continue their education at government expense, even then John R. and the boys would say that the years when Jess was with them were the happiest time of their life and that Jess was the best servant Helen Ruth had ever had. They said that, and then there would be a silence, during which they were probably thinking about the summer morning just before the war when Jess received a telephone call.

When the telephone rang that morning, Helen Ruth and John R. and the boys had just sat down to breakfast. As was usual in the summertime, they were eating at the big dropleaf table in the sun parlor. Jess had set the coffee urn by Helen Ruth's place and was starting from the room when the telephone rang. Helen Ruth, supposing the call was for a member of the family, and seeing that Jess lingered in the doorway, said for her to answer it there in the sun parlor instead of running to the telephone in the back hall.

Jess answered it, announcing whose residence it was in a voice so like Helen Ruth's that it made the boys grin. For a moment, everyone at the table kept silent. They waited for Jess's eyes to single out one of them. John R., Jr., and Kenneth even put down their grapefruit spoons. But the moment Jess picked up the instrument, she fixed her eyes on the potted fern on the window seat across the room. At once her nostrils began to twitch, her lower lip fell down, and it seemed only an act of will that she was twice able to say, "Yes, ma'am," in answer to the small, unreal, metallic voice.

When she had replaced the telephone on its cradle, she turned quickly away and started into the dining room. But Helen Ruth stopped her. "Jess," she asked, her voice full of courtesy, "was the call for you?"

Jess stopped, and they all watched her hands go up to her face. Without turning around, she leaned against the door jamb and began sobbing aloud. Helen Ruth sprang up from the table, saying, "Jess, honey, what *is* the matter?" John R. and the boys stood up, too.

"It was a telegram for me--from Brownsville."

Helen Ruth took her in her arms. "Is someone dead?"

Between sobs, Jess answered, "My little brother--our baby brother--the only one of 'em I cared for." Then her sobs became more violent.

Helen Ruth motioned for John R. to move the morning paper from the big wicker chair, and she led Jess in that direction. But Jess would not sit down, and she could not be pulled away from Helen Ruth. She held fast to her, and Helen Ruth continued to pat her gently on the back and to try to console her with gentle words. Finally, she said, "Jess, you must go to Brownsville. Maybe there's been some mistake. Maybe he's not dead. But you must go, anyway."

Presently, Jess did sit in the chair, and dried her eyes on Helen Ruth's napkin. The boys shook their heads sympathetically and John R. said she certainly must go to Brownsville. She agreed, and said she believed there was a bus at ten that she would try to catch. Helen Ruth patted her hand, telling her to go along to her room when she felt like it, and said that *she* would finish getting breakfast.

"I want to go by to see Mary first," Jess said, "so I better make haste." She stood up, forcing a grateful smile. Then she burst into tears again and threw her arms about Helen Ruth, mumbling, "Oh, God! Oh, God!" The three boys and their father saw tears come into Helen Ruth's eyes, and through her tears Helen Ruth saw a change come over their faces. It was not exactly a change of expression. It couldn't be that, she felt, because it was exactly the some on each of the four faces. It hardly seemed possible that so similar a change could reflect four men's individual feelings. She concluded that her own emotion, and probably the actual tears in her eyes, had made her imagine the change, and when Jess now pulled away and hurried off to her room, Helen Ruth's tears had dried and she could see no evidence of the change she had imagined in her husband's and her sons' faces.

While Jess was in her room preparing to leave, they finished breakfast. Then Helen Ruth began clearing the table, putting the dishes on the teacart. She had said little while they were eating, but in her mind she was all the while going over something that she knew she must tell her family. As she absent-mindedly stacked the dishes, her lips moved silently over the simple words she would use in telling them. She knew that they were watching her, and when Robbie offered to take Jess to the bus station, she knew that the change she had seen in all their faces had been an expression of sympathy for *her as* well as of an eagerness to put this whole episode behind them. "I'll take Jess to her bus," he said.

But Helen Ruth answered, in the casual tone she had been preparing to use, that she thought it probably wouldn't be the thing to do.

"Why, what do you mean, Helen Ruth?" John R. asked her.

"It was very touching, mother," Kenneth said in his new, manly voice, "the way she clung to you." He, too, wanted to express sympathy, but he also seemed to want to distract his mother from answering his father's question.

At that moment, Jess passed under the sun-parlor windows, walking down the driveway, carrying two large suitcases. Helen Ruth watched her until she reached the sidewalk. Then, very quietly, she told her family that Jess McGehee had no baby brother and had never had one. "Jess and Mary are leaving for California. They think they're going to find themselves jobs out there."

"You knew that right along?" John R. asked.

"I knew it right along."

"Did she know you did, Helen Ruth?" he asked. His voice had in it the sternness he used when questioning the boys about something.

"No, John R., she did not. I didn't learn it from her."

"Well, I don't believe it's so," he said. "Why, I don't believe that for a minute. Her carrying on was too real."

"They're going to California. They've already got their two tickets. Mrs. Dunbar got wind of it somehow, by accident, from Mrs. Lon Thompson's cook, and she called me on Monday. They've saved their money and they're going."

"And you let Jess get away with all that crying stuff just now?" John R. said.

Helen Ruth put her hands on the handle bar of the teacart. She pushed the cart a little way over the tile floor but stopped when he repeated his question. It wasn't to answer his question that she stopped, however. "Oh, my dears!" she said, addressing her whole family. Then it was a long time before she said anything more. John R. and the three boys remained seated at the table, and while Helen Ruth gazed past them and toward the front window of the sun parlor, they sat silent and still, as though they were in a picture. What could she say to them, she kept asking herself. And each time she asked the question, she received for answer some different memory of seemingly unrelated things presented themselves as answers to her question, and each of them seemed satisfactory to her. But how little sense it would make to her husband and her grown sons, she reflected, if she should suddenly begin telling them about the long hours she had spent waiting in that apartment at the Vaux Hall while John R. was on the road for the Standard Candy Company, and in the same breath should tell them about how plainly she used to talk to Jane Blakemore and how Jane pretended that the baby made her nervous and went back to Thornton. Or suppose she should abruptly remind John R. of how ill at ease the wives of his hunting friends used to make her feel and how she had later driven Sarah's worthless husband out of the yard, threatening to call a bluecoat. What if she should suddenly say that because a woman's husband hunts, there is no reason for her to hunt,

201

any more than because a man's wife sews, there is reason for him to sew. She felt that she would be willing to say anything at all, no matter how cruel or absurd it was, if it would make them understand that everything that happened in life only demonstrated in some way the lonesomeness that people felt. She was ready to tell them about sitting in the old nursery at Thornton and waiting for Carrie and Jane Blakemore to come out of the cabin in the yard. If it would make them see what she had been so long in learning to see, she would even talk at last about the "so much else" that had been missing from her life and that she had not been able to name, and about the foolish mysteries she had so nobly accepted upon her reconciliation with John R. To her, these things were all one now; they were her loneliness, the loneliness from which everybody, knowingly or unknowingly, suffered. But she knew that her husband and her sons did not recognize her loneliness or Jess McGehee's or their own. She turned her eyes from the window to look at their faces around the table, and it was strange to see that they were still thinking in the most personal and particular terms of how they had been deceived by a servant, the ignorant granddaughter of an ignorant slave, a Negro woman from Brownsville who was crazy about the movies and who would soon be riding a bus, mile after mile, on her way to Hollywood, where she might find the friendly faces of the real Neil Hamilton and the real Irene Rich. It was with effort that Helen Ruth thought again of Jess McGehee's departure and the problem of offering an explanation to her family. At last, she said patiently, "My dears, don't you see how it was for Jess? How else can they tell us anything when there is such a gulf?" After a moment she said, "How can I make you understand this?"

Her husband and her three sons sat staring at her, their big hands, all so alike, resting on the breakfast table, their faces stamped with identical expressions, not of wonder but of incredulity. Helen Ruth was still holding firmly to the handle of the teacart. She pushed it slowly and carefully over the doorsill and into the dining room, dark and cool as an underground cavern, and spotlessly clean, the way Jess McGehee had left it.

STRONG HORSE TEA

Alice Walker

Rannie Toomer's little baby boy Snooks was dying from double pneumonia and whooping cough. She sat away from him gazing into the low fire, her long crusty bottom lip hanging. She was not married. Was not pretty. Was not anybody much. And he was all she had.

"Lawd, why don't that doctor come on here?" she moaned, tears sliding from her sticky eyes. She had not washed since Snooks took sick five days ago and a long row of whitish snail tracks laced her ashen face.

"What you ought to try is some of the old home remedies," Sarah urged. She was an old neighboring lady who wore magic leaves round her neck sewed up in possum skin next to a dried lizard's foot. She knew how magic came about, and could do magic herself, people said.

"We going to have us a doctor," Rannie Toomer said fiercely, walking over to shoo a fat winter fly from her child's forehead. "I don't believe in none of your swamp magic. The 'old home remedies' I took when I was a child come just short of killing me."

Snooks, under a pile of faded quilts, made a small oblong mound in the bed. His head was like a ball of black putty wedged between the thin covers and the dingy yellow pillow. His eyes were partly open as if he were peeping out of his hard wasted skull at the chilly room, and the forceful pulse of his breathing caused a faint rustling in the sheets near his mouth like the wind pushing damp papers in a shallow ditch.

"What time you reckon he'll git here?" asked Sarah, not expecting an answer. She sat with her knees wide apart under three long skirts and a voluminous Mother Hubbard heavy with stains. From time to time she reached down to sweep her damp skirts away from the live coals. It was almost spring, but the winter cold still clung to her bones, and she had to almost sit in the fireplace to get warm. Her deep, sharp eyes had aged a moist hesitant blue that gave her a quick dull stare like a hawk. She gazed coolly at Rannie Toomer and rapped the hearthstones with her stick.

"White mailman, white doctor," she chanted skeptically.

"They gotta come see 'bout this baby," Rannie Toomer said wistfully. "Who'd go and ignore a little sick baby like my Snooks?"

"Some folks we don't know well as we *thinks* we do might," the old lady replied. "What you want to give that boy of yours is one or two of the old home remedies, arrowsroot or sassyfrass and cloves, or sugar tit soaked in cat's blood."

"We don't need none of your witch's remedies!" said Rannie Toomer. "We going to git some of them shots that makes people well. Cures 'em of all they ails, cleans 'em out and makes 'em strong, all at the same time." She grasped her baby by his shrouded toes and began to gently twist, trying to knead life into him the same way she kneaded limberness into flour dough. She spoke upward from his feet as if he were an altar.

"Doctor'll be here soon, baby. I done sent the mailman." She left him reluctantly to go and stand by the window. She pressed her face against the glass, her flat nose more flattened as she peered out at the rain.

She had gone up to the mailbox in the rain that morning, hoping she hadn't missed the mailman's car. She had sat down on an old milk can near the box and turned her drooping face in the direction the mailman's car would come. She had no umbrella, and her feet shivered inside thin, clear plastic shoes that let in water and mud.

"Howde, Rannie Mae," the red-faced mailman said pleasantly as he always did, when she stood by his car waiting to ask him something. Usually she wanted to ask what certain circulars meant that showed pretty pictures of things she needed. Did the circulars mean that somebody was coming around later and would give her hats and suitcases and shoes and sweaters and rubbing alcohol and a heater for the house and a fur bonnet for her baby? Or, why did he always give her the pictures if she couldn't have what was in them? Or, what did the words say? . . . Especially the big word written in red: "S-A-L-E!"?

He would explain shortly to her that the only way she could get the goods pictured on the circulars was to buy them in town and that town stores did their advertising by sending out pictures of their goods. She would listen with her mouth hanging open until he finished. Then she would exclaim in a dull amazed way that *she* never had any money and he could ask anybody. *She* couldn't ever buy any of the things in the pictures--so why did the stores keep sending them to her?

He tried to explain to her that *everybody* got the circulars whether they had any money to buy with or not. That this was one of the laws of advertising, and he couldn't do anything about it. He was sure she never understood what he tried to teach her about advertising, for one day she asked him for any extra circulars he had, and when he asked what she wanted them for--since she couldn't afford to buy any of the items advertised--she said she needed them to paper the inside of her house to keep out the wind.

Today he thought she looked more ignorant than usual as she stuck her dripping head inside his car. He recoiled from her breath and gave little attention to what she was saying about her sick baby as he mopped up the water she dripped on the plastic door handle of the car.

"Well, never *can* keep'em dry; I mean warm enough, in rainy weather like this here," he mumbled absently, stuffing a wad of circulars advertising hair dryers and cold creams into her hands. He wished she would stand back from his car so he could get going. But she clung to the side gabbing away about "Snooks" and "pneumonia" and "shots" and about how she wanted a "*real* doctor!"

To everything she said he nodded. "That right?" he injected sympathetically when she stopped for breath, and then he began to sneeze, for she was letting in wetness and damp, and he felt he was coming down with a cold. Black people as black as Rannie Toomer always made him uneasy, especially when they didn't smell good and when you could tell they didn't right away. Rannie Mae, leaning in over him out of the rain, smelled like a wet goat. Her dark dirty eyes clinging to his with such hungry desperation made him nervous.

"Well, ah, *mighty* sorry to hear 'bout the little fella," he said, groping for the window crank. "We'll see what we can do!" He gave her what he hoped was a big friendly smile. God! *He didn't want to hurt her feelings*; she did look so pitiful hanging there in the rain. Suddenly he had an idea.

"Whyn't you try some of old Aunt Sarah's home remedies?" he suggested brightly. He half believed along with everybody else in the county that the old blue-eyed black woman possessed magic. Magic that if it didn't work on whites probably would on blacks. But Rannie Toomer almost turned the car over shaking her head and body with an emphatic NO! She reached in a wet hand to grasp his shoulder.

"We wants us a doctor, a real doctor!" she screamed. She had begun to cry and drop her tears on him. "You git us a doctor from town!" she bellowed, shaking the solid shoulder that bulged under his new tweed coat.

"Like I say," he drawled patiently, although beginning to be furious with her, "we'll do what we can!" And he hurriedly rolled up the window and sped down the road, cringing from the thought that she had put her nasty black hands on him.

"Old home remedies! Old home remedies!" Rannie Toomer had cursed the words while she licked at the hot tears that ran down her face, the only warmth about her. She turned backwards to the trail that led to her house, trampling the wet circulars under her feet. Under the fence she went and was in a pasture surrounded by dozens of fat whitefolks' cows and an old gray horse and a mule. Cows and horses never seemed to have much trouble, she thought, as she hurried home.

Old Sarah dug steadily at the fire; the bones in her legs ached as if they were outside the flesh that enclosed them.

"White mailman, white doctor. White doctor, white mailman," she murmured from time to time, putting the poker down carefully and rubbing her shins.

"You young ones *will* turn to them," she said, " when it is *us* what got the power."

"The doctor's coming, Aunt Sarah. I know he is," Rannie Toomer said angrily.

It was less than an hour after she had talked to the mailman that she looked up expecting the doctor and saw old Sarah tramping through the grass on her walking stick. She couldn't pretend she wasn't home with the smoke from her fire climbing out the chimney, so she let her in, making her leave her bag of tricks on the porch.

Old woman old as that ought to forgit trying to cure other people with her nigger magic. Ought to use some of it on herself! she thought. She would not let Sarah lay a finger on Snooks and warned her if she tried anything she would knock her over the head with her own cane.

"He coming, all right," Rannie Toomer said again firmly, with prayerful looking, eyes out through the rain.

"Let me tell you, child," the old woman said almost gently, sipping the coffee Rannie Toomer had given her. *"He ain't."*

She had not been allowed near the boy on the bed, and that had made her angry at first, but now she looked with pity at the young woman who was so afraid her child would die. She felt rejected but at the same time sadly *glad* that the young always grow up hoping. It *did* take a long time to finally realize that you could only depend on those who would come.

"But I done told you," Rannie Toomer was saying in exasperation, "I asked the mailman to bring a doctor for my Snooks!"

Cold wind was shooting all around her from the cracks in the window framing; faded circulars blew inward from the walls.

"He done fetched the doctor," the old woman said, softly stroking her coffee cup. "What you reckon brung me over here in this here flood? It wasn't no desire to see no rainbows, I can tell you."

Rannie Toomer paled.

"*I's* the doctor, child. That there mailman didn't git no further with that message of yours then the road in front of my house. Lucky he got good lungs--deef as I is I had myself a time trying to make out *what* he was yelling."

Rannie began to cry, moaning.

Suddenly the breathing from the bed seemed to drown out the noise of the downpour outside. The baby's pulse seemed to make the whole house shake.

"Here!" she cried, snatching the baby up and handing him to Sarah. "Make him well! Oh, my lawd, make him well!"

Sarah rose from her seat by the fire and took the tiny baby, already turning a purplish blue around the eyes and mouth.

"Let's not upset the little fella unnecessarylike," Sarah said, placing the baby back on the bed. Gently she began to examine him, all the while moaning and humming a thin pagan tune that pushed against the sound of the wind and rain with its own melancholy power. She stripped him of his clothes, poked at his fiberless baby ribs, blew against his chest. Along his tiny flat back she ran her soft old fingers. The child hung on in deep rasping sleep, and his small glazed eyes neither opened fully nor fully closed.

Rannie Toomer swayed over the bed watching the old woman touching the baby. She mourned the time she had wasted waiting for a doctor. Her feeling of guilt was a stone.

207

"I'll do anything you say do, Aunt Sarah," she cried, mopping at her nose with her dress. "Anything you say, just, please God, make him git better."

Old Sarah dressed the baby again and sat down in front of the fire. She stayed deep in thought for several minutes. Rannie Toomer gazed first into her silent face and then at the baby whose breathing seemed to have eased since Sarah picked him up.

"Do something, quick!" she urged Sarah, beginning to believe in her powers completely, "Do something that'll make him rise up and call his mama!"

"The child's dying," said the old woman bluntly, staking out beforehand some limitation to her skill. "But," she went on, " there might be something still we might try . . ."

"What?" asked Rannie Toomer from her knees. She knelt before the old woman's chair, wringing her hands and crying. She fastened herself to Sarah's chair. How could she have thought anyone else could help her Snooks, she wondered brokenly, when you couldn't even depend on them to come! She had been crazy to trust anyone but the withered old magician before her.

"What can I *do*?" she urged fiercely, blinded by her new faith, driven by the labored breathing from the bed.

"It going to take a strong stomach," said Sarah slowly. "It going to take a mighty strong stomach, and most of you young peoples these days don't have'em!"

"Snooks got a strong stomach," Rannie Toomer said, peering anxiously into the serious old face.

"It ain't him that's got to have the strong stomach," Sarah said, glancing at the sobbing girl at her feet. "*You* the one got to have the strong stomach . . . he won't know *what* it is he's drinking."

Rannie Toomer began to tremble way down deep in her stomach. It sure was weak, she thought. Trembling like that. But what could she mean her Snooks to drink? Not cat's blood! and not any of the other messes she'd heard Sarah specialized in that would make anybody's stomach turn. What did she mean?

"What is it?" she whispered, bringing her head close to Sarah's knee. Sarah leaned down and put her toothless mouth to her ear.

208

"The only thing that can save this child now is some good strong horse tea!" she said, keeping her eyes turned toward the bed. "The *only* thing. And if you wants him out of that bed you better make tracks to git some!"

Rannie Toomer took up her wet coat and stepped across the porch to the pasture. The rain fell against her face with the force of small hailstones. She started walking in the direction of the trees where she could see the bulky lightish shapes of cows. Her thin plastic shoes were sucked at by the mud, but she pushed herself forward in a relentless search for the lone gray mare.

All the animals shifted ground and rolled big dark eyes at Rannie Toomer. She made as little noise as she could and leaned herself against a tree to wait.

Thunder rose from the side of the sky like tires of a big truck rumbling over rough dirt road. Then it stood a split second in the middle of the sky before it exploded like a giant firecracker, then rolled away again like an empty keg. Lightning streaked across the sky, setting the air white and charged.

Rannie Toomer stood dripping under her tree hoping not to be struck. She kept her eyes carefully on the behind of the gray mare, who, after nearly an hour had passed, began nonchalantly to spread her muddy knees.

At that moment Rannie Toomer realized that she had brought nothing to catch the precious tea in. Lightning struck something not far off and caused a cracking and groaning in the woods that frightened the animals away from their shelter. Rannie Toomer slipped down in the mud trying to take off one of her plastic shoes, and the gray mare, trickling some, broke for a clump of cedars yards away.

Rannie Toomer was close enough to the mare to catch the tea if she could keep up with her while she ran. So, alternately holding her breath and gasping for air, she started after her. Mud from her fall clung to her elbows and streaked her frizzy hair. Slipping and sliding in the mud she raced after the big mare, holding out, as if for alms, her plastic shoe.

In the house Sarah sat, her shawls and sweaters tight around her, rubbing her knees and muttering under her breath. She heard the thunder, saw the lightning that lit up the dingy room, and turned her waiting face to the bed. Hobbling over on stiff legs, she could hear no sound; the frail breathing had stopped with the thunder, not to come again.

Across the mud-washed pasture Rannie Toomer stumbled, holding out her plastic shoe for the gray mare to fill. In spurts and splashes mixed with rainwater she gathered her tea. In parting, the old mare snorted and threw up one big leg, knocking her back into the mud. She rose trembling and crying, holding the shoe, spilling none over the top but realizing a leak, a tiny crack, at her shoe's front. Quickly she stuck her mouth there over the crack, and, ankle deep in the slippery mud of the pasture, and freezing in her shabby wet coat, she ran home to give the good and warm strong horse tea to her baby Snooks.

IN SEARCH OF OUR MOTHERS' GARDENS

Alice Walker

> I described her own nature and temperament. Told how they needed a larger life for their expression. . . . I pointed out that in lieu of proper channels, her emotions had overflowed into paths that dissipated them. I talked, beautifully I thought, about an art that would be born, an art that would open the way for women the likes of her. I asked her to hope, and build up an inner life against the coming of that day. . . . I sang, with a strange quiver in my voice, a promise song.

--Jean Toomer, "Avey,"

CANE

The poet speaking to a prostitute who falls asleep while he's talking--

When the poet Jean Toomer walked through the South in the early twenties, he discovered a curious thing: black women whose spirituality was so intense, so deep, so *unconscious*, that they were themselves unaware of the richness they held. They stumbled blindly through their lives: creatures so abused and mutilated in body, so dimmed and confused by pain, that they considered themselves unworthy even of hope. In the selfless abstractions their bodies became to the men who used them, they became more than "sexual objects," more even than mere women: they became "Saints." Instead of being perceived as whole persons, their bodies became shrines: what was thought to be their minds became temples suitable for worship. These crazy Saints stared out at the world, wildly, like lunatics--or quietly, like suicides; and the "God" that was in their gaze was as mute as a great stone.

Who were these Saints? These crazy, loony, pitiful women?

Some of them, without a doubt, were our mothers and grandmothers.

In the still heat of the post-Reconstruction South, this is how they seemed to Jean Toomer: exquisite butterflies trapped in an evil honey, toiling away their lives in an era, a century, that did not acknowledge

211

them, except as "the *mule* of the world." They dreamed dreams that no one knew--not even themselves, in any coherent fashion--and saw visions no one could understand. They wandered or sat about the countryside crooning lullabies to ghosts, and drawing the mother of Christ in charcoal on courthouse walls.

They forced their minds to desert their bodies and their striving spirits sought to rise, like frail whirlwinds from the hard red clay. And when those frail whirlwinds fell, in scattered particles, upon the ground, no one mourned. Instead, men lit candles to celebrate the emptiness that remained, as people do who enter a beautiful but vacant space to resurrect a God.

Our mothers and grandmothers, some of them: moving to music not yet written. And they waited.

They waited for a day when the unknown thing that was in them would be made known; but guessed, somehow in their darkness, that on the day of their revelation they would be long dead. Therefore to Toomer they walked, and even ran, in slow motion. For they were going nowhere immediate, and the future was not yet within their grasp. And men took our mothers and grandmothers, "but got no pleasure from it." So complex was their passion and their calm.

To Toomer, they lay vacant and fallow as autumn fields, with harvest time never in sight: and he saw them enter loveless marriages, without joy; and become prostitutes, without resistance; and become mothers of children, without fulfillment.

For these grandmothers and mothers of ours were not Saints, but Artists; driven to a numb and bleeding madness by the springs of creativity in them for which there was no release. They were Creators, who lived lives of spiritual waste, because they were so rich in spirituality--which is the basis of Art--that the strain of enduring their unused and unwanted talent drove them insane. Throwing away this spirituality was their pathetic attempt to lighten the soul to a weight their work-worn, sexually abused bodies could bear.

What did it mean for a black woman to be an artist in our grandmothers' time? In our great-grandmothers' day? It is a question with an answer cruel enough to stop the blood.

Did you have a genius of a great-great-grandmother who died under some ignorant and depraved white overseer's lash? Or was she required to bake biscuits for a lazy backwater tramp, when she cried out in her soul to paint watercolors of sunsets, or the rain falling on the green and peaceful pasturelands? Or was her body broken and

212

forced to bear children (who were more often then not sold away from her)--eight, ten, fifteen, twenty children--when her one joy was the thought of modeling heroic figures of rebellion, in stone or clay?

How was the creativity of the black woman kept alive, year after year century after century, when for most of the years black people have been in America, it was a punishable crime for a black person to read or write? And the freedom to paint, to sculpt, to expand the mind with action did not exist. Consider, if you can bear to imagine it, what might have been the result if singing, too, had been forbidden by law. Listen to the voices of Bessie Smith, Billie Holiday, Nina Simone, Roberta Flack, and Aretha Franklin, among others, and imagine those voices muzzled for life. Then you may begin to comprehend the lives of our "crazy," "Sainted" mothers and grandmothers. The agony of the lives of women who might have been Poets, Novelists, Essayists, and Short-Story Writers (over a period of centuries), who died with their real gifts stifled within them.

And, if this were the end of the story, we would have cause to cry out in my paraphrase of Okot p'Bitek's great poem:

> O, my clanswomen
> Let us all cry together!
> Come,
> Let us mourn the death of our mother,
> The death of a Queen
> The ash that was produced
> By a great fire!
> O, this homestead is utterly dead
> Close the gates
> With *lacare* thorns,
> For our mother
> The creator of the Stool is lost!
> And all the young women
> Have perished in the wilderness!

But this is not the end of the story, for all the young women--our mothers and grandmothers, *ourselves*--have not perished in the wilderness. And if we ask ourselves why, and search for and find the answer, we will know beyond all efforts to erase it from our minds, just exactly who, and of what, we black American women are.

One example, perhaps the most pathetic, most misunderstood one, can provide a backdrop for out mothers' work: Phillis Wheatley, a slave in the 1700s.

Virginia Woolf, in her book *A Room of One's Own*, wrote that in order for a woman to write fiction she must have two things, certainly:

A room of her own (with key and lock) and enough money to support herself.

What then are we to make of Phillis Wheatley, a slave, who owned not even herself? This sickly, frail black girl who required a servant of her own at times--her health was so precarious--and who, had she been white, would have been easily considered the intellectual superior of all the women and most of the men in the society of her day.

Virginia Woolf wrote further, speaking of course not of our Phillis, that "any woman born with a great gift in the sixteenth century [insert "eighteenth century," insert "black woman," insert "born or made a slave"] would certainly have gone crazed, shot herself, or ended her days in some lonely cottage outside the village, half witch, half wizard [insert "Saint"], feared and mocked at. For it needs little skill and psychology to be sure that a highly gifted girl who had tried to use her gift for poetry would have been so thwarted and hindered by contrary instincts [add "chains, guns, the lash, the ownership of one's body by someone else, submission to an alien religion"], that she must have lost her health and sanity to a certainty."

The key words, as they relate to Phillis, are "contrary instincts." For when we read the poetry of Phillis Wheatley--as when we read the novels of Nella Larsen or the oddly false-sounding autobiography of that freest of all black women writers, Zora Hurston--evidence of "contrary instincts" is everywhere. Her loyalties were completely divided, as was, without question, her mind.

But how could this be otherwise? Captured at seven, a slave of wealthy, doting whites who instilled in her the "savagery" of the Africa they "rescued" her from . . . one wonders if she was even able to remember her homeland as she had known it, or as it really was.

Yet, because she did try to use her gift for poetry in a world that made her a slave, she was "so thwarted and hindered by . . . contrary instincts, that she . . . lost her health. . . ." In the last years of her brief life, burdened not only with the need to express her gift but also with a penniless, friendless "freedom" and several small children for whom she was forced to do strenuous work to feed, she lost her health, certainly. Suffering from malnutrition and neglect and who knows what mental agonies, Phillis Wheatley died.

So torn by "contrary instincts" was black, kidnapped, enslaved Phillis that her description of "the Goddess"--as she poetically called the Liberty she did not have--is ironically, cruelly humorous. And, in fact, has held Phillis up to ridicule for more than a century. It is usually read prior to hanging Phillis's memory as that of a fool. She wrote:

> The Goddess comes, she moves divinely fair,
> Olive and laurel binds her *golden* hair.
> Wherever shines this native of the skies,
> Unnumber'd charms and recent graces rise. [My italics]

It is obvious that Phillis, the slave, combed the "Goddess's" hair every morning; prior, perhaps, to bringing in the milk, or fixing her mistress's lunch. She took her imagery from the one thing she saw elevated above all others.

With the benefit of hindsight we ask, "How could she?"

But at last, Phillis, we understand. No more snickering when your stiff, struggling, ambivalent lines are forced on us. We know now that you were not an idiot or a traitor; only a sickly little black girl, snatched from your home and country and made a slave; a woman who still struggled to sing the song that was your gift, although in a land of barbarians who praised you for your bewildered tongue. It is not so much what you sang, as that you kept alive, in so many of our ancestors, *the notion of song*.

Black women are called, in the folklore that so aptly identifies one's status in society, "the *mule* of the world," because we have been handed the burdens that *everyone* else--everyone else--refused to carry. We have also been called "Matriarchs," "Superwomen," and "Mean and Evil Bitches." Not to mention "Castraters" and "Sapphire's Mama." When we have pleaded for understanding, our character has been distorted; when we have asked for simple caring, we have been handed empty inspirational appellations, then stuck in the farthest corner. When we have asked for love, we have been given children. In short, even our plainer gifts, our labors of fidelity and love, have been knocked down our throats. To be an artist and a black woman, even today, lowers our status in many respects, rather than raises it: and yet, artists we will be.

Therefore we must fearlessly pull out of ourselves and look at and identify with our lives the living creativity some of our great-grandmothers were not allowed to know. I stress *some* of them because it is well known that the majority of our great-grandmothers knew, even without "knowing" it, the reality of their spirituality, even if they didn't recognize it beyond what happened in the singing at church--and they never had any intention of giving it up.

How they did it--those millions of black women who were not Phillis Wheatley, or Lucy Terry or Frances Harper or Zora Hurston or Nella Larsen or Bessie Smith; or Elizabeth Catlett, or Katherine Dunham, either--brings me to the title of this essay, "In Search of Our Mothers' Gardens," which is a personal account that is yet shared, in its theme and its meaning, by all of us. I found, while thinking about the far-reaching world of the creative black woman, that often the truest answer to a question that really matters can be found very close.

In the late 1920s my mother ran away from home to marry my father. Marriage, if not running away, was expected of seventeen-year-old girls. By the time she was twenty, she had two children and was pregnant with a third. Five children later, I was born. And this is how I came to know my mother: she seemed a large, soft, loving-eyed woman who was rarely impatient in our home. Her quick, violent temper was on view only a few times a year, when she battled with the white landlord who had the misfortune to suggest to her that her children did not need to go to school.

She made all the clothes we wore, even my brothers' overalls. She made all the towels and sheets we used. She spent the summers canning vegetables and fruits. She spent the winter evenings making quilts enough to cover all our beds.

During the "working" day, she labored beside--not behind--my father in the fields. Her day began before sunup, and did not end until late at night. There was never a moment for her to sit down, undisturbed, to unravel her own private thoughts; never a time free from interruption--by work or the noisy inquiries of her many children. And yet, it is to my mother--and all our mothers who were not famous--that I went in search of the secret of what has fed that muzzled and often mutilated, but vibrant, creative spirit that the black woman has inherited, and that pops out in wild and unlikely places to this day.

But when, you will ask, did my overworked mother have time to know or care about feeding the creative spirit?

The answer is so simple that many of us have spent years discovering it. We have constantly looked high, when we should have looked high--and low.

For example: in the Smithsonian Institution in Washington, D.C., there hangs a quilt unlike any other in the world. In fanciful, inspired, and yet simple and identifiable figures, it portrays the story of the Crucifixion. It is considered rare, beyond price. Though it follows no known pattern of quilt-making, and though it is made of bits and pieces of worthless rags, it is obviously the work of a person of powerful imagination and deep spiritual feeling. Below this quilt I saw a note that says it was made by "an anonymous Black woman in Alabama, a hundred years ago."

If we could locate this "anonymous" black woman from Alabama, she would turn out to be one of our grandmothers--and artist who left her mark in the only materials she could afford, and in the only medium her position in society allowed her to use.

As Virginia Woolf wrote further, in *A Room of One's Own*:

> Yet genius of a sort must have existed among women as it must have existed among the working class. [Change this to "slaves" and "the wives and daughters of sharecroppers."] Now and again an Emily Brontë or a Robert Burns [change this to "a Zora Hurston or a Richard Wright"] blazes out and proves its presence. But certainly it never got itself on to paper. When, however, one reads of a witch being ducked, of a women possessed by devils [or "Sainthood"], of a wise woman selling herbs [our root workers], or even a very remarkable man who had a mother, then I think we are on the track of a lost novelist, a suppressed poet, of some mute and inglorious Jane Austen. . . . Indeed, I would venture to guess that Anon, who wrote so many poems without signing them, was often a woman. . . .

And so our mothers and grandmothers have, more often than not anonymously, handed on the creative spark, the seed of the flower they themselves never hoped to see: or like a sealed letter they could not plainly read.

And so it is, certainly, with my own mother. Unlike "Ma" Rainey's songs, which retained their creator's name even while blasting forth from Bessie Smith's mouth, no song or poem will bear my mother's name. Yet so many of the stories that I write, that we all write, are my mother's stories. Only recently did I fully realize this: that through years of listening to my mother's stories of her life, I have absorbed not only the stories themselves, but something of the manner in which she spoke, something of the urgency that involves the knowledge that her stories--like her life--must be recorded. It is probably for this reason that so much of what I have written is about characters whose counterparts in real life are so much older than I am.

But the telling of these stories, which came from my mother's lips as naturally as breathing, was not the only way my mother showed herself as an artist. For stories, too, were subject to being distracted, to dying without conclusion. Dinners must be started, and cotton must be gathered before the big rains. The artist that was and is my mother showed itself to me only after many years. This is what I finally noticed:

Like Mem, a character in *The Third Life of Grange Copeland*, my mother adorned with flowers whatever shabby house we were forced to live in. And not just your typical straggly country stand of zinnias, either. She planted ambitious gardens--and still does--with over fifty different varieties of plants that bloom profusely from early March until late November. Before she left home for the fields, she watered her flowers, chopped up the grass, and laid out new beds. When she returned from the fields she might divide clumps of bulbs, dig a cold pit, uproot and replant roses, or prune branches from her taller bushes or trees--until night came and it was too dark to see.

Whatever she planted grew as if by magic, and her fame as a grower of flowers spread over three counties. Because of her creativity with her flowers, even my memories of poverty are seen through a screen of blooms--sunflowers, petunias, roses, dahlias, forsythia, spirea, delphiniums, verbena . . . and on and on.

And I remember people coming to my mother's yard to be given cuttings from her flowers; I hear again the praise showered on her because whatever rocky soil she landed on, she turned into a garden. A garden so brilliant with colors, so original in its design, so magnificent with life and creativity, that to this day people drive by our house in Georgia--perfect strangers and imperfect strangers--to ask to stand or walk among my mother's art.

I notice that it is only when my mother is working in her flowers that she is radiant, almost to the point of being invisible--except as Creator: hand and eye. She is involved in work her soul must have. Ordering the universe in the image of her personal conception of Beauty.

Her face, as she prepares the Art that is her gift, is a legacy of respect she leaves to me, for all that illuminates and cherishes life. She has handed down respect for the possibilities--and the will to grasp them.

For her, so hindered and intruded upon in so many ways, being an artist has still been a daily part of her life. This ability to hold on, even in very simple ways, is work black women have done for a very long time.

This poem is not enough, but it is something, for the woman who literally covered the holes in our walls with sunflowers:

> They were women then
> My mama's generation
> Husky of voice--stout of
> Step
> With fists as well as
> Hands
> How they battered down
> Doors
> And ironed
> Starched white
> Shirts
> How they led
> Armies
> Headragged Generals
> Across mined
> Fields
> Booby-trapped
> Kitchens
> To discover books
> Desks
> A place for us
> How they knew what we
> *Must* know
> Without knowing a page
> Of if
> Themselves.

Guided by my heritage of a love of beauty and a respect for strength--in search of my mother's garden, I found my own.

And perhaps in Africa over two hundred years ago, there was just such a mother; perhaps she painted vivid and daring decorations in oranges and yellows and greens on the walls of her hut, perhaps she sang--in a voice like Roberta Flack's--*sweetly* over the compounds of her village; perhaps she wove the most stunning mats or told the most ingenious stories of all the village storytellers. Perhaps she was herself a poet--though only her daughter's name is signed to the poems that we know.

Perhaps Phillis Wheatley's mother was also an artist.

Perhaps in more than Phillis Wheatley's biological life is her mother's signature made clear.

ELIZABETH BISHOP

Over 2,000 Illustrations and a Complete Concordance

Thus should have been our travels:
serious, engravable.
The Seven Wonders of the World are tired
and a touch familiar, but the other scenes,
innumerable, though equally sad and still,
are foreign. Often the squatting Arab,
or group of Arabs, plotting, probably,
against our Christian Empire,
while one apart, with outstretched arm and hand
points to the Tomb, the Pit, the Sepulcher.
The branches of the date-palms look like files.
The cobbled courtyard, where the Well is dry,
is like a diagram, the brickwork conduits
are vast and obvious, the human figure
far gone in history or theology,
gone with its camel or its faithful horse.
Always the silence, the gesture, the specks of birds
suspended on invisible threads above the Site,
or the smoke rising solemnly, pulled by threads.
Granted a page alone or a page made up
of several scenes arranged in cattycornered rectangles
or circles set on stippled gray,
granted a grim lunette,
caught in the toils of an initial letter,
when dwelt upon, they all resolve themselves.
The eye drops, weighted, through the lines
the burin made, the lines that move apart
like ripples above sand,
dispersing storms, God's spreading fingerprint,
and painfully, finally, that ignite
in watery prismatic white-and-blue.

Entering the Narrows at St. Johns
the touching bleat of goats reached to the ship.
We glimpsed them, reddish, leaping up the cliffs
among the fogsoaked weeds and butter-and-eggs.
And at St. Peter's the wind blew and the sun shone madly.
Rapidly, purposefully, the Collegians marched in lines,
crisscrossing the great square with black, like ants.
In Mexico the dead man lay
in a blue arcade; the dead volcanoes
glistened like Easter lilies.
The jukebox went on playing "Ay, Jalisco!"
And at Volubilis there were beautiful poppies

splitting the mosaics; the fat old guide made eyes.
In Dingle harbor a golden length of evening
the rotting hulks held up their dripping plush.
The Englishwoman poured tea, informing us
that the Duchess was going to have a baby.
And in the brothels of Marrakesh
the little pockmarked prostitutes
balanced their tea-trays on their heads
and did their belly-dances; flung themselves
naked and giggling against our knees,
asking for cigarettes. It was somewhere near there
I saw what frightened me most of all:
A holy grave, not looking particularly holy,
one of a group under a keyhole-arched stone baldaquin
open to every wind from the pink desert.
An open, gritty, marble trough, carved solid
with exhortation, yellowed
as scattered cattle-teeth;
half-filled with dust, not even the dust
of the poor prophet paynim who once lay there.
In a smart burnoose Khadour looked on amused.

Everything only connected by "and" and "and."
Open the book. (The gilt rubs off the edges
of the pages and pollinates the fingertips.)
Open the heavy book. Why couldn't we have seen
this old Nativity while we were at it?
--the dark ajar, the rocks breaking with light,
an undisturbed, unbreathing flame,
Colorless, sparkless, freely fed on straw,
and, lulled within, a family with pets,
--and looked and looked our infant sight away.

Elizabeth Bishop

At the Fishhouses

Although it is a cold evening,
down by one of the fishhouses
an old man sits netting,
his net, in the gloaming almost invisible,
a dark purple-brown,
and his shuttle worn and polished.
The air smells so strong of codfish
it makes one's nose run and one's eyes water.
The five fishhouses have steeply peaked roofs
and narrow, cleated gangplanks slant up
to storerooms in the gables
for the wheelbarrows to be pushed up and down on.
All is silver: the heavy surface of the sea,
swelling slowly as if considering spilling over,
is opaque, but the silver of the benches,
the lobster pots, and masts, scattered
among the wild jagged rocks,
is of an apparent translucence
like the small old buildings with an emerald moss
growing on their shoreward walls.
The big fish tubs are completely lined
with layers of beautiful herring scales
and the wheelbarrows are similarly plastered
with creamy iridescent coats of mail,
with small iridescent flies crawling on them.
Up on the little slope behind the houses,
set in the sparse bright sprinkle of grass,
is an ancient wooden capstan,
cracked, with two long bleached handles
and some melancholy stains, like dried blood,
where the ironwork has rusted.
The old man accepts a Lucky Strike.
He was a friend of my gandfather.
We talk of the decline in the population
and of codfish and herring
while he waits for a herring boat to come in.
There are sequins on his vest and on his thumb.
He has scraped the scales, the principal beauty,
from unnumbered fish with that black old knife,
the blade of which is almost worn away.

Down at the water's edge, at the place
where they haul up the boats, up the long ramp
descending into the water, thin silver
tree trunks are laid horizontally
across the gray stones, down and down
at intervals of four or five feet.

222

Cold dark deep and absolutely clear,
element bearable to no mortal,
to fish and to seals . . . One seal particularly
I have seen here evening after evening.
He was curious about me. He was interested in music;
like me a believer in total immersion,
so I used to sing him Baptist hymns.
I also sang "A Mighty Fortress Is Our God."
He stood up in the water and regarded me
steadily, moving his head a little.
Then he would disappear, then suddenly emerge
almost in the same spot, with a sort of shrug
as if it were against his better judgment.
Cold dark deep and absolutely clear,
the clear gray icy water . . . Back, behind us,
the dignified tall firs begin.
Bluish, associating with their shadows,
a million Christmas trees stand
waiting for Christmas. The water seems suspended
above the rounded gray and blue-gray stones.
I have seen it over and over, the same sea, the same,
slightly, indifferently swinging above the stones,
icily free above the stones,
above the stones and then the world.
If you should dip your hand in,
your wrist would ache immediately,
your bones would begin to ache and your hand would burn
as if the water were a transmutation of fire
that feeds on stones and burns with a dark gray flame.
If you tasted it, it would first taste bitter,
then briny, then surely burn your tongue.
It is like what we imagine knowledge to be:
dark, salt, clear, moving, utterly free,
drawn from the cold hard mouth
of the world, derived from the rocky breasts
forever, flowing and drawn, and since
our knowledge is historical, flowing, and flown.

Arrival at Santos

Here is a coast; here is a harbor;
here, after a meager diet of horizon, is some scenery:
impractically shaped and--who knows--self-pitying
    mountains,
sad and harsh beneath their frivolous greenery,

with a little church on top of one. And warehouses,
some of them painted a feeble pink, or blue,
and some tall, uncertain palms. Oh, tourist,
is this how this country is going to answer you

and your immodest demands for a different world,
and a better life, and complete comprehension
of both at last, and immediately,
after eighteen days of suspension?

Finish your breakfast. The tender is coming,
a strange and ancient craft, flying a strange and brilliant
    rag.
So that's the flag. I never saw it before.
I somehow never thought of there *being* a flag,

but of course there was, all along. And coins, I presume,
and paper money; they remain to be seen.
And gingerly now we climb down the ladder backward,
myself and a fellow passenger named Miss Breen,

descending into the midst of twenty-six freighters
waiting to be loaded with green coffee beans.
Please, boy, do be more careful with that boat hook!
Watch out! Oh! It has caught Miss Breen's

skirt! There! Miss Breen is about seventy,
a retired police lieutenant, six feet tall,
with beautiful bright blue eyes and a kind expression.
Her home, when she is at home, is in Glens Fall,

s, New York. There. We are settled.
The customs officials will speak English, we hope,
and leave us our bourbon and cigarettes.
Ports are necessities, like postage stamps, or soap,

but they seldom seem to care what impression they make,
or, like this, only attempt, since it does not matter,
the unassertive colors of soap, or postage stamps--
wasting away like the former, slipping the way the latter

do when we mail the letters we wrote on the boat,
either because the glue here is very inferior
or because of the heat. We leave Santos at once;
we are driving to the interior.

                          January, 1952

Elizabeth Bishop

Questions of Travel

There are too many waterfalls here; the crowded streams
hurry too rapidly down to the sea,
and the pressure of so many clouds on the mountaintops
makes them spill over the sides in soft slow-motion,
turning to waterfalls under our very eyes.
--For if those streaks, those mile-long, shiny, tearstains,
aren't waterfalls yet,
in a quick age or so, as ages go here,
they probably will be.
But if the streams and clouds keep travelling, travelling,
the mountains look like the hulls of capsized ships,
slime-hung and barnacled.

Think of the long trip home.
Should we have stayed at home and thought of here?
Where should we be today?
Is it right to be watching strangers in a play
in this strangest of theatres?
What childishness is it that while there's a breath of life
in our bodies, we are determined to rush
to see the sun the other way around?
The tiniest green hummingbird in the world?
To stare at some inexplicable old stonework,
inexplicable and impenetrable,
at any view,
instantly seen and always, always delightful?
Oh, must we dream our dreams
and have them, too?
And have we room
for one more folded sunset, still quite warm?

But surely it would have been a pity
not to have seen the trees along this road,
really exaggerated in their beauty,
not to have seen them gesturing
like noble pantomimists, robed in pink.
--Not to have had to stop for gas and heard
the sad, two-noted, wooden tune
of disparate wooden clogs
carelessly clacking over
a grease-stained filling-station floor.
(In another country the clogs would all be tested.
Each pair there would have identical pitch.)
--A pity not to have heard
the other, less primitive music of the fat brown bird
who sings above the broken gasoline pump
in a bamboo church of Jesuit baroque:
three towers, five silver crosses.
--yes, a pity not to have pondered,

blurr'dly and inconclusively,
on what connection can exist for centuries
between the crudest wooden footwear
and, careful and finicky,
the whittled fantasies of wooden cages.
--Never to have studied history in
the weak calligraphy of songbirds' cages.
--And never to have had to listen to rain
so much like politicians' speeches:
two hours of unrelenting oratory
and then a sudden golden silence
in which the traveller takes a notebook, writes:

*Is it lack of imagination that makes us come
to imagined places, not just stay at home?
Or could Pascal have been not entirely right
about just sitting quietly in one's room?*

*Continent, city, country, society:
the choice is never wide and never free.
And here, or there . . . No. Should we have stayed at home,
wherever that may be?"*

Elizabeth Bishop

Sestina

September rain falls on the house.
In the failing light, the old grandmother
sits in the kitchen with the child
beside the Little Marvel Stove,
reading the jokes from the almanac,
laughing and talking to hide her tears.

She thinks that her equinoctial tears
and the rain that beats on the roof of the house
were both foretold by the almanac,
but only known to a grandmother.
The iron kettle sings on the stove.
She cuts some bread and says to the child,

It's time for tea now; but the child
is watching the teakettle's small hard tears
dance like mad on the hot black stove,
the way the rain must dance on the house.
Tidying up, the old grandmother
hangs up the clever almanac

on its string. Birdlike, the almanac
hovers half open above the child,
hovers above the old grandmother
and her teacup full of dark brown tears.
She shivers and says she thinks the house
feels chilly, and puts more wood in the stove.

It was to be, says the Marvel Stove.
I know what I know, says the almanac.
With crayons the child draws a rigid house
and a winding pathway. Then the child
puts in a man with buttons like tears
and shows it proudly to the grandmother.
But secretly, while the grandmother
busies herself about the stove,
the little moons fall down like tears
from between the pages of the almanac
into the flower bed the child
has carefully placed in the front of the house.

Time to plant tears, says the almanac.
The gandmother sings to the marvellous stove
and the child draws another inscrutable house.

First Death in Nova Scotia

In the cold, cold parlor
my mother laid out Arthur
beneath the chromographs:
Edward, Prince of Wales,
with Princess Alexandra,
and King George with Queen Mary.
Below them on the table
stood a stuffed loon
shot and stuffed by Uncle
Arthur, Arthur's father.

Since Uncle Arthur fired
a bullet into him,
he hadn't said a word.
He kept his own counsel
on his white, frozen lake,
the marble-topped table.
His breast was deep and white,
cold and caressable;
his eyes were red glass,
much to be desired.

"Come," said my mother,
"Come and say good-bye
to your little cousin Arthur."
I was lifted up and given
one lily of the valley
to put in Arthur's hand.
arthur's coffin was a little frosted cake,
and the red-eyed loon eyed it
from his white, frozen lake.

Arthur was very small.
He was all white, like a doll
that hadn't been painted yet.
Jack Frost had started to paint him
the way he always painted
the Maple Leaf (Forever).
He had just begun on his hair,
a few red strokes, and then
Jack Frost had dropped the brush
and left him white, forever.

The gracious royal couples
were warm in red and ermine;
their feet were well wrapped up
in the ladies' ermine trains.
They invited Arthur to be
the smallest page at court.

Elizabeth Bishop

But how could Arthur go,
clutching his tiny lily,
with his eyes shut up so tight
and the roads deep in snow?

Elizabeth Bishop

In the Waiting Room

In Worcester, Massachusetts,
I went with Aunt Consuelo
to keep her dentist's appointment
and sat and waited for her
in the dentist's waiting room.
It was winter. It got dark
early. The waiting room
was full of grown-up people,
arctics and overcoats,
lamps and magazines.
My aunt was inside
what seemed like a long time
and while I waited I read
the *National Geographic*
(I could read) and carefully
studied the photographs:
the inside of a volcano,
black, and full of ashes;
then it was spilling over
in rivulets of fire.
Osa and Martin Johnson
dressed in riding breeches,
laced boots, and pith helmets.
A dead man slung on a pole
--"Long Pig," the caption said.
Babies with pointed heads
wound round and round with string;
black, naked women with necks
wound round and round with wire
like the necks of light bulbs.
Their breasts were horrifying.
I read it right straight through.
I was too shy to stop
And then I looked at the cover:
the yellow margins, the date.
Suddenly, from inside,
came an *oh!* of pain
--Aunt Consuelo's voice--
not very loud or long.
I wasn't at all surprised;
even then I knew she was
a foolish, timid woman.
I might have been embarrassed,
but wasn't. What took me
completely by surprise
was that it was *me:*
my voice, in my mouth.
Without thinking at all
I was my foolish aunt,

--we--were falling, falling,
our eyes glued to the cover
of the *National Geographic,*
February, 1918.

I said to myself: three days
and you'll be seven years old.
I was saying it to stop
the sensation of falling off
the round, turning world
into cold, blue-black space.
But I felt: you are an *I,*
you are an *Elizabeth,*
you are one of *them.*
Why should you be one, too?
I scarcely dared to look
to see what it was I was.
I gave a sidelong glance
--I couldn't look any higher--
at shadowy gray knees,
trousers and skirts and boots
and different pairs of hands
lying under the lamps.
I knew that nothing stranger
had ever happened, that nothing
stranger could ever happen.
Why should I be my aunt,
or me, or anyone?
What similarities--
boots, hands, the family voice
I felt in my throat, or even
the *National Geographic*
and those awful hanging breasts--
held us all together
or made us all just one?
How--I didn't know any
word for it--how "unlikely". . .
How had I come to be here,
like them, and overhear
a cry of pain that could have
got loud and worse but hadn't?

The waiting room was bright
and too hot. It was sliding
beneath a big black wave,
another, and another.

Then I was back in it.
The War was on. Outside,
in Worcester, Massachusetts,
were night and slush and cold,
and it was still the fifth
of February, 1918.

One Art

The art of losing isn't hard to master;
so many things seem filled with the intent
to be lost that their loss is no disaster.

Lose something every day. Accept the fluster
of lost door keys, the hour badly spent.
The art of losing isn't hard to master.

Then practice losing farther, losing faster:
places, and names, and where it was you meant
to travel. None of these will bring disaster.

I lost my mother's watch. And look! my last, or
next-to-last, of three loved houses went.
The art of losing isn't hard to master.

I lost two cities, lovely ones. And, vaster,
some realms I owned, two rivers, a continent.
I miss them, but it wasn't a disaster.

--Even losing you (the joking voice, a gesture
I love) I shan't have lied. It's evident
the art of losing's not too hard to master
though it may look like (*Write* it!) like disaster.

Notes on Contributors

Andrews, William L.

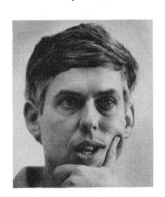

Chairman of the English Department, University of Kansas--Lawrence; formerly Professor of English at the University of Wisconsin, where he served as Director of Introductory Literature courses for undergraduates and Director of the Graduate Program in English. He is the editor/author of *Sisters of the Spirit: Three Black Women's Autobiographies of the 19th Century* and *To Tell a Free Story: The First Century of Afro-American Autobiography*. Awards he has received include fellowships from the American Council of Learned Societies and an Excellence in Teaching Award from the University of Wisconsin. As a member of the Modern English and American Literature faculty team, he contributed written and audio material for the units on Faulkner, Contemporary Southern Writers, and Malcolm X.

Archibald, Douglas N.

Professor of English at Colby College, he has served as Department Chair and member of the Educational Policy and Performing Arts Committees. He has edited the *Colby Library Quarterly* since 1986. His publications include *John Butler Yeats and Yeats,* as well as a series of articles on the poet. He is currently working on *Autobiographies* and on *The Collected Works of William Butler Yeats.*

Auerbach, Emily

Assistant Professor of English at the University of Wisconsin--Madison, where she directs the Division of University Outreach's programs in English and American literature for nontraditional students. Her publications include *Maestros, Dilettantes, and Philistines,* a study of music and literature supported by grants from the Newberry Library and the University of Wisconsin Graduate School; articles on women writers; and her own poetry and short fiction. She served as chief coordinator/editor of the Modern English and American Literature I and II courses, winning the NUCEA Meritorious Independent Study Course Award for the nineteenth-century series.

Baker, Houston A., Jr.

Director of the Center for the Study of Black Literature and Culture at the University of Pennsylvania. His publications include *Afro-American Politics,* poetry, and texts on Black American Literature. His work has been funded by the fellowships from the Guggenheim Foundation and the National Humanities Center. He is currently working on "The Achievement of Gwendolyn Brooks."

Brown, Rosellen

Former faculty member of the Creative Writing Program at the University of Houston. Her publications include collections of stories, poetry, and three novels, including *Civil Wars,* which in 1984 won the Janet H. Kafka Prize for the best novel by an American woman. She has held a Guggenheim Fellowship, two creative writing grants from the National Endowment for the Arts, and an award from the American Academy and Institute of Arts and Letters.

Clayton, Jay

Associate Professor of English at Vanderbilt University; formerly associate professor at the University of Wisconsin-- Madison. His publications include the award-winning *Romantic Vision and the Novel,* articles on contemporary literature and theory, and his own short fiction. Recipient of the University of Wisconsin Distinguished Teaching Award, he also has won fellowships to support both his research and creative writing. As a member of the Modern English and American Literature faculty team, he contributed written and audio material for the units on Hemingway, Frost, and Morrison.

Doody, Terrence

Professor of English at Rice University, he has won awards for teaching courses on nineteenth and twentieth century British and American literature. His publications include *Confessions and Commentary on the Novel* and numerous articles on the novel from Cervantes to Updike. A forthcoming book on the novel will be called *Among Other Things: Language, Presence, and the Structure of the Novel.* As a member of the Modern English and American Literature faculty team, he contributed written and audio material for the units on Eliot and Modernism, Yeats, and Roth.

Field, David

Associate Professor of English at DePauw University, he teaches courses in nonfiction, creative writing, contemporary American literature, the novel, modern continental literature, Milton and Nabokov. He has published a dozen essays on natural history as well as scholarly articles on the work of Vladimir Nabokov and is currently working on a book about fluid worlds in romantic fiction.

Froula, Christine

Associate Professor of English and Comparative Literature and Theory at Northwestern University, she has served on the Comparative Literature and *Tri-Quarterly* Committees. She has published *A Guide to Ezra Pound's Selected Poems* and *To Write Paradise: Style and Error in Pound's Cantos*, as well as articles on Milton, Browning, Woolf, Joyce, and Eliot. Awards she has received include fellowships from the National Endowment for the Humanities and Yale University. She is currently working on *Joyce and Woolf: Gender, Culture, and Literary Authority*.

Hobson, Fred C., Jr.

Professor of English at Louisiana State and co-editor of *The Southern Review*. He has published *Tell About the South: The Southern Rage to Explain; Serpent in Eden: H.L. Mencken and the South*, and articles on William Faulkner, Thomas Wolfe, and Lillian Smith. Awards he has received include the Pulitzer Prize for Meritorious Public Service and a National Endowment for the Humanities Fellowship. He is currently working on *The Savage South: History of an Image*.

Mason, Theodore O., Jr.

Assistant Professor of English at Kenyon College, where he teaches American and Afro-American literature; formerly on the faculty at Trinity College and a visiting lecturer at Mount Holyoke College. He has published articles on Alice Walker and Toni Morrison and is at work on a book-length study of African-American literature and literary theory entitled *Culture and the Historicity of Fiction: Three African-American "Moderns."*

McKay, Nellie

Associate Professor of American and Afro-American Literature at the University of Wisconsin--Madison, where she has received teaching and "star faculty" awards. Her publications include books on Toni Morrison, Jean Toomer, and the black autobiography. The Rockefeller Foundation, Ford Foundation, and National Research Council have funded her research work, and she has taught as a visiting lecturer at Harvard University and M.I.T.

Merrill, James

Born in New York City, he now lives in Stonington, Connecticut, and has achieved a worldwide reputation for his many volumes of poetry. He has won National Book Awards (for *Nights and Days* and *Mirabell*), the Bollingen Prize in Poetry (for *Braving the Elements*), the Book Critics Circle Award in Poetry (for *Scripts for the Pageant*), and the Pulitzer Prize (for *Divine Comedies*). He has also written two novels, *The (Diblos) Notebook* and *The Seraglio*; two plays, *The Immortal Husband* and *The Bait*; and a book of essays, *Recitative*.

Nkondo, Gessler Moses

Associate Professor of English and Africana Studies at Vassar College. A native of South Africa, he has served as visiting lecturer at Yale and Harvard Universities, teaching Afro-American literature, African literature in English, and other courses. His publications include *Turfloop Testimony: The Dilemma of a Black University in South Africa* and numerous articles on South African literature and politics.

Pondrom, Cyrena

Professor of English at the University of Wisconsin--Madison, where she also served as Assistant Chancellor. With research support from the American Council of Learned Societies and the University of Wisconsin, she has pursued her interests in modern literature and women's literature in English. Her publications include *The Contemporary Writer: Interviews with Sixteen Novelists and Poets, The Road from Paris: French Influence on English Poetry, 1900-1920*, and articles on Franz Kafka, H.D., Zora Neale Hurston, Gertrude Stein, and Marianne Moore.

Rivkin, Julie

Associate Professor of English at Connecticut College, she teaches courses in American literature and women's studies. She is the author of a forthcoming book, *False Positions: The Representational Logic of Henry James's Later Fiction*, and has published articles and reviews on Henry James, Virginia Woolf, and other modern and contemporary writers. Her role as a faculty team member included contributing written and audio material for units on Virginia Woolf, Nadine Gordimer, and Elizabeth Bishop.

Roberts, Sheila

Professor of English at the University of Wisconsin-- Milwaukee. An expatriate South African, she is the author of *Dan Jacobson: An Analytical and Critical Study* as well as many articles on South African literature. She is herself a published fiction writer and the recipient of both the Olive Schreiner and Thomas Pringle Awards from the English Academy of Southern Africa, and the Teacher-Scholar Award from Michigan State University.

Wyatt, David M.

Associate Professor at the University of Maryland. He has published *Prodigal Sons* and *The Fall into Eden*, as well as articles on Robert Frost, Ernest Hemingway, and Robert Penn Warren. His awards include the Phi Beta Kappa Book Prize and the University of Virginia Sesquicentennial Fellowship.

Special Mention

We gratefully thank Dr. Laurel Yourke, research associate in the Department of Liberal Studies, University of Wisconsin, for contributing valuable material and suggestions for this Study Guide. Barry Carlsen, University of Wisconsin Publications Office, contributed the fine sketches of the fourteen writers featured in this course.

Readings from the literature are an essential part of all twelve audio programs. We wish to acknowledge the many professional readers and faculty members whose voices helped capture the eloquence of twentieth-century literature: LeWan Alexander, Anna Branigan-Sweeney, Jay Clayton, Carol Cowan, Jeffrey Golden, Yolanda Henderson, Kargaletta Jackson, Teal Ann Major, Aisha McDaniel, Nellie McKay, Brian O'Dougherty, Sybil Robinson, Karl Schmidt, Hans Sturm, and Joseph Wiesenfarth. Musicians Alison Bush, Vincent Fuh, Jacqueline Lee, Douglas Quimby, and Louis Webster also contributed their artistry.

This project would not have been possible without the cooperation of Wisconsin Public Radio, the University of Wisconsin—Madison Division of University Outreach (Howard Martin, Dean), and the University of Wisconsin—Extension Independent Study Program. We wish to thank Donald Kaiser, past director of the U.W. Independent Study Program, for the essential role he played in initiating this cooperative project.